Neuroscience-based Cognitive Therapy

Neuroscience-based Cognitive Therapy

New Methods for Assessment, Treatment, and Self-Regulation

Tullio Scrimali

WILEY-BLACKWELL

A John Wiley & Sons, Ltd., Publication

This edition first published 2012
© 2012 John Wiley & Sons, Ltd.

This book is a revised and extended version of: Scrimali, Tullio (2010) *Neuroscienze e Psicologia Clinica. Dal Laboratorio di Ricerca al Setting con i Pazienti*. Milano: FrancoAngeli.

Wiley-Blackwell is an imprint of John Wiley & Sons, formed by the merger of Wiley's global Scientific, Technical and Medical business with Blackwell Publishing.

Registered office: John Wiley & Sons, Ltd, The Atrium, Southern Gate, Chichester, West Sussex, PO19 8SQ, UK

Editorial offices: 350 Main Street, Malden, MA 02148-5020, USA
9600 Garsington Road, Oxford, OX4 2DQ, UK
The Atrium, Southern Gate, Chichester, West Sussex, PO19 8SQ, UK

For details of our global editorial offices, for customer services, and for information about how to apply for permission to reuse the copyright material in this book please see our website at www.wiley.com/wiley-blackwell.

The right of Tullio Scrimali to be identified as the author of this work has been asserted in accordance with the UK Copyright, Designs and Patents Act 1988.

Library of Congress Cataloging-in-Publication Data

Scrimali, Tullio.
   [Neuroscienze e psicologia clinica. English]
   Neuroscience-based cognitive therapy : new methods for assessment, treatment, and self-regulation / Tullio Scrimali.
      p. ; cm.
   Includes bibliographical references and index.
   ISBN 978-1-119-99375-9 (hardback) – ISBN 978-1-119-99374-2 (pbk.)
   I. Title.
   [DNLM: 1. Cognitive Therapy–methods.   2. Mental Processes–physiology.
3. Neurosciences–methods.   4. Psychophysiology.   WM 425.5.C6]
   616.89′1425–dc23   2011053427

A catalogue record for this book is available from the British Library.

Set in 10.5/13pt Minion by Aptara Inc., New Delhi, India

Printed in Singapore by Ho Printing Singapore Pte Ltd

1   2012

This monograph is dedicated to my wife Wiola, Star of the East, *who decided to share her life with me, without regard for common sense or any apparent logic. In this case, the most intense emotion, that of love, took charge and overcame all rational knowledge.*

All our knowledge has its origins in emotions
Leonardo da Vinci

Contents

Contents

Foreword by Arthur Freeman

In the late 1880s, an obscure Viennese physician began his scientific work in neurology by studying the phylogenetic association between the central nervous systems of lower vertebrates and humans. He gained moderate success as a basic science researcher, even developing a gold chloride stain for nerve tissue. His goal was simple: he wanted an academic career that would allow him to study and teach about neurological disorders in lower vertebrates and in humans. His earliest publications were on basic neuroanatomy but ultimately evolved into his studies and publications on infantile and child cerebral paralysis. His plans for an academic career were, however, not to be fulfilled, for a variety of reasons. A mentor suggested that this young man look elsewhere for a career. With a growing family and the need to support them, this physician, one Sigismund Freud, began to treat a variety of disorders that he judged, at the time, to be neurologically based. Although Freud's work over the years encompassed his views on religion, anthropology, psychology, and psychopathology, his neurological interests and roots were always a backdrop for his thinking. Cozolino (2010, p.1) quotes Freud: "We must recollect that all of our provisional ideas in psychology will presumably one day be based on an organic substructure."

The rest we know to be history. Freud's psychotherapeutic insights and developments became the basis for some of the most brilliant, controversial, and illuminating psychological work of the twentieth century. Freud's legacy continues today and has been the basis for all contemporary psychotherapy, whether its models were developed to support or oppose his ideas of the origins of psychopathology and the treatment of those "nervous disorders."

Though there were opposing voices to Freud's in the early twentieth century (functionalism, gestaltism, introspectionism, and behaviorism), they did not carry the weight, or influence philosophy, medicine, sociology, or even religion, to the same degree and with the same power that Freud did.

Freud's journey was, however, not an easy one. As he explored possibilities regarding the etiology of psychopathology, he ran afoul of the psychiatric establishment, who believed his theories to be unsavory (e.g., those regarding infantile sexuality), and the psychological establishment, who rejected his ideas because they were derived from clinical observation rather than experimental data.

Starting in the 1930s, a significant movement emerged in psychology that focused on directed behavioral change. Salter, Jacobson, and others experimented and treated a broad range of emotional/behavioral disorders with direct interventions designed to alter behavior. Their seminal work was derided by the psychoanalytic establishment as simplistic and naïve. The behavioral group did not address the basic (and hypothesized) core unconscious conflicts that were believed by the psychoanalytic group to be the key issues in the development and maintenance of psychopathology. If one looks at the first two volumes of the *Diagnostic and Statistical Manual* (DSM-I, 1952; and DSM-II, 1968), the influence of psychoanalytic thinking is clear and abundant. Behavioral descriptions, much less targets, were all but missing. Neurological etiology was barely evident.

The behavioral work of the early pioneers laid the foundation for the growth of a behavioral focus in psychology in the 1950s and 1960s. Joseph Wolpe and later Arnold A. Lazarus began treating patients with behavioral technology. Although trained in a psychoanalytic model, Wolpe made brilliant observations regarding the obvious. If an individual were anxious, they were hard-pressed to be calm. Conversely, an individual in a state of relaxation would be hard-pressed to experience anxiety. Looked down upon by the psychoanalysts as simplistic and inelegant, these pioneers persisted. Their work, and that of their students and colleagues, can be viewed as the "first wave" in the growth of contemporary behavioral and cognitive behavioral therapies. In the 1950s another young and unknown physician working in a ward for the neurologically damaged was told that in addition to his neurological training he would also have to seek some training in psychiatry. This was not something that he wanted to do, inasmuch as he saw psychiatry at that time as far too "soft" and unscientific. This young doctor, one Aaron T. Beck, has gone on to rival Freud as a major proponent of a new model of psychotherapy. This model, based, in part, on Beck's psychoanalytic training, marked the beginning of the "second wave" of cognitive behavioral therapy (CBT). The addition of a cognitive focus rooted in an information processing model was not new. The ideas that underlay his model were espoused by the Stoic philosophers, many researchers, and clinicians, notably George Kelly and Albert Ellis. In 1977, Michael Mahoney called cognitive therapists the "barbarians at the gates" of the psychoanalytic establishments. The cognitivists were pounding on the gates and demanding entrance, but in those early days their calls fell on deaf ears. In the twenty-first century, however, cognitive behavioral work is firmly in place well within the establishment, and trying, as is the custom in our field, to deny access to other possible differing treatments. (Our pattern has been that when we as clinicians and researchers perceive someone or something different, we follow the model set up by nomadic tribes centuries ago: we circle our wagons for protection, and then the tribes shoot at each other.)

In the 1960s another important revolution occurred: the pharmacological revolution. Starting almost by accident, Dr Nathan S. Kline became a spokesperson for the use of pharmacotherapy for all of the major psychiatric disorders. As with any movement, there were those who opposed it, believing that medication masked the symptoms of disorders and did not allow the disorders to be available for psychotherapeutic treatment. Therefore, they argued, medication was to be minimized or even avoided.

Through the 1970s and 1980s the cognitive and behavioral models grew in terms of their following, sophistication, and importance. In the late 1980s and into the 1990s a "third wave" was developing within the CBT establishment. This new wave, lead by Marsha Linehan, Steven Hayes, and their collaborators, has grown significantly. Within the CBT movement, there have been a number of variants, some focusing on a specific problem, such as anxiety, while others have been more ubiquitous and offered models applicable to many different disorders. Some variants focus on discrete patient groups, such as children or elders, while others are more wide-ranging. Some, intending to be ground-breaking, have cut bits and pieces from other models and then offered their new "model" to the field. We have CBT models that have discovered the work of Ainsworth and Bowlby, while others have rediscovered and integrated the interpersonal psychiatry of Harry Stack Sullivan into their CBT model. Others still have even rediscovered Alfred Adler without, unfortunately, any recognition or citation. Often, the model may die or decline with the death of the founder. Witness what happened to gestalt therapy when Fritz Perls died.

One of the models that emerged in the 1980s was what was termed a "constructivist" approach. The underlying idea behind it was that each individual constructs their own reality. While this was not a new idea, it drew major interest from many quarters. We have been inundated by waves; some bigger than others, some more powerful than others.

In directing a doctoral program in clinical psychology, we have adjusted the curriculum to make sure that our graduates are familiar with the social bases of behavior, the cognitive bases of behavior, and, possibly the most important element, the biological bases of behavior. This area is one that has grown exponentially since 2000 with the development of more and better technology for assessing neurological functioning. For example, I completed a degree in neuropsychology over twenty years ago as part of my postdoctoral study but what I learned, I am embarrassed to say, is not only outdated, but naïve, given today's data. Our understanding of neurology, neuropsychology, neuropharmacology, and neuropsychiatry is an essential ingredient in understanding the development and maintenance of "emotional" problems. This neuroscientific focus must be viewed as the "fourth wave" in CBT. What we have been lacking is a voice that can integrate all of these apparently diverse elements. Fortunately there is such a person. For many years, Dr Tullio Scrimali has been developing and honing his ideas. I have worked and collaborated with Tullio over the past twenty years or more. I have heard his learned papers, read his excellent texts, attended his workshops at major international congresses, sat for hours with him discussing his work, and witnessed his growth as a scientist/clinician. I have also heard him chided or even derided for his ideas. Admittedly, Tullio has never been shy to voice an opinion, or to tackle big problems. Despite setbacks, like a true scientist, Tullio has been undeterred.

The current volume is the result of that life and professional mission, of that clinical observation, data, and insights. There is very little that he has left out. He has written a book for the experienced CBT clinician, for the academic, and for the novice in CBT. This neuroscientific model is well laid out and beautifully explicated.

Tullio starts by exploring some basic ideas, that is, the interface between neuroscience, clinical psychology, and cognitive therapy (CT). He next addresses the classic mind–brain problem. He then moves on to more biological issues that involve motor theories of the mind and the coalitional mind and we are taken on an exploration of the central nervous system. He then addresses the issues of memory and internal representational systems that include both imagery and internal dialog. The next chapter requires careful reading because of its centrality to his thesis and the fact that it is crammed with information. It deals with knowledge processes that include the unconscious and tacit dimension, process coding, tacit and explicit knowledge, procedural knowledge, and social knowledge. He then moves on to an exploration and explanation of the phylogenesis of the brain and ontogenesis of the mind, and discusses biological and cultural evolutionism.

In his chapters on psychophysiology, clinical psychophysiology, and neuroscience-based CT, Tullio begins his integration of the neurosciences model with CT. His descriptions of electroencephalography (EEG) and quantitative electroencephalography (QEEG), electrodermal activity (EDA), and quantitative electrodermal activity (QEDA) set out new tools for the clinical scientist. He describes complex psychological diagnosis with QEEG in identifying dementia, schizophrenia, depression, and attention deficit hyperactivity disorder (ADHD). He offers data regarding specific disorders including generalized anxiety disorder, panic attack disorder, post-traumatic stress disorder, phobias, obsessive-compulsive disorder, depression, eating disorders, addictions, schizophrenia, episodic mania, ADHD, stuttering, hypertension, irritable bowel syndrome, and premenstrual syndrome. Further, Tullio describes the neurobiology of relational processes such as attachment, reciprocity, and the "strange family situation." He then describes the use of meditation, mindfulness, and Biofeedback-Based Mindfulness.

Finally, there is an excellent and integrative chapter on training and continuing education in the field of neuroscience-based CT.

There are few scientist/clinicians who could have written this book, and even fewer who could do so with the tenacity of Professor Tullio Scrimali. I am grateful for his years of friendship, his clinical insights, and his collaboration. To be allowed even the small job of writing this foreword is a great honor for me.

Preface

In accordance with a personal tradition, now almost thirty years old, this book begins with an epigraph. However, one novelty is that this is the first time I have taken inspiration from modern times, having referred to ancient Greek scholars such as Plato, Protagoras, Heraclitus, and Thucydides in my previous books.

There are various reasons for this unprecedented choice. The most important is that Leonardo da Vinci's aptitude for exploring diverse fields in the sum of human knowledge, such as poetry and music, painting and sculpture, engineering and architecture, as well as medicine, means that he completely embodies the complex man. From the time I fell in love with complexity and established it as the epistemological foundation for my research, I understood that Leonardo could be the perfect reference for work that constantly evolves in tandem with the brain, mind, and society, requiring analysis and synthesis in fields ranging from neuroscience, information technology, and analog and digital microelectronics to medicine, psychology, psychiatry, psychotherapy, sociology, politics, and humanistic sciences. Not even art is unrelated to my work, and while guitarist-singer Joseph LeDoux performs with his Amygdaloides group in New York, I have formed a band called Entropy of Mind, holding concerts in various cities in Sicily. Music, dramatization, and painting are also an integral part of the emotional "Tacita . . . Mente" lab that I developed and tested with Desirée Arena, Ileana Milano, and Simona Ingrà at the ALETEIA Clinical Center in Enna.

There is another reason for my linking myself to da Vinci's genius. Having specialized in psychiatry and trained in Milan, I sensed Leonardo's spirit in his *Last Supper* and in his garden, painted in the rooms of the Sforzesco Castle. During my training in the city of Navigli, I breathed the presence of the master who lived and worked there for a considerable time. Several years ago, I went to Amboise, France, to visit the places where Leonardo spent the last days of his life. In that French village, I saw his home, the objects of his everyday life, his deathbed, and, above all, his last writings. Among them, the aphorism I quote at the opening to this book moved me profoundly and seems to have anticipated epistemological choices in Italian cognitivism (Guidano and Liotti, 1983; Guidano, 1987, 1991; Scrimali, 2008). Emotion or perception comes before rational knowledge and, in any case, always guides and determines it. I then resolved to adopt this phrase for one of my next books. With this volume, the moment to call on da Vinci's aphorism seemed to have arrived. A book that sought to merge brain, mind, and technology seemed very appropriate, though inadequate, to honor the great man.

Purely by coincidence, this choice proved particularly timely. A recent opinion poll of 140,000 European Union citizens on the occasion of the fiftieth anniversary of the Treaty of Rome asked who was the European genius par excellence. The poll provided a clear-cut response: Leonardo da Vinci, distantly followed by Shakespeare, Mozart, Einstein, and Socrates. From the celebrated European genius Leonardo, the epigraph for this small book written in Sicily, island in the middle of a sea of history, serves as the perfect metaphor for complexity.

Tullio Scrimali
tscrima@tin.it

Acknowledgments

Many people collaborated in the clinical work and research described in this book. So as not to be too verbose, I will mention only those that made the largest contributions.

Enrico Adorno, Claudio Cantone, Roberto Caputo, Antonino Alain Catalfamo, Villiam Giroldini, and Salvatore Messina provided substantial support for developing the original hardware and software systems described here. Giuseppe Castro, Giacomina Cultrera, Danielle Mancuso, Sonya Maugeri, and Katia Polopoli played important roles in performing research in psychophysiology. Under my supervision at the ALETEIA Clinical Center laboratories, Angela Miccichè implemented the research program relating to the use of MindLAB Set in documenting the effects of meditation techniques on brain processes. A warm thank you to all the colleagues and associates who, on a progressively larger scale, experimented with my MindLAB Set, supplying valuable feedback.

Even two nonhumans, though with good souls – Baika, my West Highland terrier, and Ghenia, my Scottish terrier – provided their support, helping me to relax during long hours spent at the computer, playing around me or cuddling up at my feet to lend encouragement and reinforcement from the depths of their diminutive eyes!

A special mention is due to my American friends James Claiborn and Arthur Freeman. Jim worked on revising the text after its translation into English. It was no easy job! Unfortunately, writing a book in one language, in this case Italian, and then translating it into another does not easily result in a text that is both well formed and fully comprehensible. Professional translators frequently do not have sufficient understanding of the specific matters on which the book is focused, especially when they have to deal with new topics such as those treated in this book. Thanks, Jim.

What can I say about Arthur Freeman and our fantastic friendship? I could tell endless stories of our adventures of the mind, while teaching, lecturing, researching, traveling, and sharing fantastic experiences all around the world. But the most important thing I can say is that meeting Art in Toronto, about twenty years ago, changed my life. I was a quite unknown "Italian" researcher and clinician. Art was already a very important author on cognitive therapy with a strong and deserved international reputation. I was a son of little Sicily and Italian culture; he was a son of great America. So many differences in our background and our personal stories. But, across these differences, a strong friendship has been built and with his help, encouragement, and support, step by step, I have been able to develop an international career, of which this book is a new stage. Thanks, Art.

The last friend I would like to thank is Darren Reed. We worked together for more than a year in developing the editorial project on which this book is based. Our collaboration and friendship have been truly "dialectic," due to our different profiles. I am a "Latin" author; he is a very "British" manager. Can you imagine anything more challenging? In the end we attuned perfectly to each other, and this book is the "complex" result of this fantastic and somewhat difficult job. Thanks, Darren.

Finally, a special thank you to my readers. If you have purchased this book with a view to implementing the new methods I discuss, you will most certainly provide a small but important contribution to the development of a new chapter in clinical psychology. Send your feedback to: tscrima@tin.it

Tullio Scrimali

Abbreviations

ATR	antidepressant treatment response
CAT	computerized axial tomography
CBT	cognitive behavioral therapy
CCT	complex cognitive therapy
CNS	central nervous system
CT	cognitive therapy
DSM	*Diagnostic and Statistical Manual of Mental Disorders*
EDA	electrodermal activity
EABCT	European Congress for Cognitive and Behavioral Therapies
EEG	electroencephalogram, electroencephalography
EMG	electromyography
fMRI	functional magnetic resonance imaging
fNIR	functional near-infrared based optical brain imaging
ICCP	International Association for Cognitive Psychotherapy
ICD	International Classification of Diseases
MANOVA	multivariate analysis of variance
NINCDS-ADRDA	National Institute of Neurological and Communicative Disorders and Stroke/Alzheimer's Disease and Related Disorders Association
NIR	near infrared
NS-EDRs	nonspecific electrodermal responses
NS-SCRs	nonspecific skin conductance responses
OCD	obsessive-compulsive disorder
PET	positron emission tomography
QEDA	quantitative electrodermal activity

QEEG	quantitative electroencephalogram, quantitative electroencephalography
REM	rapid eye movement
SCL	skin conductance level
SCRs	skin conductance responses
SPECT	single photon emission computed tomography
SSRIs	selective serotonin re-uptake inhibitors
TOTE	test, operate, test, and exit
WCBCT	World Congress of Behavioral and Cognitive Therapies

Introduction

The research and data described in this book are the result of the studies, experiments, and conceptual interpretations that have engaged me for many years. In fact, my interest in neuroscience and psychotherapy was sparked as I was preparing my graduate thesis between 1975 and 1977 at the Department of Psychiatry of the University of Catania, under the supervision of Professor Vincenzo Rapisarda. It dealt with experimental work based on recording electrodermal activity and biofeedback. At the University of Milan's Resident School of Psychiatry, where I studied for four years under the eminent psychiatrist Carlo Lorenzo Cazzullo, whom I consider one of my most important mentors, and under the supervision of Professor Silvio Scarone, I devoted myself to studying electroencephalographic activity with specific reference to evoked potentials, the subject matter for my specialty thesis.

Therefore, neuroscience was a profound passion at the foundation of my scientific education and clinical training. In 1980, at the Department of Psychiatry, with the encouragement and support of its director Vincenzo Rapisarda, a man truly impassioned by new technology, I established a laboratory for clinical psychophysiology and launched into a teaching role in psychophysiology at the Resident School of Psychiatry.

Up until 2002, my scientific and academic career developed primarily in the psychiatric field, but from that year on, I took on a new university experience teaching clinical psychology to undergraduate students in the psychology curriculum, and later, to master's-level students in psychology at the University of Catania and at Kore University in Enna. Thus, as I entered a new scientific and clinical world, I quickly realized that while the importance of neuroscience could be considered to be accepted in psychiatry, in the clinical psychologists' community, things were still different. In the field

Neuroscience-based Cognitive Therapy: New Methods for Assessment, Treatment, and Self-Regulation, First Edition. Tullio Scrimali.
© 2012 John Wiley & Sons, Ltd. Published 2012 by John Wiley & Sons, Ltd.

of psychology, psychophysiology is still considered a science solely for the very specialized, and the idea of introducing equipment into this setting always met with strong resistance. So I began working on developing a new body of knowledge and core competencies that would bring neuroscience and clinical psychology closer together. The first step on this road was the publication of a book named *Sulle Tracce della Mente* ("On the Trail of the Mind") (Scrimali and Grimaldi, 1991). At that time I proposed a new constructivistic approach in clinical psychophysiology.

With the publication of this book, I hope to bring to fruition the project of creating a new perspective in cognitive therapy, which I have called "neuroscience-based cognitive therapy." Standard cognitive therapy (CT) had its roots in human information processing and computer science. Thanks to the more recent developments of neuroscience, with particular reference to the epistemology of complexity, it is possible today to create a new perspective in CT based on neuroscience, according to a complex systems approach.

The main topics of such a new orientation in CT are constructivism and motor theories of mind, complexity and chaos theories, neuroscience, and clinical psychophysiology. This book is devoted to focusing on and fully explaining this new approach. The aim is to enable the reader to discover the new scientific foundations and so develop an innovative clinical practice in the area of mental disorders.

The book represents an intellectual journey which can be divided into three parts. In Part I, Neuroscience in Context, which includes Chapters 1 to 6, I describe the contemporary neuroscience background with specific reference to complex epistemology. In Part II, Clinical Psychophysiology and its Parameters (Chapters 7 to 10), the bases of the most important psychophysiological parameters are illustrated. Finally, in Part III, Neuroscience-based Methods in the Clinical Setting (Chapters 11 to 20), I describe in detail the methods, the hardware, and the software used to record and analyze electrodermal activity (EDA) in the clinic.

By following this book, the reader can not only become familiar with a new background for CT but also acquire new methods for client assessment, therapy, and self-regulation. The neuroscience-based CT that I present has the capacity to develop rapidly, due to the wide availability of economic and intuitive methodologies coming from neuroscience laboratories and usable in the clinical setting. This will allow for the collection of a larger and even more detailed series of data in the coming years. This book serves to guide those who are interested in taking a similar fascinating journey from the laboratory to the patient therapy setting.

Buon viaggio!

1

Neuroscience in Context

1

Neuroscience, Clinical Psychology, and Cognitive Therapy

Neuroscience constitutes one of the most important components in contemporary scientific development. Due to the introduction, on the one hand, of increasingly more sophisticated techniques and, on the other, of those that are progressively easier to learn and apply as well as more economic to acquire and utilize, neuroscience is no longer either the exclusive heuristic method for understanding the brain and comprehending the mind typically employed in costly professional research labs, or the tool of mental disorder clinics. The purpose of this book, and of the research and applications described in it, is to propose a series of methodologies that, though coming from neuroscience laboratories, still provide concrete clinical applications today.

At the outset, we must quickly tackle a problem that Paul Grobstein focused on in an interesting article, asking whether psychotherapists and clinicians of the mind were genuinely interested in neuroscience today, or whether they were inclined to consider it an annoying and intrusive approach (Grobstein, 2003). I myself have had to confront, in Italy and abroad, some spirited colleagues, clinical psychologists, and psychotherapists who were highly annoyed by neuroscience, often becoming openly hostile to it. In the minds of some clinicians, there must be a vision similar to that humorously represented in Figure 1.1.

This book shows how neuroscience is now already available to clinical psychologists, not only as a valuable new brain and mind heuristics, but also as valid application methods with which I have personally worked for

Neuroscience-based Cognitive Therapy: New Methods for Assessment, Treatment, and Self-Regulation,
First Edition. Tullio Scrimali.
© 2012 John Wiley & Sons, Ltd. Published 2012 by John Wiley & Sons, Ltd.

Figure 1.1 How clinicians imagine the psychophysiological setting.

many years. To begin with, let's define exactly what neuroscience is and what it concerns.

The term "neuroscience" indicates a set of disciplines, both heuristic and applicational. The objectives of these studies range from structural, both macroscopic and microscopic, to functional aspects, examined from the biochemical, biophysical, and physiological viewpoint. Neuroscience also includes the study of the phylogenetic and ontogenetic development of the brain. From an applications viewpoint within the clinical setting, neuroscience predetermines the identification of etiologic pathogenetic processes of neurological and mental diseases and the development of new methodologies for the diagnosis and treatment of psychic distress.

The Society for Neuroscience was officially founded in 1969 but, from a strictly historical point of view, we can say that the macroscopic morphological study of the brain began in ancient Egypt. Until some years ago, neuroscience was considered largely as a biological branch of human knowledge, while more recently, due to the development of new disciplines such as cognitive psychology, neuropsychology, scientific philosophy, and theories of complexity, a very solid bridge to the human sciences has been created.

The most typical investigational methods in contemporary neuroscience are built on all those techniques that make possible a morphological, and above all functional, accurate, objective, and replicable, study of the central, peripheral, and autonomic nervous systems. In this book the concept of imaging is used broadly, referring to the development of a model or an understanding of the brain, rather than in the narrow sense of a visual image provided by brain imaging techniques such as CAT. Among these techniques of cerebral imaging, those relating to recording electroencephalographic (EEG) activity and studying electrodermal activity (EDA) are the most frequently employed today.

Methods of cerebral imaging that were developed in the last thirty years of the twentieth century, due to the advent of information systems technology methodologies, brought a series of important contributions to the comprehension of dysfunctional processes and structural alterations in the nervous system over the course of psychiatric disorders, particularly in the area of schizophrenia. Introduced into a clinical setting at the beginning of the 1970s, the first brain imaging technique was computerized axial tomography (CAT), which evolved into computed tomography with the development of brain analysis methodologies that allowed the study of various cross-sections in addition to the axial.

Godfrey Hounsfield, the English engineer who fine-tuned the technique, obtained the Nobel Prize in 1979 (Hounsfield, 1973). In the following decade, at the start of the 1980s, nuclear magnetic resonance was developed and introduced into the clinical setting, permitting better definition than computed tomography. In this case, the inventor and technique developer was a researcher of Armenian descent and a naturalized United States citizen, Rayon Damadian, who obtained the Nobel Prize in 2003 for this revolutionary invention (Mattson and Simon, 1996).

A real revolution in the area of brain imaging techniques took place with the development of new methodologies that were capable not just of identifying structural alterations in the cerebral mass but also of directly viewing in real time the biochemical modifications occurring in various parts of the brain as they are stimulated for action. We can say that, with the finalization of such methodologies, the age-old dream of having a tool for direct observation of brain activity in a living human being was finally realized. The principal techniques in functional brain imaging are single positron emission tomography (SPECT), positron emission tomography (PET), and functional magnetic resonance imaging (fMRI).

The first two methodologies make it possible to view functional cerebral activation by highlighting blood flow. In particular, PET allows the dynamic study of cerebral metabolism, by viewing both regional blood flow and local consumption of glucose. Additionally, functional analysis of the different brain systems that utilize different neurotransmitters is possible.

From the 1990s, the technique that signaled a real leap in studies using dynamic functional viewing of the central nervous system (CNS) was fMRI. In particular, a specific fMRI method utilizes blood as a means of natural contrast based on the fact that hemoglobin is diamagnetic and oxyhemoglobin is paramagnetic. In functionally activated areas of the brain, an increase in oxygen consumption and oxygenated blood flow occurs, resulting in an increase of oxygenated hemoglobin and a reduction in deoxyhemoglobin. The fMRI thus allows us to view activated areas of the brain without the necessity of administering any other means of contrast. Therefore, the method is extremely manageable apart from the need to have the patient enter the MRI tunnel.

Morphological and functional imaging techniques applied to the CNS remain, for now, confined to the laboratory, even though a recent development looks promising for application in the clinical setting in the near future. In the United States, BIOPAC has recently marketed a new functional analysis system limited to the frontal lobe that no longer requires the patient to enter the MRI tunnel lying down, but can be used simply by applying small sensors to the patient's forehead (BIOPAC, 2009). Via a screen placed in front of the patient, this system is also able to activate the cognitive and executive functions typical of the frontal lobes and record the internal functional correlates of nerve activity patterns under both normal and pathological conditions, all in a quasi-clinical setting with the patient comfortably seated and minimally disturbed. The system cost of about €30,000 (about US$42,600) is quite accessible, making it, at least on paper, a tool that can promote the development of research in clinical psychology founded on analysis of functional modification in the frontal lobes.

This new technology is called functional optical brain imaging, or functional near-infrared (NIR) based optical brain imaging (fNIR). Like fMRI, it is based on the potential for analyzing in real time the metabolic changes relative to neuron activity by quantifying regional levels of oxyhemoglobin and deoxyhemoglobin. Analysis is based not on a methodology related to the magnetic behavior of hemoglobin molecules but on the application of spectral techniques. Since only a cap with 16 integrated sensors is needed, the fNIR appears truly revolutionary and boasts great potential for the study of cognitive processes. Due to the fact that it predominantly analyzes the functional activity of the frontal lobes, it appears quite promising for research in mental disorders, specifically autism and schizophrenia (McCarthy *et al.*, 1997).

Some medical specialties, such as neurology, neurosurgery, and neuropathology, have already established strong links with neuroscience, applying new methods for diagnosis and treatment (Waxman, 2004).

In psychiatry (the discipline to which the subject matter of this book is most closely related), many exchanges with the field of neuroscience have been developed and concerning a range of disorders such as schizophrenia, depression, and anxiety (Lepage *et al.*, 2011; Berlim *et al.*, 2010; Killgore *et al.*, 2011; Gabbard, 2005). Some branches of neuroscience seem to be closer to cognitive therapy (CT), such as behavioral neuroscience (Breedlove, Rosenzweig, and Watson, 2007), cognitive neuroscience (Holyoak and Morrison, 2005), and developmental neuroscience (Nadarajah *et al.*, 2003). Furthermore, if we consider my own complex approach to CT then social neuroscience (Harmon-Jones and Beer, 2009) and Systems Neuroscience (Hemmen and Sejnowski, 2006) must also be considered.

The aim of this book is to create a new branch of science that can be a link between neuroscience and CT. But what are the actual applications that we can transfer from the neuroscience lab to the clinical psychology setting, and what use do they have? I maintain that there are primarily two applications: complex psychological diagnosis and psychotherapy. Both are discussed in subsequent chapters, and both are based on my research and applications experience.

In neuroscience, the discipline that bridges the laboratory and the clinical setting is known as clinical psychophysiology. This discipline involves methods and procedures that constitute a true interface system between the brain, the mind, and their relational context. In the clinical context, it thus deals with implementing objective analysis methodologies of the functioning of the central, neurovegetative, and autonomic nervous systems. As we will see later, the techniques that are now more readily available in the clinical setting are computerized EEG and digital analysis of EDA.

As I describe, the idea of utilizing psychophysiological techniques in the clinical psychology setting is in the same vein as the most recent positions documented in psychotherapy and contemporary neuroscience, such as that of Nobel Prize winner Erik Kandel, who sees the clinic, and particularly clinical psychology, psychiatry, and psychotherapy, as more and more closely flanking the lab. Scholars such as Cozolino and Siegel propose a neurobiology of psychotherapy and relational processes, including the crucial one of reciprocity and attachment (Kandel, 1998; Cozolino, 2002; Siegel, 1999; 2007). Before moving on to describe the range of applications in clinical psychology, it is important to focus, even if briefly, on a series of conceptual and theoretical topics that form the basis for the rational and consistent clinical use of the techniques coming out of the neuroscience laboratories.

2

The Mind–Brain Problem

The relationship of the mind to the brain, or mind–brain problem, constitutes a question that has been debated for centuries and which was confronted organically for the first time in the modern age by René Descartes, who proposed a dualistic solution. To the great French philosopher, the mind was an extracorporeal entity (*res cogitans* or mental substance) structured by a spiritual reality, not a material one. The brain, on the other hand, belonged to the physical dimension (*res extensa* or corporeal substance). The two entities interacted via the pineal gland's role as mediator, which represented the critical interface between the immaterial world of the mind and the physical world of the brain (Descartes, 1984–1991).

The mind–brain problem is, however, quite a bit older, and reflection on this theme began with the birth of western thought. In Greece, within the brief course of the fifth and fourth centuries BCE, there was a profound philosophical development focused on the human psyche that formed the conceptual foundation for all further development in theories concerning the mind–brain problem. The three key positions in the conception of the problem are clearly identifiable in the reflections of Greek philosophers such as Democritus, Plato, and Aristotle. These ideas then travel through twenty-five hundred years of history to resurface today with the same strong impact. We can only be impressed by the incredible modernity of ancient Greek philosophical content which still forms a solid epistemological foundation for modern thought in the western world.

Democritus may be considered the founder of the materialist-substantialist concept of the human psyche. He considered that both spirit

Neuroscience-based Cognitive Therapy: New Methods for Assessment, Treatment, and Self-Regulation,
First Edition. Tullio Scrimali.
© 2012 John Wiley & Sons, Ltd. Published 2012 by John Wiley & Sons, Ltd.

and body constitute entities in the same way as do atoms, even though those entities forming the psyche would be more dynamic and ethereal. Therefore, the body is material and the mind is material; however, both are rather transitory, as they require the energy that respiration supplies. To Democritus, with the cessation of breathing and death, both the body and psyche decompose and decay, following an inexorable course of increasing entropy, as we would term it today. To the great philosopher, even cognition occurred through material channels, via interaction between the atoms the material emits and the sensory organs (Diels and Kranz, 1976). We can ultimately identify in Democritus the true originator of the biologist-physicalist-reductionist tradition, one that is clearly present in contemporary neuroscience conceptualizations today.

Some years later, Plato firmly opposed Democritus' view, asserting that the psyche, though also endowed with substantive properties, was made up of different material from that of the body. To the great Athenian philosopher, the psyche was in fact an entity alien to the body, residing there as prisoner yet always aspiring to transcend it. To Plato, the human spirit is also immortal and survives the death of the body. Souls receive reward and punishment in the afterlife according to their behavior during earthly existence, as described in the *Phaedo* (Reale and Antiseri, 1997). Therefore, Plato may be considered the real originator of substantialist theories of the mind and the soul, which find full recognition within the framework of many religious doctrines such as Christianity, Islam, and Buddhism. In addition to this substantialist view on which modern religions were founded, Plato offered a description of the human psyche as made up of three different entities, well represented in the very beautiful metaphor of the charioteer on the chariot pulled by two horses, one black, ugly, angry, and unfaithful, the other white, intelligent, and gentle. To get the chariot to move, the charioteer must mediate between the two very different animals and, more than that, master the black horse, which represents the carnal, emotional, and impulsive part of the mind as opposed to the intellectual part, or the metaphorical white steed.

A truly critical scientific revolution occurred some years later when Aristotle became the first to introduce a functionalist-dualist yet non-substantialist view of the mind–brain connection (Ackrill, 1972–3). Aristotle considered the mind not as an ontological entity distinct from the biological entity of the brain but rather as a function of the latter. Aristotle thus proposed a functionalist approach to the study of the mind that differed profoundly from that of his master Plato, who had arrived, as we saw, at deeming the mind a real substance, distinct from the body and capable of autonomous existence (Plato, 1900–1907).

Aristotle then discerned three components in the human psyche but did so with impressive modernity in referring to biological concepts. In fact, he discussed a vegetative mind tied to basic biological functions, a sensitive mind connected to the perception of reality, and an intellectual or rational mind (Reale and Antiseri, 1997). The extraordinary acuity of this view, which anticipated current advances in neuroscience, seems incredible. Aristotle's "vegetative mind" can be identified in the hypothalamic and limbic systems, and more generally in that which we now define as the autonomic brain, the "sensitive" structural region belongs to human information processing, and finally the intellectual or rational area corresponds to the frontal lobes, responsible for the higher processes of the human mind.

Plato's concept of the mind as an ontological autonomous reality separate from the brain was criticized by other philosophers and subsequently by materialist neuroscientists, who preferred to consider the mind not as both an autonomous and a heteronymous entity but rather as a process that derives from the brain. In the modern era, it was the English philosopher Thomas Hobbes who worked out a first materialist concept of the mind according to which mental processes would be nothing more than manifestations of brain matter activity. Hobbes then tried to move beyond Descartes' dualism by also endowing the mind with those characteristics that Descartes had maintained were essentially material (Hobbes, 1994). Over the course of the nineteenth century, the materialist orientation expressed in Hobbes' philosophy found new life thanks to contributions from the biologist Thomas Henry Huxley, who, in the wake of Charles Darwin's biological research, considering himself both pupil and disciple, proposed limiting the interference of spiritualistic and religious thought within science. From his work in biology, he coined the term "epiphenomenon" for the mind; in ancient Greek, literally something that appears above – in this case in the upper brain (Huxley, 1874).

It seems timely to highlight the modern quality of Huxley's theories. In proposing the concept and term of epiphenomenon, he anticipated present-day positions elaborated in the area of complexity. In this context, in fact, the concept of emergence is considered critical, consistent with the human mind deriving from the phylogenetic and ontogenetic evolution of the brain as a result of its ongoing process of complexity.

Developing his psychodynamic and psychoanalytical theories in the late nineteenth century, Sigmund Freud adopted a partially functionalist concept concerning the problem of the mind: he conceived the mind as a function of the brain while also stressing the inaccessibility and uncontrollability of the unconscious, thereby attributing to it a quasi-substantive character. According to some authors, his positions come close to those of Plato and substantialism (Plato, 1900–1907). However, also in accordance with his medical training, Freud confirmed that the knowledge that scholars then possessed about the brain did not yet allow psychoanalysis to be based on biological foundations. This limitation has largely been overcome today with developments in neuroscience, psychophysiological techniques, and brain imaging.

Erik Kandel, winner of the 2000 Nobel Prize, furthered study and research in the psychodynamic and neuroscience areas, confirming many of the Freudian insights on mind processes (Kandel, 2001). If I may be allowed a humorous aside, I imagine that if it were available in his time, perhaps Freud would have called on a MindLAB Set (the neuroscience device I developed and which will be described in Chapter 9) and used a laptop computer when sitting by the patient's couch in his renowned Viennese office. His disciple Carl Jung partially achieved something approaching this, during the height of the development of the psychodynamic movement, by systematically utilizing a psychogalvanometer, which we may consider to be the precursor to the MindLAB Set. Yet we still had to wait some years for the introduction of the computer into the setting.

A new scientific, reductionist, and materialist approach that was very critical of psychoanalysis developed between the end of the nineteenth and the first part of the twentieth century, with the emergence of the behavioral movement. The behaviorists immediately proposed eliminating the mind concept from scientific discussion in psychology, considering it harmful and superfluous, and instead limiting study to observable behavior only (Pavlov, 1927). From this position, Ivan Pavlov also tried to use rudimentary psychophysiological techniques to obtain objective information about the mind, which may be considered the first point of departure from modern reductionist psychophysiology. Interactionist dualism and its critical lockout of biological reductionism nevertheless returned in the second part of the twentieth century with the contributions of Karl Popper and John Eccles, who again established the principle of mind and brain as different entities. Popper described the existence of three realities: World 1, composed of the entire class of material universes, both inorganic and organic; World 2, including the emotional, perceptive, and creative experience connected to each individual self; and finally World 3, identifying with the cultural reality constructed by humanity over the course of its development. Popper further emphasizes: "biological processes are self-transcendent, producing thoughts, intentions, and a whole world of products from the human mind like language that cannot be understood and explained only in terms of neurophysiological mechanisms" (Popper, 1972). Thus mind became part of World 2 while the brain belonged to World 1 (Popper and Eccles, 1977).

In the search for a new nonreductionist approach, the contribution of Eccles and Popper to the mind–brain problem was a turning point in modern philosophical science and neuroscience, at least with regard to work methods, sanctioning the inescapable need for interdisciplinary collaboration between scholars in various disciplines (physics, epistemology, neuroscience, psychology, psychotherapy, and psychiatry). In any case, it should be stressed that, on a content level, many critical positions today that address the dualist-interactionist paradigm regarding the mind–brain connection must be documented. For example, Gerald Edelman maintains that he has already gone beyond the problem of the conscious, developing a definitive neuronal Darwinist concept (Edelman, 1987), while Francis Crick asserted categorically: "Your joy, your pain, your memories, your ambitions, your sense of personal identity and free will are nothing more than the behavior of the group of countless nerve cells and molecules composing them" (Crick, 1994).

From the 1980s, John Searle's highly monistic position also proved to be well thought-out. Searle considers mental phenomena as a mere epiphenomenon of cerebral processes, developing an epistemological position that defines biological naturalism. He further asserts that dualistic positions, which derive from a Cartesian view, are not compatible with the laws of physics and are inclined to permanently eliminate the problem of the ghost in the machine. In short, to Searle, the mind is nothing more than a brain state (Searle, 2005). Daniel Dennett, scientific philosopher and co-director of the Center for Cognitive Studies at Tufts University, also dedicated himself to the attempt to develop a monistic-type organic mind philosophy that was well rooted in results from scientific research, with particular reference to computer technologies and artificial intelligence. He defines himself as a teleofunctionalist, confirming that he considers the human mind the final and most complex function of the human brain (Dennett, 1991). By contrast, Roger Penrose, a physicist at Oxford University, worked out a new interactionist concept of the mind–brain dynamic, referring to quantum physics studies while criticizing the computational paradigm of the mind (Penrose, 1989).

In his last book, *How the Self Controls Its Brain*, published shortly before his death in 1997, John Eccles devoted himself to the final goal of his long scientific career – to resolve the fundamental problem of mind–brain interaction, namely as immaterial or mental events that can modify material structures or physical neuron structures and vice versa. Nobel Prize winner Eccles agreed with Penrose that it may be possible to overcome such problems with new developments in quantum theory, arriving at the conclusion that some quantum mechanics areas such as probability consist neither of energy nor of matter. Eccles thereby asserted that the mind can be considered a non-material area equivalent to a probability area. The anatomical center of mind–brain interaction would be, according to him, identifiable in the presynaptic vesicle cells (Eccles, 1994).

The controversy continued, however, and John G. Taylor radically criticized the quantum approach to the study of mind–brain interaction, highlighting some excessively simplified formulations from Penrose (Taylor, 1992). Other authors immediately fell prey to a highly discouraging impulse, thinking and asserting publicly that perhaps the mind problem surpassed human observational capacities. In his book *The Problem of Consciousness*, Colin McGinn maintained that the gnosiological limits of our brains are attributable, in his opinion, to the evolutionary dynamic. "If mice and monkeys cannot even conceive of quantum mechanics then perhaps Homo sapiens are not evolved enough to resolve the problem of mind–brain interaction," he argued (McGinn, 1991).

David J. Chalmers echoed McGinn, asserting that any physics theory can arrive at describing, at most, single mental functions, but no current concept could explain how the execution of cognitive activity may generate the subjective experience of the self. However, Chalmers confirmed the necessity and opportunity of working on developing a scientific theory of the consciousness. To this end, he attempted to formulate the concept of a computational matrix consciousness in line with developing quite a complex program on physical computers that could invent a phenomenon similar to a rudimentary mind. After confirming that to date it was still not possible to anticipate the typology and characteristics of an artificial intelligence program capable of originating the simulation of consciousness, he nevertheless concluded that such a theory should still not be rejected. Finally, Chalmers expressed himself in favor of a dualist hypothesis of the mind–brain problem in line with a computational paradigm. The brain would be a physical machine and the mind a program built from information (Chalmers, 1995).

As is evident, we are still some way from an all-encompassing solution to the problem of the mind–brain connection. A unique thread of development is starting to be spun across the various epistemological positions, documentable among the diverse authors working in neuroscience. This direction is summed up in the assertion that it does not seem currently possible to propose any modality for the study of the human brain that considers it as an entity separate from environmental context, historical reality, and cultural background. For this reason, there is a positive documentable convergence between neuroscientists and clinicians today, directed toward identifying a concept of the mind–brain problem that offers promising prospects for the applied as opposed to the speculative arena.

As a conclusion to this summary of the history and development of the mind–brain problem, it is time to put forward my own current position. I emphasize "current," as I consider theories and convictions as completely temporary and transient processes; I strongly adhere to Popper's falsification paradigm.

My personal reflection on this key topic dates from the start of the 1980s (Scrimali and Grimaldi, 1982) and began to fully take shape in the 1990s. An important stage was the publication of my book *Sulle Tracce della Mente* ("On the Trail of the Mind"), where I took a position against the biological reductionism that, until that time, had for the most part characterized the development of neuroscience, proposing instead a constructivist and complex psychophysiology that takes its place in Italian systemic and constructivist cognitivism (Scrimali and Grimaldi, 1991; Guidano, 1987; Guidano and Liotti, 1983). The position that resulted – and that I maintain – is the following: in accordance with Popper's falsification epistemology of scientific research and in line with constructivism, I formulated a concept consistent with the problem of the mind–brain dynamic not having to interest us as clinicians and neuroscientists, except from the viewpoint that our adopted theory yields operational results. Therefore I refuse, a priori, to establish what may ontologically be the mind and whether it may be some entity or substance endowed with autonomous life, although, in truth, that seems rather improbable to me. Regarding the brain, in contrast, I have quite clear ideas: I consider it, in light of the science of complexity, as a complex, nonlinear system that is far from a state of equilibrium, capable of self-organization, and above all constantly developing from one state to another according to an orthogenetically irreversible gradient.

I tend to consider the mind, then, not as a material entity (for this, there are religions that assure us of the presence of a soul inside us and of its immortality) but as a *process* that emerges from the phylogenetic and ontogenetic development of the human brain, or simply the brain. I say "simply the brain" because it is important to me to underline my personal conviction that even animals, and particularly more evolved mammals, have a mind that, though different from our own, is largely based on analogous processes, consistent with less complexity and minimal organization in their brains as well as decreased mass in their frontal lobes. The comparison between humans and animals that many religions have intentionally put forward seems truly pessimistic to me, as they scorn the latter as inferior creatures or absolutely negative entities (typical examples are the snake in Christianity and the dog in Islam). As a neuroscientist as well as a scholar and clinician of the human mind, I would like to reassert my view that among us *Homo sapiens* and the other creatures that inhabit our blue planet, there exists an evolutionary continuum and therefore a continuum of minds.

In his 2008 book *Le Culture degli Altri Animali. È Homo L'Unico Sapiens?* ("The Cultures of Other Animals. Are Humans the Only Sapiens?"), Michelangelo Bisconti asked the very interesting question of whether *Homo* was the only *sapiens* on our planet. His response was negative and constitutes the point of departure for a fascinating report on the cultures of other animals. According to Bisconti, many mammals are capable of accumulating innovative knowledge through each generation and of non-genetically transmitting it to offspring, through a teaching process that passes for parenting, exactly as happens in the species *Homo sapiens*. The difference would consist only in the fact that, not having a written language available to them, direct communication through the parents modeling processes to their offspring is necessary.

I have always found arrogant the concept that considers us to be the only thinking creatures living on this planet, or the only ones to be absolutely endowed with a divine soul. Such a view, in my opinion, is fatalistic and prevents us from understanding humans and from loving animals as they deserve to be loved. I have raised, cared for, and loved many dogs and cats, and I can assure you that they have brilliant souls. They also play, work, fall in love, care for others, cooperate, can be sad, cry, become jealous, and give up all hope. Primates even seem capable of a strong sense of humor, of playing practical jokes and pranks, and of having a lot of fun with them, even behind the backs of us humans (DeWaal, 2009).

If the minds of *sapiens* are processes emerging from the phylogenetic evolution of the human brain, it must be stressed that in reality many different minds emerge over the course of ontogenetic development of every single *Homo sapiens*, as our brains become increasingly more complex, as Jean Piaget demonstrated (1954). A mind that is capable of abstraction, for example, emerges only after adolescence, as a result of reorganization in the frontal areas established in this crucial phase of the life cycle. A never-before-encountered and mysterious paleognostic mind emerges instead during psychotic apophania, taking the unfortunate person that lives through such a process back to a paleological bicameral mind phase (Scrimali, 2008).

A metaphor that is helpful when I use it with patients – though I do not think it rings altogether true, as it is reductionist – is that of computer information systems and programs. I explain that the brain is the hardware and that the mind represents a sort of software. In light of this metaphor, I describe myself then as their Norton (from the name of one of the best-known and most complete anti-virus software packages), able to identify viruses in the human mind that enter through the network of social interactions, especially via parents during dysfunctional parenting (not through the internet in this case!). After identifying viruses, worms, and Trojan horses in their brains (plans, beliefs, and dysfunctional internal operational models), I move on to reprogramming the mind for positive and developed functioning. Naturally, things do not occur exactly like that, and psychotherapy is among the most complex and sophisticated of intervention methods in which emotional and relational variables play a vital role.

In clinical intervention with patients afflicted with mental disorders and in research in the context of clinical psychophysiology, the two areas in which I have been active for my whole career, I maintain that, in any case, new discoveries in neuroscience must be utilized, whether for psychodiagnostic or therapeutic purposes, and I therefore propose a psychodiagnostic tool and techniques for emotional self-regulation based on the recording of biological feedback from psychophysiological parameters such as psychofeedback and Biofeedback-Based Mindfulness. In conclusion, I consider adopting clinical psychophysiological techniques as one of the methodologies able to achieve a process of integration between mind and brain. The data supplied with regard to dynamic conditions of cerebral structures allow the mind to acquire new information and to subsequently develop capabilities never before encountered. Such competence entails the emergence of innovative attitudes and a more integrated balance that are intrapsychic as well as relational and social.

3

Motor Theories of Mind and a Complex Biocybernetic Model in Neuroscience

The epistemology of most of the neurosciences has developed along a path involving the progressive abandonment of associative and sensory concepts of the mind in favor of adopting motor theories and a complex biocybernetic model. Since the second half of the 1980s, I have dedicated myself to developing a constructivist psychophysiology to be incorporated into the clinical foundation of Italian cognitivism. This is primarily oriented, with Guidano, Liotti, and Perris, to a constructivist, developmental, and systemic focus, defining a frame of reference that may be summarized in the following points (Guidano and Liotti, 1983; Guidano, 1987; Perris, 1989; Scrimali and Grimaldi, 1982; 1991, 2003; Scrimali, 2008):

- Human beings are not reactive but proactive with respect to their environment.
- A wide range of existing mind processes that operate inherently, and therefore are not conscious, constitute a powerful form of cognition.
- Personal human experiences and their development are strictly individual and completely unique self-organizational processes, and self-organizational patterns show a strong tendency toward self-maintenance.
- Although self-referential, organizational patterns of the self reflect the influence of relational and social systems in their developmental history and active functional patterns.

A crucial transformation in the field of cognitive psychology was documented in the second half of the 1960s with the contributions of Miller,

Neuroscience-based Cognitive Therapy: New Methods for Assessment, Treatment, and Self-Regulation, First Edition. Tullio Scrimali.
© 2012 John Wiley & Sons, Ltd. Published 2012 by John Wiley & Sons, Ltd.

Galanter, and Pribram, now included in the historic *Plans and the Struc-ture of Behavior* (1960). These three authors clearly asserted that, between stimulus and behavioral or psychophysiological response, there was much more than could be explained by a simple process of associations. Accord-ing to this model, a process of central origin moderates all nervous system inputs. In fact, sensory receptors are active, independent of any stimulus deriving from the environment, and efferent nerve fibers constantly mod-ulate their processes, the most paradigmatic example being that of stretch receptors present in the muscles. Originating in the motor neurons, efferent fibers (gamma fibers) control the degree of extension of muscle spindles. Therefore, the afferent message pattern depends on the degree of muscular extension as well as on the control that the central nerve structures exert on the receptor. In other words, in order to determine the actual degree of muscle spindle extension from inputs external to the body, the nervous system must integrate information about the level of control that the CNS itself exerts on the muscle spindles. Fundamentally, the brain is therefore relying not on a passive interpretation of inputs, but rather on information entering the mind's neuronal structures, which is always the result of eval-uating and comparing external data and spontaneous patterns of activity inside the body.

Miller, Galanter, and Pribram thus replaced the reflex arc concept with that of the TOTE unit. From the words "test, operate, test, and exit," TOTE describes an operational unit in which any nerve process, whether focused on the transfer of energy or information, or on exerting control, includes two processors: one that can conduct a test and the other programmed to carry out operational activity. The unit is therefore made up of both an op-erational and a verification element, introducing into psychophysiology the cybernetic hypothesis, according to which one of the fundamental mecha-nisms in nervous system functioning is feedback. The operational activity is thereby inseparably tied to information processing. The mechanism trig-gers where there is incongruence, that is, any discrepancy between internal models and external stimulation patterns, and terminates with congruence. Therefore, each piece of information coming from outside the nervous sys-tem acts not on the basis of its energy but on that of its informational content. This information takes on specific characteristics, due not so much to its intrinsic properties as to the greater meaning it acquires in relation to the internal condition of the nervous system itself.

Miller and colleagues then went on to develop motor theories of the mind in which the nervous system would function not as a passive receptor and associator of sensory data but, on the contrary, as an active organizer and selector of reality. Motor theories of the mind are the specific development in constructivist epistemology within the scope of neurophysiology that allowed the formation of a new scenario, based no longer on the sensory or reflexological study of the human brain but rather on a biocybernetic, systemic, and procedural one. Where the human mind is motor and proactive, as opposed to sensory and reactive, it seems clear that reality is not passively registered but structured with available heuristic factors that rely on mind programs, in part innate and in part built during the development and learning process. A subject regarding the constructivist and motor orientation of the mind in psychophysiology that has provided an important contribution is the conception and explanation of emotional phenomenology.

Advances in the cognitivist sphere have demonstrated that the qualitative connotation of emotional factors depends primarily on the cognitive processing of somatic feedback and the environmental situation. I refer to the theory of Schachter and Singer, constructed from a now famous experiment. The conclusions reached by these authors were that, given a physiological state of activation for which an individual may not have an immediate explanation, they will label this state and describe their feelings in terms of the knowledge available to them (Schachter and Singer, 1962). As is clear, Schachter and Singer introduced the element of cognitive evaluation of somatic data.

We must nevertheless observe that cognitive evaluation interferes not only with decoding arousal but with the interpretation of stimuli as well (Lindsay and Norman, 1977). In fact, Pribram formulated the key concept that every perceptual stimulus coming from the environment does not provoke somatic modifications per se, but determines their extent and quality as they derive from the cognitive processes' interpretation of the situation, guided by memory (Pribram, 1971). This system attaches the significance of information to the stimulus, and the significance of the final result of a complex cognitive evaluation to the response. From this viewpoint, we can also understand how the sudden absence of a stimulus, and therefore a piece of information, is often received as information in the absence of other information. This concept highlights how the activation of somatic effectors is not a direct consequence of environmental stimulation but the effect and result of processing informational content from the situational stimulus (Leventhal, 1979).

Quite a lot of experimental data supported this theory (Sokolov, 1963; Averill, 1980; Lang, 1979), some of which came from my laboratory. In one of these experiments conducted by my work group, I administered to 8 subjects (6th-year medical students and doctors, 4 males and 4 females) 10 unpleasant acoustic stimuli in a frequency envelope, recording the endosomatic EDA (electrodermal potential).

The instructions provided to subjects were the following:

> "We will now have you listen to some sounds that will perhaps be annoying but certainly not harmful to your ears."

At the end of the experiment, subjects were asked to describe the tones they heard by selecting one of the following definitions:

1. all unpleasant but not unbearable;
2. all unpleasant and difficult to tolerate;
3. all unpleasant at the beginning but then quite tolerable.

The orienting response (Figure 3.1a) is defined as that characterized by decreased positive electrodermal potential (the recording needle swings to the left). and the defensive response (Figure 3.1b) as that where an increased positive potential is shown (the needle swings to the right). In our experiment we observed significant agreement between subjective evaluation of the stimulus and psychophysiological response modality. When the subject evaluated the stimulus as detrimental, we recorded a defensive reflex, while when categorizing the stimulus as simply unpleasant, the subject experienced an orienting response.

The data just described fits well into a constructivist point of view. Emotional activation, deriving from analog acquisition of real data, shown in the electrodermal response is categorized by the explicit knowledge system, which processes it serially and expresses it in digital and declarative terms. From the time that the real data acquisition system, according to a tacit and unconscious modality, continuously and quickly processes an enormous amount of data, provoking incessant psychobiological variations (arousal, orientation, defense), the explicit knowledge system constantly faces the need to decipher these emotional variations and factor them into a declarative and narrative dimension. This processing occurs within the scope of available theories based on the general orientation of each individual person's knowledge organization. Thus, an arousal reaction is categorized as threatening and harmful to the security of the self where the general orientation of knowledge is based on a phobic

Figure 3.1 An experiment to elicit orienting responses (3.1a) and defensive responses (3.1b).

criterion. The subject who is inclined to gambling, in contrast, constantly seeks an arousal reaction that they would categorize as that which makes more sense to their existence.

Specific clinical implications regarding theory and assessment derive from such a conception of emotional phenomenology. From one point of view, such a model of the emotive dynamic allows us to explain the experimental data, also documented in my laboratory, concerning the dissociation that is often found in subjective evaluation of the anxious state obtained via test-based tools such as the State-Trait Anxiety Inventory (Spielberger, Gorsuch, and Lushene, 1970), and the degree of nerve and biochemical arousal evaluated via psychophysiological parameters such as EDA and thermal activation index (Scrimali and Grimaldi, 1991).

In fact, we encounter cases where the patient describes themselves as having a high level of anxiety without that having any correlation to the psychophysiological level measured; and vice versa, cases in which intense nervous activation is not considered in the subjective evaluation. In the first situation, we would find a redundant cognitive process in line with psychophysiological and biochemical activation, and in the second we would instead find elevated arousal that the patient does not categorize as anxiety. The obvious need for a complex and integrated multifactor assessment of the emotional problem derives from this observation.

On the therapy side, the observation that it can act at different levels and with diverse modalities derives from the model illustrated. A therapy based on an anti-anxiety psychotropic drug influences, for example, the activity of limbic structures as well as the psychophysiological arousal that the psychoactive drug mediates (Costa *et al.*, 1983). Psychotherapy acts alternatively and primarily on the cognitive structures (Emery, Hollon, and Bedrosian, 1981). The rewriting of cognitive programs and restructuring of belief systems that are also achieved via rebalancing the psychophysiological condition are pursued systematically in cognitive psychotherapy. In this therapeutic context, it seems to me that a valid operative synthesis between psychophysiological, psychopathological, and psychotherapeutic models is established.

Adoption of the constructivist orientation and motor theories of the mind permitted me to achieve a revolution in schizophrenia psychopathology, for which I developed a new model called Entropy of Mind (see Chapter 4). The innovation largely relates to themes of delusional hallucination (Scrimali, 2008). When reflecting on this topic, in fact, given that the information reaches specific visual or acoustic sensory areas, the largest part coming from within the nervous system itself, it appears clear that hallucination is made up of information present in the patient's brain and that the patient does not recognize it as such, but considers it instead a product of the outside world. Abandoning the rationalistic standpoint to adopt a constructivist view, the delusion immediately appears to be a legitimate construct of reality that finds full explanation in light of the personal and family history of the subject and their narrative (Scrimali, 2008).

4

Complexity, Chaos, and Dynamical Systems

4.1 Introduction

A very important transition occurred during the 1980s in the field of CT, from a standard associative and rationalistic approach to constructivism and motor theories of the mind (Mahoney, 1991; Guidano, 1987). I enthusiastically participated in this revolution, working together with Michael Mahoney and Vittorio Guidano. From the second half of the 1990s to today a second revolution has taken place in neuroscience and CT. This last revolution has been based on complexity, chaos, and nonlinear dynamical systems (Chamberlain and Butz, 1998).

4.2 Complexity

The most important theorist of complexity is today considered to be Edgar Morin. His ongoing reflections seem to provide an ideal response to the present historical phase in human development, where everything is becoming more chaotic and less linear. The enormous amount of information in our world means that every one of us faces a very difficult challenge in negotiating a path between order and disorder, and in the way we organize and utilize new knowledge. According to Morin (2008):

> A well-made head is one that is apt to organize knowledge in such a way as to avoid its stagnant accumulation. Every piece of information is a translation and simultaneously a reconstruction of representations, ideas, theories, and

Neuroscience-based Cognitive Therapy: New Methods for Assessment, Treatment, and Self-Regulation, First Edition. Tullio Scrimali.
© 2012 John Wiley & Sons, Ltd. Published 2012 by John Wiley & Sons, Ltd.

discourse (from signals, signs, and symbols). The process is circular and it transitions from separation to connection, from connection to separation, and then, from analysis to synthesis and from synthesis to analysis.

In addition to the in-depth description of the well-made head, we are in debt to Morin for his marvelous metaphor of complexity. The distinguished French author points out that, in its Latin root, "complex" means woven like fabric. In fabric, every single thread in the weave maintains its individuality but, intertwining with others, also forms a new structure, the fabric itself.

A first epistemology of complexity was invented, or intuited at least, by ancient Greek philosophers, in particular the great Heraclitus of Ephesus, who can rightfully be considered the first author in western culture to formulate and clearly express the basic principles of a dynamic view articulated from reality and existence (Heraclitus, 1954). In fact, Heraclitus identified in change and evolution the distinctive character of complex systems. He created this wonderful image: "Everything flows and nothing stays. . . You can't step twice into the same river." It is a profound insight that fully captures the dynamism of reality and, at the same time, it offers the appearance of phenomenic stability to the naive mind of *sapiens*, who is spurred on by order, expectation, and permanence. Heraclitus beautifully describes the crisscrossing of diverse elements in the phenomenon of life with his iconic assertion that "one dies in life and lives in death," pointing out that parts of our bodies die daily in order to make life possible. For that matter, death is caused by the progressive change and compromise in the same processes that generate life.

Ex morte vita! In the training room at the University of Catania's Department of Anatomy, this was an inscription that stood out, both encouraging and admonishing us. I remember that it was this particular phrase that helped me when, barely in my twenties, I had to confront the horror of being in a room with many slabs on which our fellow *sapiens* of all ages were lying and whom we students, still fresh from adolescence and literally brimming with life, had to cut, dissect, and destroy in order to one day understand as doctors, and so learn to help our patients. When strength was about to abandon me and my vision was blurring, and when scalpels trembled a little too much in my faltering hands, I repeated to myself: *Ex morte vita!* I comforted myself that way and moved forward, but it was an experience that touched me deeply. From death comes life, then, but life is necessarily tied to death, as I better understood when I studied the phenomenon of carcinogenesis. Cancer is a disease in which the cells seem to have found unrestrained vitality, reproducing tumultuously while refusing to die, and it is this very surplus of life that becomes pathology and destroys the living system, along with the cancer cells themselves.

What, though, are the fundamental axioms of complex systems science, and how do they correlate with the information paradigm that, as I've already mentioned, seems to constitute a critical topic in current science? Before moving on to summarize the basic principles of the epistemology of complexity, I would, however, like to quote some words from Heraclitus that still seem far-reaching although they were written about 2,500 years ago.

> Conflict is the father of all things.
> That which is in opposition is reconciled and the most beautiful harmony derives from things that are different.
> Everything is generated through contrast.
> Ignorant men do not understand that what is different agrees with itself: harmony derives from opposites.
> One thing derives from all things and from one thing, all others.

In contemporary writings on complexity one important component is the criticism of determinism and the proposal of a probabilistic logic in which uncertainty constitutes the basic variable. Where, in their classic formulation, the laws of physics describe an idealized, symmetrical, stable, and foreseeable world, Prigogine's interest focuses on a world that is considered unstable, uncertain, and capable of evolution (Prigogine, 1980). An understanding of chaotic systems can therefore be pursued only in probabilistic and not deterministic terms (Prigogine, 1996).

The fundamental dimension of irreversibility develops from probability, starting from classic thermodynamics and, in particular, from Clausius' second principle, according to which the entropy of the universe constantly increases toward a maximum. The continuous increment in entropy therefore delineates an arrow in time, an irreversible directionality of dynamic processes from the past to the future. The nonlinear physics of dynamical systems is thus the physics of chaos, unstable processes, probabilistic behaviors, and multiple choices.

4.3 Chaos Theory

The term "chaos" has been, for a long time, synonymous with something mythic and not scientific. But a science of chaos does exist and has many implications today for psychology, psychiatry, clinical psychology, and psychotherapy (Chamberlain and Butz, 1998). Chaos theory was born at the beginning of the twentieth century, thanks to the work of the French mathematician Henri Poincaré (Poincaré, 1904). Chaos should be seen not as an absence of order, but as the presence of a great amount of information. The topics coming from chaos theory that have most implications for neuroscience-based CT are mainly dynamical and nonlinear systems theory and self-organization theory (Strogatz, 1994).

Chaos theory can be considered an epistemology based on the idea that reality is not the realm of order, stability, and equilibrium but rather the field of irregularity, disorder, and spontaneous changes. The epistemology of chaos finds a place in many different disciplines, such as mathematics, physics chemistry, engineering, and biology. Some applications of chaos theory can be found in meteorology, medicine, and psychology. We will see, as we go on, that psychology, psychiatry, and psychotherapy can be considered the area in which chaos theory can find one of its most useful applications.

4.4 Complex Systems

A complex system is composed of many different and rather heterogeneous elements that interact in terms of nonlinearity. Complex systems are usually open systems, able to exchange matter and energy with the exterior world. Due to this constant flux, complex open systems are able to remain unchanged and, over time, retain a constant level of entropy as reconstruction and reorganization of structures compensates for their continuous degradation.

It would seem useful at this point to insert a summary of the most important characteristics of a complex system; a veritable rulebook, if you will.

1. Complex systems include a large number of elements.
2. The elements must be able to interact and the interaction must not be purely physical but must also involve information transfer.
3. Interactions appears quite active in the sense that each element influences a certain number of other elements in the system.
4. Interactions are nonlinear. This means that a small action can yield results of great magnitude. The image of the beat of a butterfly's wing that creates a tornado after complex interactions is well known.
5. Interaction must occur normally at short range, although long-range interactions are possible through other mediating components of the system.

6. Recursive circuits exist in each element.
7. Complex systems are open systems (closed systems cannot be complex, just complicated). Complex systems acquire matter, energy, and information.
8. Complex systems operate in self-organizational conditions and are far from being in equilibrium.
9. Complex systems have a history. This means that they evolve over time and that their past conditions are responsible for their present ones. Evolution occurs according to the law of irreversibility. Every state condition always creates a new balance over time, which proceeds unidirectionally from the past to the future. A complex system may evolve toward more organized conditions (a progressive shift) or collapse into states of lesser evolution (a regressive shift). However, it can never return to the exact same conditions as those that preceded it. This aspect differentiates complex from noncomplex physical systems quite clearly. Changes that intervene in noncomplex physical systems are reversible and those that intervene in complex systems are irreversible.
10. Each single element of the system is unaware of the behavior of the entire system.

Based on these points, it appears evident that the nervous system itself can be considered a complex system, as it is acknowledged that the nervous system exhibits all the characteristics of a structure of this type. Many authors even consider the nervous system of *sapiens* the most complex system known to us in the universe.

Another very important aspect of complex systems theory is that of autopoiesis, developed and proposed from the 1970s by Maturana and Varela (1980). These two great authors introduced this concept to describe a system that continuously redefined the identity of self through ceaseless states of change, as when it was able to maintain itself in disequilibrium while constantly rebuilding and re-forming itself over the complete life cycle. The autopoietic system is even capable of reproducing itself. Overall, an autopoietic system can thus be described as one characterized by a perpetually active series of building, transformational, and destructive processes, which, maintained in dynamic balance, ceaselessly support and regenerate the system itself. An autopoietic system draws energy and material from the environment, and releases degraded energy and waste. Therefore, autopoietic systems can exist through the constant extraction of energy and matter from their environment.

A very important corollary is that an autopoietic system is a living one or, if you prefer, that the living being is an autopoietic system. In practice, the distinct criterion for life, according to the autopoietic principle, is the maintenance of its own organization, and the capacity for reproduction and evolution. Any system that has such characteristics can to all intents and purposes be called a living being (Maturana and Varela, 1980). The logic of autopoiesis thus moves neuroscientific research and reflection away from the logic of the computer and information systems in order to progressively move it closer to the logic of complexity. Indeed, the computer is not only not autopoietic but, on the contrary, typically appears to be an allopoietic system, in the sense that it is not able to maintain, evolve, or reproduce itself.

4.5 From Complexity to a Neuroscience-based Cognitive Therapy

A new orientation in contemporary neuroscience is developing from the theories of complexity, one that introduces the concept of chaos into the study of the brain. Skarda and Freeman stress how it may be possible to initiate a valuable new phase in neuroscience by introducing new approaches into the study of the human brain, such as that of the theory of dynamic nonlinear systems, theories of the self, and theories of chaos (Skarda and Freeman, 1990). Such new and compelling concepts seem to provide a glimpse into some remarkable progress in understanding the functioning of the human brain, definitively archiving the metaphor of the information systems era. The new, complex approach to neuroscience naturally opens a debate with reductionist orientations, projecting us toward a new, complex science of the brain (Izhikevich, 2007).

From the theory of chaos in neuroscience, a theory of chaos in psychiatry is then derived (Skarda and Freeman, 1990). I personally created a complex model of schizophrenia, based on the concept of dynamic nonlinear systems, and which I termed Entropy of Mind (Scrimali, 2008). Also very interesting is the formulation of Perna and Masterpasqua regarding two large systems in the brain that continually interact; one is chaotic and probabilistic, while the other is ordered and deterministic (Perna and Masterpasqua, 1997). The former is characterized by a logic of associative functioning that is synthetic and syncretic; the second is tied to formal and logical sequential processes. From the perspective of entropy (understood in terms of an informative indeterminacy), the chaotic and probabilistic system is one of high entropy, while the ordered and deterministic system appears to continually create order from disorder; thus it is a teleological system based on the goal of systematically reducing indeterminacy and, therefore, entropy. In a condition of good integration, the two systems function in perfect harmony; in a pathological state, however, a discrepancy is created between environmental pressures with an excessive input of information and the capacity of the ordered and deterministic system to lower the level of entropy. In this way, the comprehensive level of entropy begins to grow dangerously. The system can no longer maintain the prior state of dynamic equilibrium and must implement a transition toward a new condition, characterized by a different set-up for the information processing systems. This new set-up may be constituted by the schizophrenic condition. According to Perna and Masterpasqua, in schizophrenia the level of entropy and chaos of the entire nervous system increases massively. This increase of disorder is reflected in the environmental niche, which also enters a condition of turbulence, with negative repercussions on the patient, creating a vicious circle that continually increases entropy.

The formulation of Perna and Masterpasqua can be easily set alongside an idea of Guidano (1991) regarding the two processes of the mind: experience (a chaotic and probabilistic process) and explanation (an ordered and deterministic process). The formulation also finds a basis in much psychophysiological data describing the two different systems of elaboration present in the CNS that are altered by the condition of schizophrenia.

Some recent experimental research has furnished data that support the hypothesis that schizophrenia can be considered a condition of high entropy and chaos of the mind. Paulus and Braff (2003) have conducted experimental research using chaos theory in order to quantify the level of entropy of the CNSs of schizophrenic patients. These authors then compared their results to a healthy control group. The working hypothesis that constituted the basis of the research is linked to a conception in which the schizophrenic condition is considered to be a state of complex disorganization of the entire nervous system, rather than a simple movement toward a less evolved and integrated state. The data that emerged from this research demonstrated a higher average level of entropy in schizophrenic patients than in the control group. This research represents one of the first attempts to apply nonlinear analytical methods to the condition of the CNS as compared to the normal measures of performance and integration of classical neuropsychology.

Another experimental contribution has been proposed by Tschacher and Scheier (1995), based on research that monitored the clinical condition of a group of schizophrenic patients for 200 or more consecutive days. Methods of nonlinear dynamic analysis were applied to the variations in the symptomatic condition. These authors demonstrated, with their sample group, that a significant majority of the patients showed a chaotic trend rather than a linear evolution in their symptomatic situations. Research on schizophrenia inspired by chaos theory and nonlinear dynamic systems is in its infancy, but it appears promising. The aim of the therapeutical, integrated protocol that I created and called "negative entropy" is to lower the entropy and to better organize information in the brain of psychotic patients.

Another major advantage to be gained from introducing into psychiatry the theory of complex systems is that it will enable us to positively cope with the negative theory of chronicity. If the brain is a complex system, it can always develop new conditions if we give it the chance, thanks to therapy. Following the seminal work of Carlo Perris (Perris, 1989), I eliminated from my vocabulary (and from that of my students and my clinical staff) the term "chronic patient" in favor of the name "difficult patient."

To finish, according to complex systems theory, we can today consider the therapeutical process not just as deterministic but also as stochastic. This means that when change in the mind of patients is initiated, thanks to therapy, we cannot be sure of the direction and extension of the changes that will be produced.

5

Modular and Gradiental Brain, Coalitional Mind

5.1 Introduction

In the dynamic context of neuroscience which is now in full development, new theories on the functioning of the mind and the most recent descriptions of the brain hold a remarkable degree of relevance. These theories have been developed primarily based on advances in morphological and functional imaging techniques of the nervous system, as well as on recordings of psychophysiological parameters correlating with the peripheral nervous system. In this chapter, I will describe a theoretical frame of reference I have developed over the course of the last decade, one that adopts the concept of a modular brain and coalitional mind. Such a conception, informed by my background in cognitivism, constructivism, and complexity, considers the brain a dynamic, nonlinear system that is far from being in equilibrium, and the mind a coalition of processes that emerge progressively over the course of the life cycle from the continuous evolution of the brain itself (Guidano and Liotti 1983; Mahoney, 1991; Freeman, 1992; Scrimali and Grimaldi, 2001).

The first formulation of a modular model of the brain is found in Freud. In fact, the human mind system was described in psychodynamic theory as organized into diverse entities, interrelating in dynamic and often conflicting terms (id, ego, superego). Freud's model of the psyche thus represents a first, admirable attempt at organically describing the structure and functions of the mind, although, in light of its being a science-based approach at the end of the nineteenth century, it is still founded predominantly on

Neuroscience-based Cognitive Therapy: New Methods for Assessment, Treatment, and Self-Regulation, First Edition. Tullio Scrimali.
© 2012 John Wiley & Sons, Ltd. Published 2012 by John Wiley & Sons, Ltd.

energy-type themes, as articulated within Freud's theory of libido (Freud, 1989). Within the scope of an 1895 psychology in *The Interpretation of Dreams*, Freud puts forward a series of interesting new perspectives regarding the relationships between emotion and thought. After focusing his attention on some mechanisms of the psyche based on energy, the great Viennese author sheds some light on cognitive processes. Subsequent scholars such as Adler and Rapaport and, more recently, clinical cognitivist authors, have contributed more extensively to this conceptualization (Adler, 1979; Rapaport, 1971; Guidano and Liotti, 1983).

From my high school days I have studied and always admired the work of Freud and Jung, and the psychodynamic movement more generally. I was convinced from the time I became a medical student that psychodynamic theory and development in the psychoanalytic movement were irretrievably tied to nineteenth-century science, and therefore already outmoded and anachronistic in the second half of the twentieth century. This juvenile embrace of such a position guided me toward my first studies at the University of Catania Institute of Physiology's neuroscience laboratory, and then later when specializing in clinical psychiatry with a specific focus on behavioralism. In those years of the late 1970s and early 1980s, my acquaintance with Paolo Pancheri and encounter with biofeedback was the perfect development, as it allowed me to merge neuroscience, psychophysiology, and psychotherapy (Pancheri, 1979; Scrimali and Grimaldi, 1982).

Over the following years I grew tired of behavioral psychology and psychotherapy that seemed to deny the study of the mind. Instead I wanted to focus my efforts on the mind, and I took a profound interest in information systems and standard cognitivism until a pivotal encounter with Guidano and Liotti in the first half of the 1980s, and the consequent adoption of a constructivist and evolutionist view. Over the course of the 1990s, I became progressively more interested in theories of complexity and the logic of dynamic nonlinear systems. My teaching in clinical psychology at Kore University's Department of Psychology from 2003 was informed by the logic of complex systems. I trained hundreds of psychology students at Kore University in Enna, introducing them to a view that was not only more psychodynamic but also complex, and where neuroscience played an important role.

As I complete the current volume, Massimo Ammaniti is clearly and concisely advocating considering psychoanalysis in the postmodern context solely as a cultural movement as opposed to a scientific one, and recognizing it is less as a clinical orientation that would be capable of responding to the complex requirements of treatment in today's world (Ammaniti, 2009). Nevertheless, some of Freud's contributions are still crucial, such as the study of the unconscious dimension of the mind; the description of a mental system composed of multiverse minds (unconscious, ego, superego); the analysis of the therapeutic bond; and the dynamics of transference and countertransference that are prolifically confirmed today in the theory of attachment and in that of interpersonal relational cycles exhibited by patients, according to the view of Safran and Muran (2000).

I progressively adopted and developed a systemic, procedural, and dynamic view of the human psyche, arriving at proposing a *second psychodynamic model* as a complex movement in clinical psychology, psychiatry, and psychotherapy that offers a dynamic concept of the mind (www.secondapsicodinamica.org). The first psychodynamic was developed at the end of the nineteenth and in the first half of the twentieth century, founded on a theory of energy. The second psychodynamic, by contrast, ties to information, to a motor, biocybernetic, and ecological view of the mind and is informed by theories of complexity. This is similar to what happened with the advent of the second cybernetics, after the development of the first.

I therefore describe a second psychodynamic model in the epistemological, scientific, and clinical movement that considers the human mind and, more generally, the mind of mammals (with particular reference to primates), as a dynamic, nonlinear, and complex process that emerges from the brain, studied and described in light of the logic of dynamic nonlinear systems. In this view, evolutionism occupies a relevant role, both biological and cultural, as does a profoundly lay concept of science and research. With the second psychodynamic model in sociology and politics, I propose a pluralistic view and a social, cooperative, and joint concept of government. A critical topic in the second psychodynamic model aligns with the theories of complexity and is built from ecology, no longer just for the mind but also, and above all, for the environment (Bateson, 1979; Morin, 2008).

5.2 The Modular and Gradiental Brain

The view of the modular brain that I adopted and have developed over the last ten years consists of considering the brain as composed of many information processing systems and the mind as a coalition of multiple processes that are articulated on different levels. I was inspired by the work of Fodor, Ornstein, and Goldberg in developing a similar conception.

Jerry Fodor hypothesized that every human is equipped with multiple minds, each specialized for different purposes and each characterized by its own functional dynamic, by a different evolutionary significance, and by a unique history of development (Fodor, 1983). On the other hand, Robert Ornstein developed the interesting concept of mind in place. According to his conception, based on environmental demands in each instance, that module within the coalition of specialized modules which is the most suited to carrying out the requested task is activated. If environmental contingencies are modified and the temporarily active mind does not prove the one best placed to carry out the requested task, it is remanded to backup and a more suitable module is activated in its place.

Goldberg identified and described the cortical components of the human nervous system as gradiental (Goldberg, 2001). While the most obsolete structures of the human brain, such as the thalamic structures, exhibit an apparent modular organization, the more recent ones, typically the cerebral cortex, appear to be the key players in very complex self-organizational processes based on a probability dynamic connected to the flow of information coming to a certain extent from the external world. Goldberg recharacterized that modular organization as determined on a genetic basis and characterized by more linear, deterministic, and modular functioning. On the contrary, the gradiental cortical brain should be considered less linear, more probabilistic and chaotic, as it creates its own balance based on evolutionary stochastic processes that are the optimal response to a different evolutionary level (Goldberg, 2001). Reptiles and birds exhibit a predominantly modular brain organization (thus the common insult "birdbrain" could be paraphrased more elegantly and accurately as "you have a largely modular brain"), and mammals, equipped with a remarkable cerebral cortex apparatus, instead appear largely dominated by teleonomic dynamics, founded on self-organizational processes that activate based on the flow of information coming from the environment. In humans, the brain has an immense cortex and therefore exhibits the most unpredictable and evolutionary dynamic according to its stochastic orientation.

Complementing that of the modular and gradiental organization of mammals' brains, a concept I'd like to introduce involves the coalitional and decentralized control of cerebral processes. A decentralized control and regulation system is one that each cerebral module contains and activates inside itself. On the other hand, the coalitional control process is that which unites the diverse decentralized control processes into a coalition of systems that work coherently.

An example of coalitional and decentralized control that comes to mind, and drawn from my study of the classics, is that which was first achieved with enormous success by the Romans. Let us begin with the motto *unus ex pluribus* ("one from many") that best represents coalitional logic. In other words, it is unity achieved through respect for multiplicity and the integration of diversity. The Roman Empire imposed few, though ironclad, rules concerning military and defense policy, the scrupulous payment of taxes, and the inflexible application of Roman law, yet it was extremely protective of civil rights in a manner quite advanced for the period. Each population that formed part of the empire was nevertheless left free to maintain its own peripheral governmental structure with its own religion, laws, practices, and customs.

Truly complex, the Roman imperial system functioned well, as does the human brain when the dynamic of decentralized and coalitional control is articulated positively. In schizophrenia, or better yet, in Entropy of Mind, coalitional processes get involved, generating disorder and increased entropy, exactly as happened during the decline of the Roman Empire when the various local governing bodies began attempting to eliminate the emperor from coalitional control, provoking revolts, secessions, and uprisings that, in the end, led to a slow but inexorable decline.

A modular description of the human brain was proposed in anatomical-functional terms by Luria, who hypothesized that the CNS may be a complex functional system within which various areas and levels operate contemporaneously and synergistically, each with a specific role (Luria, 1973). In the context of such a complex anatomical and functional system, it is possible to first identify a structure dedicated to maintaining and regulating the biological homeostasis of the entire body that includes the brainstem, reticular formation, the most obsolete parts of the limbic cortex, and the hypothalamus. This structure is described as the *vital nervous system*. Yet another system is charged with the development, control, and integration of motor behavior and is described as *myostatic*. This system possesses a sophisticated, dedicated, decentralized control unit that is the cerebellum. Finally, a complex structure that is particularly evolved in humans is the *pro mundo system*, dedicated to fostering and managing the exchange of information and actions. This system is responsible for connecting to the external world, and therefore for relationships with the environment and peers. The following form a part of the pro mundo system:

- a system connected to the sensory receptors, which receives, decodes, and, in the short term, stores information coming from the outside world. The cortical centers of such a system are largely distributed throughout the occipital lobe (with particular reference to visual information), the temporal lobe (aural information), and parietal lobe (somatic sensitivity);
- a system of voluntary motion, whose principal cortical area was identified in the prerolandic sulcus; and
- a system located in the frontal and prefrontal lobes, charged with unifying strategic planning and long-term storage of knowledge processes. The higher processes of the mind are headquartered in this last system.

Lesions in the vital system, morphological or functional alterations in the sensory system, and dysfunctions in the motor system do not significantly compromise the higher functions of the mind such as self-consciousness, a sense of personal identity, and formulation of action plans and strategies.

The frontal lobes are a gradiental system rather than a modular one. From the phylogenetic viewpoint, the remarkable development of the frontal lobes constitutes a very recent achievement unique to *Homo sapiens*. These lobes maintain close connections with the sensory cortex, the motor cortex, and the language areas, but their processes are not directly tied to the acquisition of sensory information or motor processes, such as movement and simple interaction with the environment.

Lesions on the frontal lobes do not provoke substantial permanent alterations in memory or short-term orientation with the environment. No deficit in perception, language, or even logic operations occurs following such lesions. Upon a more in-depth examination, we can, however, observe that patients with these lesions are not able to develop long-term plans. Their conduct, in fact, shows they are having difficulty with strategically planning their behavior and staying focused on the here and now, and their conduct includes implementing recursive tactics that do not adapt to changing scenarios, environments, or logic. We can observe an obvious example of such a characteristic in the behavior of patients afflicted with neurological lesions on the frontal lobes when they are administered the Wisconsin Card Sorting Test (Psychological Assessment Resources, 2003). The patient must sort cards drawn from a deck of stimulus cards. Sorting is on the basis of different criteria such as shape, color, and number. The patient must get ten sorts for each criterion. Patients with lesions on the frontal lobes show perseveration, that is, the patient continues to use the same criterion even after being informed that the sort is incorrect. We see this same perseverative behavior in schizophrenic patients on the Wisconsin Card Sorting Test.

The frontal lobes exhibit notable functional synergy with the limbic system formations, and particularly with the amygdala, thereby appearing to be closely connected to the emotional dimension as well. The human brain's limbic system primarily includes the modular structures of the thalamus, amygdala, hippocampus, and hypothalamus. The hemispheric functional specialization process seems especially evidenced in the frontal lobes. In right-handed subjects, the left hemisphere specializes in semantic and language-based processes, while the right hemisphere specializes in spatial decoding processes and largely oversees emotional phenomena.

Supplementing Luria's model, I will report some considerations on important aspects of cerebral functioning that have been the focus of recent developments in contemporary neuroscience. They concern the concepts of both the emotional and social brains, as well as the description of the morphological and, more importantly, primarily functional organization of the central and peripheral, sympathetic and parasympathetic nervous systems.

5.3 The Social Brain

In recent years conceptual work on cooperative, relational, and social processes was advanced particularly by an important contribution from the development of an ethological dimension in the work of Bowlby, Ainsworth, and other authors, with particular reference to our own work (Bowlby, 1988; Ainsworth, 1989; Guidano and Liotti, 1983).

Freud's view of the human being was as an egocentric creature stimulated by problematic conflicts from childhood. Freud's first formulation, centering on a relationship with parental figures and focused on the dynamics of erotic love for the opposite-sex parent as well as hatred and competition for the same-sex parent, seems unconvincing, and generated a remarkable amount of confusion even among his closest disciples, including Jung. In the post-World War II era, a powerful movement developed in psychotherapy that adopted the theory of attachment to conceptualize and experimentally study the relations of young people with their parental figures. In the late 1980s, Cindy Hazan and Phillip Shaver applied the attachment theory to adult romantic relationships (Hazan and Shaver, 1987).

Ultimately, the theory of attachment addressed the study of the therapeutic bond in psychotherapy. This relationship involves a specific form of attachment and parenting, even re-parenting, between adults.

In this book, I outline only the pivotal role of Gianni Liotti in developing an evolutionary model in psychopathology and psychotherapy, based specifically on the conception and study of interpersonal motivational systems such as attachment and upbringing as it relates to gender, cooperation, and competition (Liotti, 2009). Liotti adopts a psychobiological perspective that gives due consideration to neuroscience's contribution and links the emotional process to the relational framework, proclaiming that the relational experience is based on the typical processes and mechanisms shared by all social mammals. In humans, cognitive modulation performs an ancillary role to the basic mechanisms of the relational dynamic that activates from paleognostic brain activity (Liotti, 2009).

Louis Cozolino, from Pepperdine University in Los Angeles, thoroughly examined the theme of the social brain from a neuroscience-related perspective, tying it to psychopathology and therapy. Cozolino identifies three areas in the social brain's structures and systems (Cozolino, 2004; 2006):

- cortical and subcortical structures (which I describe as gradiental and modular);
- sensory, motor, and affective systems; and
- regulatory systems.

The *cortical and subcortical structures* include a gradiental component consisting of the orbitomedial prefrontal cortex, the somatosensory cortex, and the cingulate cortex, as well as the modular structures of the amygdala, hippocampus, and hypothalamus.

It must be emphasized here that the *sensory, motor, and affective systems* are responsible for the recognition of faces and facial expressions. The role of systems composed of mirror neurons is also important, and its discovery is the result of research by Rizzolati, Fogassi, and Gallese (2000). Capable of producing internal patterns of relational actions and processes observed in other individuals of the same species, mirror neuron systems carry out a key role in behavioral, emotional, and relational synchronization in higher primates and human beings. The topic of facial recognition and facial expression recognition takes on remarkable importance in the entropy of mind model and negative entropy protocol that I developed for schizophrenia and its therapy. My experimental research demonstrated, in fact, that facial recognition appears compromised, as does the ability to read emotion on the faces of others, in the schizophrenic patient (Scrimali, 2008).

The *regulatory systems* relate to:

- stress;
- fear;
- social commitment (the role of the vagal autonomic nervous system is important); and
- social motivation (this deals with interpersonal motivational systems as described by Liotti).

This summary of the systems and processes involved in the social brain dynamic takes account of the enormous importance of interpersonal relations in the human species and the need to include consideration of Machiavellian intelligence in a complex model of the mind. I firmly believe that by giving sufficient attention to the emotional and relational processes of the mind we arrive at the requisite superstructure of clinical cognitivism. In standard cognitive psychotherapy, unfortunately, the analysis of mental processes rests firmly at the cognitive level, with an evident incapacity to adequately describe the complex dynamic of the human mind and the psychic distress that is inseparably tied to the emotional and relational process.

Based on this analysis, there is a need to propose a post-standard cognitivist model in psychotherapy. My complex cognitive therapy (CCT) (Scrimali, 2010b) puts forward just such a model, in the face of quite deep-seated resistance within the standard cognitivist movement. The cognitivist model currently employed in the United States, which is reductionist, easy to use, lacks neurophysiological and epistemological bases, and employs an ahistoric view of humans based on a continuous present without past or future, seems to promise complete success in the international context. However, we are seeing some hints of crisis and a new movement in cognitive psychotherapy, distinguishing itself from the standard model, is beginning to unobtrusively establish itself. This has happened in Italy and is now in its final stages with the work of authors such as Guidano, Liotti, Perris (Guidano, 1991; Guidano and Liotti, 1983; Perris, 1989), and, to some extent, with my own work. In the United States, Jeffrey Young's schema therapy, which starts from an equally rationalistic view of the connection to reality but introduces emotion, history, and relations into the psychotherapeutic process, is another example (Young, 1999).

5.4 The Central Nervous System, Neurovegetative Nervous System, and Visceral Brain

In discussing the modular and gradiental brain, I have thus far largely referred to the CNS, which is just one, though probably the most important, of the various nervous systems with which we are endowed. There exist at least two others: the neurovegetative nervous system, and the visceral brain or autonomic nervous system, with specific connection to the digestive tract.

5.4.1 The Neurovegetative Nervous System

Let's start with the definition of this important component of the nervous system. I find it unhelpful to use the term peripheral nervous system, because the CNS also possesses peripheral structures such as the motor and sensory nerves, and because, in reality, the neurovegetative nervous system is equipped with decentralized control structures allocated to the neuro-cranium, including the hypothalamus. I also believe the term "autonomic" to be inappropriate because this component is anything but autonomous in function, since it responds to decentralized control centers like the hypothalamus and amygdala, and because coalitional control comes from the cortical structures. This is evident when we generate modifications in the functional conditions of the neurovegetative nervous system with internal representation activity, when intentionally thinking about positive conditions. In this case, the gradiental cortical structures instigate central and conscious regulation of the neurovegetative nervous system.

The vegetative nervous system is divided into two branches, which are in continuous functional balance. The sympathetic system activates in order to increase the body's levels of functioning, empowering it to respond to challenge, conflict, and danger. On the other hand, the parasympathetic system's activities prevail when the body relaxes and conserves energy, activating processes of maintenance of wellbeing as well as morphological and functional rebuilding. Many diseases derive from a negative functional dynamic between the two systems, from the most serious and insidious, such as arterial hypertension, to the most benign but unfortunately quite socially debilitating, such as hyperhidrosis.

An interesting conception was recently proposed describing the vagal parasympathetic system's functions when involved in one of its important roles in the socialization process (Cozolino, 2006). When the cooperative interpersonal motivational systems of parenting, attachment, and sexuality are activated, a very specific functional condition must be created in the vegetative nervous system. On the one hand, it must be stimulated, and on the other, it must be calm and relaxed. In this case, the vagal system is able to optimally modulate the physiological condition. This does not happen in people who live in a constant state of tension and conflict in social and personal relationships, however, as such conditions do not permit the vagal brake to activate (Cozolino, 2006). These are individuals who have the characteristics described by Friedman as Type A – always activated, hostile, critical, ready to go on the defense or attack, and who are eroding their bodies until they are at high risk for development of cardiovascular disease (Friedman, 1996).

It seems that competent and proficient regulation of the vagal system, which includes the gradiental and modular structures or those cortical areas in the right hemisphere connected to socialization processes, the right amygdala and nucleus ambiguus, may be determined in part by the individual's genetics – and therefore may conform to the above-mentioned temperament – and in part by parenting and life events during development (Cozolino, 2006). In children and adolescents, insufficient vagal competence could mean they have difficulty synchronizing themselves with their peers and being relaxed in their company. This dysregulation may also be implicated in attention deficit hyperactivity disorder (ADHD). In adulthood, inefficient vagal regulation gives rise to difficulty in letting go of relationships with others, starting with family and couple relationships. Thus, when disagreement and conflict occurs, a person may not be able to control the fight-or-flight syndrome, causing breakups and further relational trauma.

It seems useful to add here that the electrodermal parameter, which I'll frequently address in this book, provides a quite accurate picture of the vagal tone. In fact, hyperactive children with attention and concentration deficit, and who exhibit excessive fear and exaggerated anger, record elevated levels of electrodermal conductance, showing continuous and excessive sympathetic activation with inadequate vagal regulation (O'Connell *et al.*, 2004).

5.4.2 The Visceral Brain

To conclude this description of the human brain, we shall look at the third and last brain with which we are equipped: the visceral brain, or autonomic nervous system, which is particularly evident in the digestive tract. Humans have always perceived that emotions play an important role in the function of the digestive system and, because of this, we often refer to the so-called gut as well as the heart when we talk about emotional situations (Pancheri, 1979).

Via the vagus nerve, the enteric autonomic nervous brain is connected to both the neurovegetative and central nervous systems. Links between the different systems seem to be reciprocal rather than unidirectional, as was thought until quite recently. In fact, the structures that make up the enteric nervous system produce neurotransmitters (95% of serotonin is produced there) and proteins that contribute to the CNS's effective functioning. Therefore, on the one hand, information coming from the external world modulates the digestive tract's activity until it arrests in case of stress and intense danger and, on the other hand, positive stomach and intestinal activity produces a condition of satisfaction and wellbeing through positive proprioceptive feedback and increased serotonin.

Data relating to the fact that the digestive tract is able to learn and therefore shows evidence of memory processes was demonstrated experimentally in Pavlov's research with dogs, when the Russian scholar was able to teach the dogs' digestive systems (in this case, the salivary glands) to respond to the presence of environmental stimuli that, per se, would have been irrelevant to digestion if the dogs had not learned that they could be related to the administering of food. The fact that the digestive tract is equipped with memory processes mediated by the enteric nervous system itself holds important implications for the therapy of many psychosomatic as well as mental disorders. In irritable bowel syndrome, for instance, the intestine learns to react negatively to stressful environmental conditions with spasms and diarrhea. Therefore, psychotherapeutic intervention that makes the patient aware of dysfunctional patterns and ineffective coping mechanisms is insufficient. For therapy to be effective the colon must be re-educated to work effectively. This can be implemented indirectly through electrodermal activity (EDA) or directly with biofeedback techniques, utilizing noninvasive tools capable of recording intestinal peristalsis.

Treatment of illnesses such as eating disorders, where the functional dynamic of the digestive tract is altered, should also strive to include special gastroenteric rehabilitation and re-education procedures. For instance, if a person induces vomiting by inserting two fingers into the throat to physically produce the regurgitation reflex at the onset of the disorder, then the stomach learns what is required of it over time. Even where the motivation to not vomit is produced through psychotherapy, once the person afflicted with the inveterate eating disorder eats something, the stomach will then promptly do its job by automatically provoking vomiting rather than activating the digestive process.

In anorexic girls, the intestine gradually learns to function in a different way, increasing its capacity to utilize even the smallest nutritional component from the small amounts of food ingested. I have personally seen girls in clinic who were so emaciated and ate so little that they seemed truly to be defying the laws of physiology. They managed to sustain themselves in a strange equilibrium, having a normal life though exhibiting a body mass index of just 13.5. Once psychotherapy had produced the motivation to eat, the phenomena of automatic vomiting and intestinal obstruction had to be confronted. The enteric nervous system of these patients had developed new programs and tended to maintain them. Nevertheless, specific gastroenteric rehabilitation techniques must be included, based on specific exercises and the extensive use of biofeedback methods. For these reasons, digestive rehabilitation is an important topic in the Fineo and Tantalo protocols (see Section 18.1.5) that I developed over time for the treatment of bulimia and anorexia respectively (Scrimali and Grimaldi, 2003).

5.5 Paleognosis and Neognosis in the Mind of *Homo sapiens*

The presence of highly developed frontal lobes and the appearance of a semantic-type system of representation of reality tied to language are the result of an evolutionary dynamic within the humanization process. Different sensory modalities also exhibit both a phylogenetic and an ontogenetic evolutionary gradient, transitioning from touch and smell to hearing and then to vision. Where nonhuman mammals explore their world primarily by sniffing and tasting, we do it largely by seeing. However, a child first develops a tactile and olfactory representation of the world that then gradually becomes auditory and finally visual, in agreement with the principle that ontogenesis recapitulates phylogenesis. In love, a partially paleognostic condition of the mind, an evolutionary regression to tactile, taste, and olfactory modalities seems to crystallize.

I intend to propose in this book, then, a new and unpublished conceptualization, defining a *Homo sapiens* whose brain functions well as neognostic. I use the term "neognostic" because this person's mind is characterized by mental processes that were acquired during recent evolutionary history, and these mental processes are compromised in a psychotic condition of Entropy of Mind, a condition that I define as paleognostic. In the case of the schizophrenic individual, in fact, it is as if they had reset the mind to a more obsolete mental way of functioning. Furthermore, from the viewpoint of human brain development in the evolutionary phases of the life cycle, in agreement with Piaget, we can identify a paleognostic phase in infancy and subsequently the development of a neognostic functioning during adolescence. I mention this briefly below; the conceptualization is thoroughly illustrated in my book *Entropy of Mind and Negative Entropy* (Scrimali, 2008).

Regarding the human mind, I adopted and developed a conceptual frame that seems ideal from which to construct a model for a complex clinical psychology. I am not asserting that the human mind truly corresponds to what I am describing at present – my description is provisional, and built according to our current knowledge. It is, therefore, a very approximate map. Yet it is an ideal model to guide successful maneuvering in the diagnostic and therapeutic operations required in the clinical psychology setting. As an example, I proposed the Entropy of Mind and Negative Entropy model based on this map, providing a new and improved interpretation for the pathology of schizophrenia and a protocol for its treatment that works quite well (Scrimali, 2008). According to this conceptualization, the human mind processes to be considered are diverse, and I will treat them accordingly in what follows, with the proviso that I will spend more time on knowledge and coalitional processes as opposed to the now classic memory and internal representational systems in cognitive neuroscience.

5.6 Memory

Memory systems are a fundamental aspect of the functioning and, even more so, the malfunctioning of the mind, capable of supporting processes suited to information storage. Within the realm of psychology and cognitive neuropsychology, memory is considered one of the pivotal processes of cognition. Any mental process, in fact, requires active participation from the various systems charged with storing information.

In-depth study of memory in the cognitive realm started with Neisser, who described the functioning of three modules simply labeled 1, 2, and 3. The first module is the sensory memory, the second would correspond to the working memory, and the third would correspond to the long-term memory. While neuronal configurations form the first two memory systems, the long-term memory seems to be best described as involving processes of nucleic acid structural modification (Neisser, 1982).

According to recent connectionist models of mnestic processes, information is stored in complex neuronal networks. It is not possible, then, to access isolated information, as each piece of information must be contextualized and frequently enhanced by other information registered on different occasions and under diverse circumstances. It is also important to stress that memory functions in constructive terms and according to a process of assimilation. Each piece of data memorized is acquired in a contextual dimension and compiled with other previously acquired knowledge. Memorization therefore occurs selectively and constructively on the basis of the subject's needs and specific objectives in any given situation or circumstance.

Memory constitutes a process and a multidimensional entity and, to date, it has not been possible to identify an all-encompassing framework for this essential subject matter. Within a cognitive model of human information processing, the memory plays a vital role in all cognitive processes. The theories developed, abilities achieved, and emotions felt together constitute a background that makes interaction with reality and acquisition of new information, and therefore construction of memories, possible.

As I have highlighted, the literature does not yet reflect comprehensive classifications and definitions of the complex processes involved in memory. Traditionally, starting with Neisser, short-term memory is distinguished from long-term. Short-term memory was, in recent years, elaborated and described as the working memory process, which comprises a set of diverse activities delegated to the short-term management of information during an actual interaction process with the external world (Neisser, 1982).

Cohene and Squire made an important qualitative distinction between two mnestic processes defined as declarative (or explicit) memory and procedural (or implicit) memory. The first relates to the conscious registration of such information as people, places, objects, numbers, words, etc. It appears evident that declarative explicit memory is located at a higher phylogenetic and ontogenetic evolutionary level, deriving from the humanization process and, therefore, from the progressive digitization of the human mind. In the realm of implicit memory that then acts outside awareness, Gazzaniga, Ivry, and Mangun describe four components: procedural, perceptive, that connected to conditioning processes, and that connected to extinction of conditioning processes (Gazzaniga, Ivry, and Mangun, 1998).

Schacter describes an implicit emotional memory as being a crucial function of the tacit mind and, as such, it is characterized by marked paleognosis, both phylogenetic and ontogenetic. In the phylogenetic area, in fact, it is the only form of memory available to nonhuman mammals while, in the personal development history of every *Homo sapiens*, it constitutes the first form of experiential registration from the time it is activated at birth (Schacter, 1996). With reference to the nervous system, this implicit memory relies on the subcortical modular structures of the amygdala, basic nuclei, and the already well-developed limbic system functioning from the very first weeks of life. The implicit memory is activated by sensory data that do not necessarily have to reach the level of awareness, either during the memorization phase or during data recall. The affective memory is also part of implicit memory.

The studies of Squire and Paller (2000) and LeDoux (1996) identified the emotive memory center as being in the amygdala, which is a very small structure in the shape of an almond, belonging to the older phylogenetic component of the human brain. The amygdala represents an important hub in the emotional brain. Perceptual stimuli coming from the environment can reach the amygdala through two circuits. The direct one is the thalamo-amygdala, apt to advance, in the very short expanse of just a few milliseconds, an adaptive response of approach and problem-solving or retreat and flight. The second, indirect and longer, circuit includes cortical structures of the executive brain, hence the frontal lobes. Such a circuit allows conscious evaluation of situations and then a slower but much more integrated behavioral response.

Any sound or image that can elicit an emotional reaction is transferred to the emotional memory but also activates a series of biological processes such as variation in heart or respiration rate, vasoconstriction and vasodilation, perspiration, etc. These states are promoted by hypothalamic centers connected to the amygdala, which, as seen earlier, is closely connected to the objectives of the memorization process and hippocampus. Therefore, every situation will be memorized along with its specific emotional overtones. Archaic and paleognostic structures always manage behavior considered important to adaptation and survival.

Related to this conceptualization, it is worth mentioning the phylogenetic and ontogenetic gradient of the sensory organs. Smell is one of the most primitive senses and one of the most useful for survival, even though its function is in part vanishing in civilized humans. Therefore, there is nothing more powerful than an odor to activate the amygdala's short circuit and resurrect an intense emotional condition, whether positive or negative.

As I have mentioned, it is understood that restructuring the physical processes tied to emotional implicit memory requires procedures that can reach the more primitive and paleognostic brain. Therefore discussion, even using Socratic questioning as is typically done in standard CT, is not enough to counsel an individual afflicted by a phobia in order to convince them, from a rational standpoint, of the real innocuousness of the event that they fear or avoid. Indeed, that individual will continue to anticipate such an event in negative terms, colored by all the anxiety and somatic reactions connected to it that were also experienced during the sensitization process. Such a process of sensitization will have created an intense emotional mnestic trace at the hippocampus level, with a parade of such negative somatic symptoms as tachycardia, perspiration, feeling cold, trembling, nausea, diarrhea, etc.

As explained, the classic psychotherapeutic dialogical process implemented through the so-called Socratic dialog in standard CT interacts solely via the semantic and digital explicit channel in the frontal lobe structures. Only real experiences that allow the amygdala to register new, positive emotions in situations once feared can profoundly restructure the emotional mind-set. For this reason, in the scope of CCT, I attach great importance to analogical techniques implemented in group therapy, as, for example, in the Tacita. . .Mente laboratory. In this relational and experiential context, the patient experiences new emotions that will remain in the hippocampus through the short amygdala pathway, driving feelings of wellbeing, emotional warmth, sharing, and security.

Within his explanation of long-term memory, Tulving further distinguishes both a semantic and an episodic memory. The first involves material processed in the linguistic sense and the second concerns real events that were experienced, and is therefore also labeled autobiographical (Tulving, 1972).

5.7 Internal Representational Systems

The human brain continuously builds from perceptual data but predominantly from that contained in the memory systems, or internal representations of reality. In our minds, it is as if there were a movie theater of sorts where we continuously project vivid films supplied with audio. Scenes in these films come from both archived material (memories) and perceptual data (the films we continually acquire via the sensory organs). Sometimes, we invent stories, and we represent them in this internal movie theater. They are our fantasies.

Internal representational systems are of two types: iconic (and therefore analog) or digital process, as in the internal dialog that Paivio (1985) emphasized. On our planet, the presence of a digital internal dialog seems to be the exclusive privilege of the human species. Internal representational processes carry out a crucial role in determining human behavior and adapting it to reality. They are characterized by serious biases in neurotic patients and, even more so, in psychotics.

5.7.1 Imagery

Kosslyn was the author who developed a neuroscience-based cognitive approach through the study of processes involved in mental imagery. He also used cerebral functional imaging techniques like fMRI. He arrived at the conclusion that mental imagery does not constitute a sort of collection of photographs stored in the memory that are reproduced as such. Instead, he emphasized that iconic material is continuously recreated, combining elements coming from diverse imagery relating to different memories (Kosslyn, 1994). Bateson stressed the importance of the iconic representational process of reality, asserting: "In as much as I am human, I am a builder of mental imagery" (Bateson, 1979).

The presence of an anticipatory internal representational process with respect to reality plays a critical role in determining human behavior. In fact, *Homo sapiens* take action based not solely on perceptual data but rather on the supply of the anticipatory imagery activating in the mind. For example, having to travel to reach a certain destination, I first visualize the route and then, traveling it, I compare what I am observing with what I am visualizing. I believe, and I customarily say this to my patients, that we humans are able to implement only that which we are first capable of imagining. Therefore, not being able to visualize a sequence in which we are competent performers prevents us from realizing and living it. In many pathologies, but primarily in depression, the patient maintains that, when asked to imagine the next day and days to come, they can visualize nothing. Only by planning one positive day, then striving to visualize it as in a film, is one able to live it.

The mental imagery that we produce does not just come from perceptual experiences that we visualize, as demonstrated in studies on people who are blind from birth but describe vivid images produced in their mind's eye. It seems, then, that the process of iconic representation of reality may be linked closely with the content of what Jung defined as the collective unconscious, and which we could define today as the most primitive component tied to the genome and phylogenesis of our brain (Jung, 1991).

The role of mental imagery and the ability to utilize the therapeutic tool of iconic and analog internal representational systems that are no longer just digital is a rapidly developing area in the sphere of cognitive psychotherapy. Actually, it was the originators of behavioral therapy, such as Wolpe, who introduced the use of the imagination as a technique for treatment of neuroses back in the 1950s (Wolpe, 1968). In particular, it was Wolpe himself who proposed the need to have the patient visualize images of fearful situations in the application of his "systematic desensitization" (Wolpe, 1958). We understood well that this method broadened the scope of behavioral therapy, without perhaps being aware of exactly how it did so. In any case, from the time Wolfe introduced cognitive processes into his therapeutic methodologies, therapy ceased to be truly behaviorist.

The use of "imagery" is now being developed organically in CT (Stopa, 2009). Useful mental imagery methods have been studied and proposed for treatment of such diverse pathologies as post-traumatic stress disorder, phobias, mood disorders, and eating disorders (Grey, 2009; Stopa, 2009; Cooper, 2009; Mansell and Hodson, 2009). As already highlighted in the description of the CCT that I formulated and am currently developing (Scrimali, 2010b), I quite often use mental imagery when working with my patients, teaching them to visualize in the therapeutic setting what they will then implement in real-life scenarios.

I conclude this section with a reflection. It seems that the many authors of standard CT do not realize that the increasingly widespread adoption of the techniques of mindfulness and imagery put their model up for debate, calling into question their very rationalist paradigm. In fact, mental imagery is a part of the analog world that they do not include in their own conceptualizations, which are based on only the digital, and therefore internal, dialog. Just as the behaviorists wanted to study and modify behavior, only to then introduce the technique of imagining fearful situations, so it seems that the standard cognitivists, after refusing to consider the analog and tacit emotional world, now wish to adopt methods that are themselves based on such aspects. Thrown out the door, complexity still comes back through the window.

5.7.2 *Internal Dialog*

Internal dialog is the second internal representational system, digital and semantic in this case, typical of the evolution from the primate to the human brain and therefore characteristic of *Homo sapiens*. We humans continually dialog with ourselves, commenting on what takes place but also formulating theories on what will or could happen. Internal dialog has great importance in determining our behavior and appears to be central in psychopathology, being at the basis of the numerous symptoms of diverse mental disorders. For example, in the panic cycle as described by Clark, every perception of any alteration in the heart's functioning, for example extrasystole, is remarked upon with such dysfunctional internal dialog as "Oh no, what's wrong with my heart?" This pessimistic attitude in the internal dialog provokes an increased heart rate and further comment in the phobic's dramatic internal dialog, for instance "I am having a heart attack and I have to go to the emergency room" (Clark, 1995).

It seems clear, then, that internal dialog analysis and modification plays an important role in cognitive psychotherapy. A typical internal dialog sequence that I identified in people afflicted with eating disorders, goes something like this. Before they consume food having complex carbohydrates like bread or pasta the dialog is: "That food will make me gain weight!" This generates a sense of guilt and physical discomfort that is a prelude to another negative phrase, such as "Somehow, I have to get rid of these calories that I should have never consumed!"

Another interesting and relevant aspect of internal dialog's psychopathology is shown in my reflections within the context of the Entropy of Mind model. In schizophrenia, the internal dialog is perceived by the patient as an external voice that most times admonishes or comments maliciously on everything that the patient does.

5.8 Knowledge Processes

5.8.1 *Introduction*

The term "knowledge" can be defined either as a process or as content. In this case, I will discuss knowledge processes, that is, those that allow the individual to acquire new information for various purposes.

An important aspect of the constructivist orientation within cognitivism is the conception that knowledge processes about reality may develop according to quite distinct modalities, otherwise defined by diverse authors and described in constructivism as tacit and explicit knowledge. In 1980, Shevrin and Dickman asserted that if behavior cannot be included without studying cognition, then conscious cognitive processes cannot be explained without accounting for unconscious cognitive processes (Shevrin and Dickman, 1980). Mahoney observed that, since behavioral therapists had been disregarding cognition for years, then perhaps cognitivists had been guilty of the same with regard to unconscious processes (Mahoney, 1980). In any event, an organic description of tacit knowledge processes, with particular reference to psychopathology and cognitive psychotherapy, is found in the work of Guidano and Liotti. At the start of the 1980s, these two authors published a book which represented an important stage in the development of constructivist cognitivism: *Cognitive Processes and Emotional Disorders* (Guidano and Liotti, 1983). Then Michael Mahoney started to collaborate with Guidano and Reda at the Department of Psychiatry, University of Rome, where I joined them, offering some contributions to the Italian Cognitive Therapy (Reda and Mahoney, 1984).

My reflection on this topic began with the conception of Guidano and Liotti, who first proposed an organic model of the mind with two processes (tacit and explicit knowledge). I integrated this conception with both procedural and Machiavellian knowledge. Such an integration appears indispensable for the formulation of a more complete and organic frame of the human mind. In fact, in light of cybernetic and ethological logic, the human being must be seen as an agent that moves through reality, pursuing goals and implementing procedures. This happens in a social context that avails itself of specific and sophisticated relational and social competence.

5.8.2 The Unconscious and Tacit Dimension

The concept of the unconscious constituted one of the crucial topics in the psychodynamic models of Freud and Jung, even though the conception of an area of the mind that was inaccessible to conscious awareness had already been formulated by philosophers such as Leibniz, Shelling, Schopenhauer, and Bergson. In the unconscious, Freud identified some components of the psyche that were tied to basic instincts such as Eros, or primal desire, and the destructive aggression of Thanatos, or the death wish. The extreme emphasis Freud placed on the erotic libido component probably derived from the climate of sexual repression typical of middle-class societies in that era (Freud, 1989).

On this important topic, Jung contributed a more wide-ranging set of concepts. In his work, along with contributions to the idea of the individual unconscious, he introduced the collective unconscious. The illustrious Swiss psychiatrist maintained that the collective unconscious was made up of the archetypes present in the human mind, independent of the culture represented in the conscious during particular mental states such as sleep or hallucination. Jung stressed that the collective unconscious constitutes a sort of historical memory of humanity from which dreams, imagery, and mysterious themes tied to the experiences of our ancestors emerge. To cite the author: "They communicate the spirit of our unknown ancestors, their way of thinking and feeling, their way of experiencing life and the world, other human beings and gods" (Jung, 1991).

Today we tend to think that the so-called collective unconscious may be made up of very primitive mental activity of the iconic type that represents basic motivations and mind processes of mammals in terms of imagery. For example, the archetype of the good mother appears to be connected to the basic example of the search for closeness, love, and protection from the nurturing feminine figure, one that is engraved on the genome of all mammals. In point of fact, then, dreams and hallucinations must be narrated, as it is acknowledged that *Homo sapiens* are compelled by their voluminous digital brains to find meaning. So dreams, hallucinations, and archetypes become histories that take on a strong connotation relating to time, space, and primarily to the personal circumstances of every human.

Maturana underscores this concept well when he asserts that all our living experience must of necessity take the form of a comment, a reflection, or, in short, an explanation. This is in synch, I would add, with the strong motivation of *Homo sapiens* to create order from disorder (Maturana, 1988).

Studies on the unconscious dimension in the cognitive arena, defined as "tacit," began with Polany (1966; 1968) in the second half of the 1960s. Asserting that "we know more than we know how to express," Polany conceptualizes the presence of two different dimensions of knowledge, again claiming that the explicit dimension is always founded on a pre-existing tacit dimension. Tacit knowledge makes its official appearance in the international CT literature with Guidano and Liotti in the now historic *Cognitive Processes and Emotional Disorders* (1983). Over his entire scientific career, Guidano elaborated the central process of the tacit dimension that he subsequently defined as "experiencing," involved in a constant dialog with the explicit dimension that he called "explaining." This dynamic soon became central to his thinking, as he pointed out that a human being is a mysterious creature to whom living is not enough and to whom creating some sense out of living itself seems obligatory. Where other mammals strive for pure and simple survival, humans instead tend largely to make sense out of their survival (Guidano, 1991).

With regard to neuroscience, the treatment of the topic of tacit knowledge still appears to be rather shallow. Daniel and Alex Bennet recently formulated a description of tacit knowledge within which they identify four different processes:

- tacit knowledge of bodily states;
- tacit knowledge as intuition with respect to reality;
- tacit knowledge relating to emotional control; and
- tacit knowledge of the spiritual type.

According to Bennet and Bennet (2008), the more thoroughly examined domain relating to tacit knowledge is that of feelings (affective tacit knowledge), within which emotions represent the affective manifestation most connected to the somatic sphere. A primitive structure of the reptilian brain, the amygdala, is an anatomical system essential to tacit knowledge.

The amygdala is closely connected to the frontal lobe. In this reciprocal interaction between the amygdala – and therefore between primitive modular and substantially paleognostic structures of decentralized control – on the one hand, and the gradient and neognostic frontal brain on the other, the anatomical and functional basis for the experience–explain dynamic described by Guidano (1991) may be identified.

5.8.3 Information Coding in the Human Brain

The human brain contains both analog and digital processors (Figure 5.1), as in current information systems there exist both analog and digital computers. The latter are those we utilize every day as personal computers and the former are employed in the speedy control of complex and parallel processes. An analog system immediately represents the functions in play, emulating the future from them. For example, in an hourglass or in an analog watch, the sand's descent from the upper to the lower chamber and the constant movement of the hands over the watch face represent the passage of time (Teasdale and Barnard, 1993).

Analog and digital processing both have advantages and disadvantages. The former is very quick and able to process enormous amounts of data at one time while making use of relatively simple and economical devices. The latter is slow and almost always requires analog-to-digital conversion

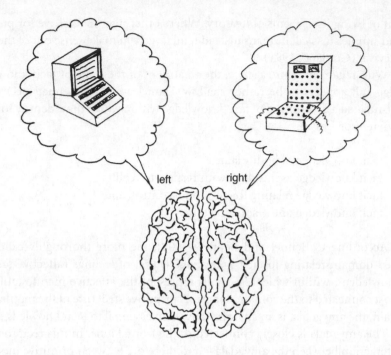

Figure 5.1 Left and right brain hemispheres as corresponding to analogical and digital computers.

because reality is rarely digital! From the viewpoint of data memory, analog is relatively unreliable, and digital can last longer without deteriorating. With regard to development, analog is older and digital more recent. Both in the biological development of living beings and in human-created technology, digital came after analog but seldom supersedes it.

When the largest part of our brain retains analog processes, this means that, due to their speed and comprehensiveness, these analog processes maintained an evolutionary advantage. The analog-to-digital conversion utilized by many common devices, such as a scanner or a digital camera, can be related to the experience–explain dynamic described by Guidano. Multiple possible biases in the human mind are identified in this complicated interface.

The analog brain can also be defined as a higher-level mind-entropy processor, while the digital one is more orderly. In schizophrenia, analog cerebral systems are more active. For this reason, I labeled the schizophrenic condition as Entropy of Mind.

I will now summarize four knowledge processes of the human mind that I include in the model of the modular and gradiental brain, and coalitional mind: tacit knowledge (experiencing); explicit knowledge (explaining); procedural knowledge (acting); and social or Machiavellian intelligence (relating).

5.8.4 Tacit Knowledge: Experiencing

- *Basic activity*: to keep the individual in constant contact with the environment, focusing his or her attention on events that have instantaneous value (in the here and now).
- *Goal*: short-term adaptation and survival.
- *Information processing modality*: analog. This is a high-capacity channel capable of the parallel processing of enormous amounts of information in very short time periods, making it available for quick environmental adaptation.
- *Memory systems*:
  - short-term and implicit, and
  - long-term and episodic.
- *Knowledge and connection to the conscious*: tacit knowledge activity is processed unconsciously and is not transferable, per se, if it does not first undergo the digitization process.
- *Relevant brain structures*: right temporal lobe, amygdala, hippocampus, thalamus, rhinencephalon, and hypothalamus.
- *Ontogenetic chronology*: information processing system that matures early. Its organization can be achieved as early as the first stages in an infant's development.
- *Phylogenetic chronology*: primitive system that is quite developed in all mammals.

5.8.5 Explicit Knowledge: Explaining

- *Basic activity*: to create conceptual order from chaotic disorder in the flow of immediate experience, and a strategically articulated concept of self and the world.
- *Goal*: to allow long-term adaptation of the individual and species by building a body of knowledge that can be transferred to peers and progeny in both spoken and, primarily, written form.

- *Information processing modality*: serial, implemented via limited-capacity channels with longer processing times than those required for analog and parallel coding.
- *Memory systems*:
  - short-term and declarative, and
  - long-term and semantic. Semantic memory can utilize supports external to the brain. This is what occurred after the invention of writing. Non-biological information processing systems can also be recruited, interfacing with the brain via specific input and output interfaces like electronic processors. Today, a brain network connection is instantaneously possible through electronic media such as the worldwide web.
- *Knowledge and connection to the conscious*: explicit knowledge activity is processed consciously. In fact, explicit knowledge continuously performs digital and semantic decoding of content from other forms of knowledge in order to make the data available to the conscious.
- *Relevant brain structures*: frontal and prefrontal lobes.
- *Ontogenetic chronology*: the frontal and prefrontal lobes are a late-developing system that begins maturing with language acquisition and represents a long evolutionary process, characterized by the progressive transition from concrete to abstract thought.
- *Phylogenetic chronology*: very recent. Such knowledge is the exclusive and unique property of *Homo sapiens*.

5.8.6 *Procedural Knowledge: Acting*

- *Basic activity*: to implement a series of behavioral sequences directed at the development of complex strategies for interacting with the environment.
- *Goal*: to interact in the environment to acquire suitable energy, material, and information to keep the system alive; to withdraw from threats in order to promote survival and wellbeing of the self; and to flexibly and developmentally optimize interaction with reality.
- *Information processing modality*: concurrent with both digital, semantic-type computational systems and parallel information processing activity.
- *Memory systems*:
  - short-term and procedural, and
  - long-term and procedural.

- *Knowledge and connection to the conscious*: procedural system activity can be controlled either consciously or automatically. Typically, learning a new executive ability develops under the strict control of conscious activity. Newly developed attitudes are implemented in terms that are increasingly automatic. In this way, a remarkable portion of digital processing, which as we've already seen has a limited capacity, is free to dedicate itself to new executive activity that must be learned.
- *Relevant brain structures*: frontal lobes and motor areas.
- *Ontogenetic chronology*: a mixed system where the most primitive systems activate in coordination with more recently developed ones.
- *Phylogenetic chronology*: on the whole, a level of coordinated activity that reaches unknown heights in humans, as it does in other mammals and primates. The latter are able to acquire great ability in manipulating objects, yet remain far less developed in executive competence than humans.

5.8.7 Social or Machiavellian Intelligence: Relating

- *Basic activity*: to implement, maintain, and optimize exchanges with peers. Language plays a primary role in the basic activity of social or Machiavellian intelligence.
- *Goal*: to maintain positive relations with peers, increasing personal power as well as the possibility of survival and wellbeing for the self and offspring; and to form a couple relationship aimed at procreation and the stable upbringing of progeny.
- *Information processing modality*: both analog and digital. Different channels of acquisition and information transmission operate simultaneously, as in verbal and nonverbal communication sequences.
- *Memory systems*:
  ○ short-term, declarative, and procedural, and
  ○ long-term, declarative, and procedural.
- *Knowledge and connection to the conscious*: some aspects of inherent social or Machiavellian intelligence activities are under the control of the conscious while others are not. Verbal communication is typically under the strict control of the conscious, but the nonverbal component of communication is much less consciously controlled, in both transmission and reception of information.

- *Relevant brain structures*: dorsolateral structures of the prefrontal cortex connected to a complex network that includes parts of the upper temporal cortex and lower parietal cortex. It also includes limbic structures, the amygdala, the caudate nucleus, and the thalamus.
- *Ontogenetic chronology*: late (subsequent to language development).
- *Phylogenetic chronology*: late, with pronounced features in *Homo sapiens*.

In the mental system, the four knowledge processes just described are organized according to dynamic and integrated mechanisms that are complex patterns of information described as schemas. Tacit, explicit, procedural, and relational elements are assembled in every schema, where they act and interact. These schemas constitute the mind's logical, computational, and cybernetic programs. The modalities deriving from the characteristics of the schemas process information and control both procedural and social behavior.

5.9 Coalitional Processes

Despite the incessant activity of differentiated and specialized knowledge systems, as well as the constant and vertiginous quantity of data that is acquired via interaction with the world, every human being has a perception of self that is both unique and stable over time. It is the continuous perception of this sense of self that is always recognizable purely through the incessant physical, mental, and relational changes that constitute the central dynamic of self and its give and take. In schizophrenia, according to my conceptualized model, dysfunctional coordination provokes entropy of mind, a frenetic increase in the disorder that I have described as "frenentropy." Therefore, schizophrenia is a disorder that seems to be a unique pathology relating to coordination of processes rather than a single mental and cerebral activity, although many of these processes are altered (Scrimali, 2008).

5.9.1 The Self

The issue of the self has seen a revival of interest on the part of various authors in recent years. These scholars come from areas that include cognitive psychology and neuroscience. In *The Self and its Brain*, Popper observed that a unique characteristic of human beings is that of being systematically aware of their own identity during their whole lifespan, even after periods of a break in consciousness that are physiological, such as during sleep, or pathological, as during a coma.

According to Popper, the sense of self is not, then, a physical reality. On the contrary, the body's physical structure changes throughout life. Therefore, the self must instead be a process tied to knowledge and memory. Popper rejects the idea that the self is formed merely from self-observational activity, and expresses his conviction that it may be the result of knowledge processes that organize information acquired from the environment as well as from innate and biologically predetermined programs. Popper and Eccles both conclude that at any given moment, although the brain is involved in many different activities, each individual perceives him or herself as a unique entity (Popper and Eccles, 1997).

Following Popper's epistemological reflection and Eccles' neurophysiological studies, in recent years the concept of self has become central to the clinical cognitive sphere. Many authors and influential thinkers have contributed their ideas to the central concept of self (Bandura, 1971; Bowlby, 1988; Goncalves, 1989; Mahoney, 1991; Guidano, 1988; 1991). Though there is great diversity in the theories, the following four statements seem fundamental and common to various theoretical developments in the cognitive models of the self:

- The self is a process of unification and internal coherence that derives from incessant abstract activity from multiple and multiform personal experiences.
- The self constitutes an entity capable of influencing the fate of the single individual as well as that of those who share its ecological niche.
- The self, once developed through the evolutionary phases of the life cycle, reaches a certain stability during adulthood.
- Within the cognitive paradigm, the self is considered a subjective entity structured from human information processing with autonomous attributes, independence, and stability, and exhibits a marked capacity for evolution.

One of the authors who conducted the most complete exploration of the self within clinical cognitive theory was Vittorio Guidano (1988; 1991). He placed an evolutionary epistemology and constructivist conception of the connection with reality at the center of his model. Guidano considered the self to be not a structure but rather an organizational process in a constant state of becoming. According to Guidano, the self is articulated on two levels and each level consists of distinct processes. The processes involve acquisition of experiential data (experience) and decoding of this data in the explicit sense through the linguistic tool (explanation). Guidano's conception of the self, then, can be defined as bi-level. The sense of self, specific and unique to every human being, would derive from a constantly changing dynamic process involving experience and explanation. The unique perceptual processing of reality interacting with equally idiosyncratic attitudes and explanatory competence creates the specific connotation of each individual self.

Consistent with the conceptualization that I previously proposed and illustrated concerning the four knowledge processes of experiencing, explaining, acting, and relating, the self assumes a multi-level connotation. The unified nature of the self derives from two unique attributes of biological systems, in this case, the brain and complex knowledge systems, or the mind. According to the theory of autopoiesis, living beings are systems capable of maintaining values of variables, within a restricted range, or limiting the fundamental variables that define the individual. In the case of the human knowledge system, the variable that is maintained within this range, despite continual disturbances, is personal identity. On the other hand, self-reference is the process via which each new piece of information the system acquires must be capable of being integrated into the system itself.

The formation of the self and its continuous state of becoming is implemented in an intersubjective dimension in relation to significant people. During the development phase, these are the parental figures, and in adulthood, they are members of the personal network. William James described his concept of self as involving the following two polarities (James, 1997):

"I" (I-self) is the primary Self who processes information;
"Me" (Me-self) is the object of the Self's own contemplation.

James further describes a series of components in the primary Self (I-self):

- *self-awareness*: monitoring its own
  - internal physical states,
  - needs,
  - thoughts, and emotions.
- *self-agency*: a sense of being the primary player in its own processes;
- *self-continuity*: the perception of continuity through change; and
- *self-coherence*: the construction of non-incongruous meaning.

The concept of self necessitates the ability to distinguish between self and non-self. Other complex systems that comprise the human body also invoke the distinction between self and non-self. The immune system shows notable similarity to the nervous system in this respect. Over the course of the life cycle, the immune system evolves, continuously self-organizing and modulating its own functions and processes. It is critical to the immune system's proper functioning that it is able to continuously distinguish between that which is part of the body (self) and that which is extraneous (non-self). That which is recognized as extraneous (non-self) is attacked and destroyed in an effort to maintain the integrity of the biological system that is the human body, which is faced with all those external noxae that could put the individual's complex organization in crisis.

Antonio Damasio describes the central theme on which the self operates as one of distinction between entities and processes that belong to it, and entities and processes that are outside its own physical and mental boundaries (Damasio, 1999). Damasio has produced a remarkably interesting model of the self, albeit one based on experimental data and research. One intriguing aspect of Damasio's thinking lies in his distinction between different levels and functions of the self, summarized as proto-self, core self, and autobiographical self.

- The *proto-self* is the collection of all the information coming from the individual's own internal biological world. As a rule, this information does not draw from the conscious. In fact, Damasio points out that the threshold of emergence of human awareness is at the boundary between the proto-self and the core self.
- The *core self* is made up of those knowledge patterns that are triggered by the external world and that will modify the condition of the CNS. It will have been structured by distributed information and will therefore recognize analog code. The core self appears to be animated by a here-and-now dynamic, oriented in such a way as to allow personal identification in actual exchanges with the external world.
- The *autobiographical self* emerges from memory processing activity that organizes information patterns coming from the external world into definitive mnesic structures. For Damasio, this component of the self reflects on the past and anticipates the future.

Damasio's model brings to mind the motto on the young Pharaoh Tutankhamen's cartouche. Carter and Carnavon discovered Tutankhamen's tomb during an intriguing excavation that has always fascinated me. Every pharaoh selected a motto for his cartouche and Tutankhamen's seems to be devoted to the autobiographical self, as conceptualized by Damasio: "I know the past and foresee the future."

Damasio's model is quite close to my own conception of the coalitional processes of the mind and is in agreement with the multi-level dynamic of self, and continuous narrative conception of the proactive as opposed to reactive brain. In certain circumstances, however, as in the case of autoimmune diseases, the capacity to accurately discern between "self" and "non-self" deteriorates. The immune system is suddenly unable to recognize entire cellular systems as self, and even attacks and neutralizes them with sophisticated destruction mechanisms. Something similar occurs in schizophrenia when the modules and coalitional processes of the nervous system suddenly reject their own activities and processes as if they were external disturbances. This seems to happen during hallucinations, traceable to nervous system activities that are erroneously coded as external processes considered threatening to the mental system's integrity, and are therefore the object of neutralization and coping processes.

According to Guidano, the dynamic of building the self derives from the basic biological and motivational processes prematurely overlapping the so-called nuclear or prototypical scenes. They form from the first significant emotional experiences, systematically recurring in interaction with parental figures, and tending to gradually structure a first constant self-perception modality. A subsequent evolutionary stage is the construction of a set of explicit rules which allow integration of analog material from the prototypical scenes into an explanatory dimension. Beck described a very similar process within his theory of schemas. According to Beck, schemas are units built from complex, emotional, and cognitive information that operate, whether as memory processes or as heuristic tools, in the analysis of reality over the life cycle. Every individual orients in space and time, attributing sense to their experiences based on gradually structured schemas (Beck, 1979). It is the rigid and dysfunctional schemas that are structured from negative experiences during the life cycle's development phase and that connote the equally dysfunctional mechanisms for information processing in neurotic or depressed patients.

5.9.2 Personal Identity

As a process, the self produces, nourishes, and maintains a structure that can be identified in personal identity. Guidano describes personal identity sometimes as a process on an equal footing with the self, and at other times as a structure built from an ordered set of explicit information. I personally prefer to consider personal identity a system (a knowledge system allocated to memory structures) that is built and continuously altered by the self's processing activity. The interface between personal identity, the self, and the external world is identifiable, in my view, in an additional process traceable to narrative.

5.9.3 Narrative

The topic of narrative has become increasingly relevant in the cognitivist sphere, primarily in the constructivist field (Russel and Wandrei, 1996). Personal narrative can be described as a heuristic program through which every individual makes their own life experience explicit and expresses their own personal identity (Bruner, 1991). Built from personal narrative, the heuristic program provides fusion of thought, motivation, memory, and the most disparate life experience in such a way that the components of ambiguity and uncertainty inevitably connected with reality diminish, while internal coherence and, therefore order and negative entropy, can increase in the mind (Bruner, 1986).

During the historical development of every single individual, narrative is structured progressively from a matrix of heuristic instances presented dramatically during childhood. As emphatically underscored by Bettelheim (1976), a child confronts a series of probing issues, such as:

- Who am I?
- Where do I come from?
- How was the universe created?
- Who created animals and humans?
- What is my purpose in life?
- What should I become?

Disturbed by these questions, the child asks itself whether it can count on benevolent influences in reality in order to escape from a scenario of uncertainty and, in particular, turn to its parents as sources of certainty and security. It is important that in the instance of creating order from uncertainty and disorder deriving from emergent abstract thought, the child finds support in parental figures and generally from the network of people that surround it.

Some children thus begin to construct a positive history centered on the perception of being able to control reality and live quite calmly through the mysterious circumstances that surround human existence. Those less fortunate enter into a history populated by uncertainty, phantoms, and negative influences that accentuate the sense of chaos and threatening danger of existence. Real-life experience and the actual identity process constantly shape each individual's personal narrative. The relationship between personal identity and the heuristic narrative program must be considered reciprocal and dialectic.

In fact, when the personal narrative is dictated by an individual's actual identity, current experience and its representation constantly remodel it. Built from the narrative, the heuristic program tends to create sense and order out of reality on the basis of past history. Every new event must be able to fit into the script that is playing out, as every new character or event introduced into a novel must find its own place in the plot of the saga the author has written.

In schizophrenia, we witness an apparent dramatic disruption in the narrative competence of the mind, and therefore one of the critical objectives in the therapeutic process must be the reconstruction and reactivation of the patient's personal narrative. Although this narrative is aimed at maintaining order and coherence in the mind and therefore still exhibits ample disposition and openness to uncertainty, ambiguity, and disorder, it triggers only temporary states of disequilibrium, subsequently overcome with the activation of new evolutionary processes and entropy control.

Narrative was the focus of discussion for neuroscientists such as Siegel, who, with his relational mind, proposes an interpersonal neurobiology of the narrative processes (Siegel, 1999). A neural structure that plays a central role in the narrative process dynamic is, according to Siegel, the hippocampus, which he defines as a cognitive organizer capable of actively creating a sense of the self, both synchronic and diachronic, integrating current as well as past, present, and future processes. Though fed by the hippocampus-dependent memory systems, narrative processes still involve numerous other structures in the two hemispheres. By means of analog representations, the right hemisphere supplies basic imagery and scenarios for the stories to be narrated, while the left hemisphere implements one of its logical and linear processes according to digital computational codes that permit communication with other humans about personal stories. Narrative activity is therefore the result of complex integrated processes between the posterior, ventral, and bilateral regions of the two hemispheres.

In this case, functional and material recursion between mental processes and brain systems is fully achieved.

Narrative activity derives from the integrity and comprehensive functional coordination of multiple cerebral structures, but this process, in turn, integrates the diverse brain modules into a positive recursion that produces and encourages organization, or negative entropy, of the human mind (Bruner, 1986). Where the processing of reality, as well as the behavior that each person exhibits when in contact with the external world, are the result of significant processes, and where such significant processes operate under the unifying aegis of narrative, then current exchanges with reality essentially represent the ultimate in a personal story. Personal narrative responds, in fact, to the irrepressible need of the minds of *Homo sapiens* to structure a sense of reality that is consistent with prior history and cultural patterns in place where that individual lives.

Narrative theorists further proposed a narrative paradigm of language that they tended to distinguish from the rational paradigm (Russel and Wandrei, 1996; Lyddon and Schreiner, 1998). In the rational paradigm, language is considered a complex system of indications used to reflect reality and communicate the relational state between people. Within the narrative paradigm, language is considered the active creator of reality as opposed to a simple mirror of existing states. Additionally, narrative scholars emphasize that human word play can lead to new levels of meaning that transcend the original functions of denotation. Thus, such authors place in question the rational paradigm and its tendency to exclude knowledge modalities not exclusively associated with logic and reason, regarding narrative instead as an appropriate form of knowledge that addresses the richness, diversity, and complexity of human life (Russel and Wandrei, 1996).

6

Phylogenesis of the Brain and Ontogenesis of the Mind: Biological and Cultural Evolutionism

Evolution is a very important topic in both contemporary biological and psychological neuroscience (Ornstein, 1992). The theory of evolution proposed by Darwin (1859) in the nineteenth century outlined a conception of phylogenetic development as a flexible and nondeterministic process, to a remarkable extent subject to the laws of probability through mutation. Some of the more recently developed disciplines, such as ecology and ethology, share many axioms and specific views with evolutionist logic (Dennet, 1996; Gintis, 2007). One of the most important is the historical approach, in which both the biological and psychological realities, as well as relational and social realities, studied at a given time are actually the result of millions of years of history. In light of this approach, it seems impossible to understand the *hic et nunc* or here and now without referring to the diachronic dimension of biological and epistemic phylogenesis and ontogenesis.

According to an effective metaphor proposed by Monod, we can say that every single human is a kind of living fossil in whose body and, particularly, in whose nervous system the history of evolution is clearly engraved. Another fundamental concept deriving from the evolutionary perspective is that of variability. Without marked variability in the individuals of one population, no factor could modify the general characteristics of one species (Monod, 1972).

Biological evolution is made possible by genetic code characteristics, or DNA, and by its modalities of replication and transfer from one generation to another. While the replication of DNA generally produces accurate transfer of information, this process can be disrupted by genetic mutations.

Neuroscience-based Cognitive Therapy: New Methods for Assessment, Treatment, and Self-Regulation,
First Edition. Tullio Scrimali.

A mutation causes a modification in the genotype that can be transmitted to offspring. Where a mutation carries an advantage in terms of adaptation to the environment and reproductive capacity, it will tend to spread progressively throughout the population. In the organizational architecture of the human brain, traces of a very clear series of evolutionary processes are observable, with a transition from the reptilian brain to that of less evolved mammals and then primates, to the point of hemispheric specialization, with the related linguistic competence that represented the most important evolutionary leap over the course of the humanization process.

In recent years, we have witnessed an impressive increase in research and studies focusing on the origin and biological evolution of humans and the origin and evolution of language and consciousness. Following the evolutionary process of hominids in his *Evolution of the Brain: Creation of the Self* (1989), John Eccles attempted to reconstruct how the advent and evolution of language had made possible the emergence of a specific mind-set in *Homo sapiens*, the capacity of self-reflection, and therefore, the birth and development of the self. Language seems to be one of the unique variables in the humanization process (Eccles, 1989).

In understanding human language we need to distinguish between different aspects or functions. The first two, consisting of the expressive and signaling functions, are in reality also present in the communication of animals; many species can communicate information about state of mind or the presence of environmental conditions that are of importance to the group to which the subject belongs. The higher categories of language include the descriptive and the critical functions that are found only in human communication. The descriptive function defines a conceptual representation of any one reality to be communicated. In the critical function, language becomes a tool and support for speculation, the highest form of cognitive functioning. These language categories, in the order cited here, demonstrate a chronological phylogenetic gradient. They further reveal a clear process of ontogenetic evolution in humans.

In the very young child, the first language functions to appear are the expressive and signaling ones, and only later in development does competency in the descriptive and critical functions develop. In the beginning, the capacity to speak appears in the child to be largely focused on building a positive interaction with the external world. Subsequently, the development of language focuses primarily on increasing abstract thought capacity and, during a third phase, achieving the mind-set for self-reflection and making sense of the subject's own life.

Language development seems to proceed in step with the phenomenon of hemispheric specialization, a characteristic unique to humans. In fact, the linguistic function corresponds to increased complexity and specialization of specific cortical areas allocated to the left hemisphere, called areas 39 and 40. Based on the study of fossil skulls, it has been possible to establish that two areas identified as being in the same location as areas 39 and 40 in *Homo sapiens* began to develop with *Homo habilis* and continued to evolve in *Homo erectus*, subsequently undergoing major development in Neanderthals. Language acquisition represents a particularly pronounced evolutionary leap forward, fraught with important consequences.

In *Homo habilis*, there existed a hominid that some authors claim was capable of essential language, in any case able to increase its competence in finding food and signaling danger. *Homo erectus* possessed a remarkable brain and demonstrated language area development, along with increased competence in environmental interaction. *Homo habilis* showed the first evidence of culturally appropriate abstract concepts, evidenced by the ornaments and fossil remains of plants and flowers in their burial sites. But it is in *Homo sapiens* that the evolutionary high point was reached with the appearance of the conscious self, where cultural development began to accelerate. Self-consciousness, then, seems to be a unique, and is probably the most marked, characteristic in the human species.

Emerging self-consciousness is an evolutionary process that also characterizes ontogenesis, in accordance with the well-known principle previously mentioned that ontogenesis recapitulates phylogenesis. An aspect of development that preceded self-consciousness and is both phylogenetic and ontogenetic is the recognition of self in reflected images and an awareness of one's own distinct identity. The recognition of self in the mirror is not present in naive chimpanzees but can be learned, as numerous studies have clearly documented. Human babies do not recognize themselves in a mirror until about eighteen months and, up to that age, behave as if they are looking at another infant (De Waal, 2008). A relationship between the competence of various animals in mirror self-recognition and their evolutionary level has been demonstrated. Primates easily learn to refer their own reflected images back to themselves, but only after the age of three years.

The awareness of self occupies a later evolutionary level than does the capacity to represent the world of physical objects, and later still than the capacity to recognize one's own physical identity in the mirror. Frith and Dolan proposed a neuropsychological theory concerning self-consciousness, distinguishing two well-differentiated types of cognitive process, defined as low-level and high-level. The first are automatic and routine and the second are aware, intentionally controlling, and above all strategically oriented. The high-level cognitive functions could be directly associated with the conscious and awareness. From an anatomical and physiological viewpoint, the high-level cognitive functions associated with the conscious are traceable to the prefrontal cortex areas while the low-level activities are attributable to the more posterior cortical areas.

The capacity to refer to self and therefore achieve higher cognitive processes represents a vital performance in the mind's functioning and one which is altered in schizophrenia. Savage-Rumbaugh stressed that the awareness of self typical of humans, in comparison to the large evolved primates, is consistent with the potential for recognizing the existence of different theories of reality and multiple differentiated operative options (Savage-Rumbaugh, 1999). The potential for consciously evaluating and choosing from such diverse possibilities and monitoring one's own achievement strategies of goals is an important characteristic of self-consciousness. Another essential aspect of self-awareness is that of building a concept of one's own mind. This evolutionary achievement, which every child attains by five years of age, first appeared, from the phylogenetic viewpoint, during the humanization process, reaching its evolutionary climax in *Homo sapiens*. We can clearly deduce, therefore, that modern humans are the synthesis of a strong symbiosis between biological and cultural evolution. At the time when the first hominid succeeded in communicating to one of its peers not so much any data concerning external reality but rather any one of its subjective experiences, the doors to a new reality opened wide to the world of culture.

From that time, biological and cultural evolution represented two dynamic and closely overlapping processes that led to the biological and epistemological dimension of humans today. For hundreds of thousands of years, a process of increasing cultural capacity, brain mass, and complexity of cerebral structure developed. The result of this evolutionary process was an enormous influence with regard to the environment that began with *Homo erectus*. Neanderthals probably no longer had to fear the rivalry of other mammals that populated their territory. Unfortunately, however, the achievement of supremacy over other living species triggered, even during the dark age of prehistory, the remarkable intra-species competition and aggression that became a quality unique to the human species, culminating in the true genocide, probably initiated by *Homo sapiens* themselves, of the less evolved Neanderthals.

With cultural evolution, the gradual development of progressively more evolved and complex social organizations led humans to drastically modify the terms of biological evolution. The capacity for adaptation in and dominance by single individuals over various historical periods and within diverse social and anthropological realities appears to be closely related to the characteristics of social organization.

As evolutionist biology and genetics have sought to clarify the modalities through which the evolutionary process was implemented, including culturally, theoretical models that can explain the formation process of new theories and their assertion or repression modalities have recently been formulated. One author to formulate a series of organic theories on cultural evolution, positioning himself among the most authoritative exponents of evolutionary epistemology, is Karl Popper. He outlined a pattern-based evolutionary process founded on both the overall and the individual knowledge level of the entire human race. The first stage is the emergence of a new explanatory theory that no longer originates from the observation of reality, as empiricists maintained, but is achieved creatively and autonomously by the mind of a human being. This phenomenon can be incorporated into gene mutation in biological evolution (Popper, 1972). Once operative, the new theory will be subjected to evolutionary pressure, with the principle of falsifiability, and will continue to be active until the governing heuristic program has identified facts that contradict it. At this point, it will be eclipsed by other conceptions produced in the interim. In order for this dynamic to be implemented in positive terms, it is therefore indispensable for the heuristic process to develop adequately; it can sometimes be affected by a series of grave errors, such as the introduction of ad hoc hypotheses or conventionalist movements that, rather than ensure the theory's survival, prevent development and lead to consequent abandonment.

According to Popper's conceptualization, humans learn from experience via the two crucial mechanisms of action and selection. Human beings can learn and increase their personal store of knowledge only by being active, having goals, and building expectations. Popper then reasserts that every evolutionary change, both biological and behavioral or cognitive, starts from the information storage structures: the genome for biological aspects and the nervous system for knowledge processes. The behavior repertoire is in part innate, in part transmitted during the early phases of development. This complex information system becomes the operating theater for mutations or random variations that are subject to the environment's selective pressure.

The evolutionary scenario on the personal knowledge system level, as outlined by Popper, therefore appears to be the following. From basic, genetic, and cultural information acquired through direct transfer from parents, society, school, and other informational agents, each individual child shows a marked tendency toward a kind of deviation. This deviation with respect to information received as a legacy from the previous generation leads them to continually modify their knowledge system in constant dynamic relation to the environment. A specific self is thereby structured in very brain and continuously remodeled according to environmental pressure. "The Self changes," Popper categorically asserts, "purely by maintaining its own identity as it may!" (Popper, 1972).

Ultimately, it seems clear that the authoritarian institutions of biological and cultural evolution and evolutionary epistemology play a very important role with regard to my own complex approach to neuroscience. The brain's differentiation into specific modular and gradiental components can also be traced to the evolutionary history of this miraculous organ, whose biological structure indelibly registers millions and millions of years of evolution.

A description of the human brain as consisting of diverse components which represent evolutionary levels was first proposed organically by MacLean (1973). This author described the human brain as made up of three systems:

- the *reptilian brain*, made up of primitive structures already present in reptiles;
- the *limbic brain*, made up of nervous centers and neural pathways that appear in less evolved mammals; and
- the *neocortex*, the typical structure of cerebral organization in more evolved mammals such as primates.

The tripartite brain as described by MacLean must also include hemispheric specialization, with particular reference to the left anterior prefrontal lobe, a cerebral structure that is typical of hominids and displays most evolutionary development in *Homo sapiens* (Sperry, 1980). We can thus describe four quite distinct brain structures in humans that operate in collaboration, according to a hierarchical logic in which the more

recent structures supervise and coordinate the activities of the more primitive ones. The presence of differentiated and hierarchically ordered structures in the brain is part of an evolutionary story millions of years old and
which witnessed the structuring of new, progressively more sophisticated,
brain centers, as they passed from reptiles to the first mammals and then to
more evolved mammals up to the humanization process.

6.1 The Reptilian Brain: The Archipallium

Territorial control, predation, and the search for a partner with which to
mate are the activities that are the responsibility of this component. Knowledge functions expressed in the reptilian brain are genetically determined,
therefore are repetitive, not very flexible, and devoted primarily to maintaining physical survival. The limited capacity to evolve found in such a brain
structure's knowledge system probably explains the difficulty experienced
by large reptiles in adapting to rapidly changing environmental situations
in the past.

6.2 The Limbic System: The Paleopallium

The first mammals displayed an incomparable capacity to learn from experience. Such a tremendously important ability must be associated with the
appearance of the limbic system. With the advent of the first mammals, this
cerebral system is no longer primarily centralized in the olfactory perceptual
system, as was the case with the reptilian brain, but rather in vision and
therefore in a much more powerful and sophisticated means of acquiring
data from reality.

Whereas the reptilian brain operated mainly on the basis of genetically
preordained programs and exhibited very little functional freedom, the
limbic system proved to be less determined by internal data and more
capable of evolving on the basis of external data acquired via new and
powerful sensory systems, such as vision and hearing. The paleopallium
appeared to be well equipped with sophisticated memory processes capable
of acquiring new information and structuring the mnestic trace that was
subsequently able to drive problem-solving strategies. Thus, it began to
develop a marked capacity for learning and its behavior tended to diversify in
every individual, based on a specific, personal knowledge-building process.

The diverse behaviors involved in reproduction in mammals compared to reptiles made the development of a sophisticated process of raising offspring necessary, which supported the birth of complex social behavior.

6.3 Brain Structures of Less Evolved Mammals: The Neopallium

The third brain structure that developed at an increased pace concurrently with the evolution of mammals is the neopallium. The neopallium experienced impressive, complex development in humans, where the brain matter constituting this component proved almost incredibly superior even to that of the more evolved primates.

6.4 Specialized Frontal Lobes

The last and most recent evolutionary stage in the development of the human brain is the hemispheric specialization that coincides with the acquisition of linguistic abilities, the optimization of abstracting representations of reality, and the creation of an articulated flexible knowledge base that was transferable not only to peers but especially to progeny.

The description of structurally and functionally diversified cerebral systems was recently completed in biochemical research and integrated in the neuroscience field, representing another important level of study in brain and mind functioning. A series of substances that can play the role of chemical mediators in the transmission of information to the nervous systems has already been identified. Among them are some amino acids (glutamic acid, aspartic acid, gamma-aminobutyric acid), some monoamines (norepinephrine, adrenaline, serotonin, and dopamine), and a series of neuropeptides (substance P and enkephalin). Most of these mediators can now be identified and mapped in the human brain. Therefore it is now possible to describe different brain systems according to which biochemical features they have.

In particular, noradrenergic, dopaminergic, and serotoninergic systems have been described. A comprehensive description of the anatomical and functional aspects of such systems is outside the scope of this book, and, moreover, these are not yet clarified in contemporary research. Therefore, I will limit myself to emphasizing that, since the 1980s, some attempts have been made at developing a complex psychobiological approach to personality structure that also considers the role of different mediators. For example, Cloninger (1994) describes three systems, as follows:

- the harm-avoidance system as a serotoninergic system;
- the novelty-seeking system as a dopaminergic system; and
- the reward-dependence system as a noradrenergic system.

Even though Cloninger's model may appear schematic and reductive, it still constitutes one of the first attempts at developing an integrated bio-psychosocial approach within the study of complex cognitive systems.

At the end of the nineteenth and in the first part of the twentieth century, diversified and hierarchically ordered brain structures were considered the basis for developing a linear paradigm for the mind in which the most recent structures, repositories of rationality, must continuously dominate those more primitive structures that are stimulated by a strong instinctual burden, characterized as substantially negative and destructive. This conception is, for example, at the basis of Freudian metapsychology and theory of conflict. According to a more modern view, the brain is instead a computational system that operates in concert, that is, an information processing system of the coalitional type. The more primitive structures carry out a very important role within human life, and work in constant cooperation with the more evolved knowledge structures. The human brain probably constitutes the most evolved, sophisticated, functional, flexible, and powerful complex system in this region of the universe. Its patterns of functioning derive from processes that animate an assemblage of billions of functional units, each one of which assumes thousands of communication configurations via multiple dendritic structures. The evolutionary possibilities are of such a magnitude that they are difficult to calculate, and are capable of rendering reason from the complexity of the human mind.

The good functioning of the human mind is the ultimate goal in a phylogenetic as well as ontogenetic evolutionary process that embraces the entire arc of existence of every single human being. The amount of information deriving from the continuous flux of experience from the external world and from perception of the internal world, relentlessly processed and reordered within the knowledge system, are integrated into the complex and self-organizing process of the self that constitutes the mind's unifying application.

An extremely complex biological system, and a particularly imbalanced one, the human brain is organized into multiple functional units equipped with decentralized control mechanisms. This means that each one of them is furnished with autonomous peripheral regulatory processes. As we have already seen, the most primitive structures exhibit a marked modularity that is genetically determined, while, from a phylogenetic and ontogenetic viewpoint, those more recent structures demonstrate distinct self-organizational postures modulated by the incoming flow of information. From the multiple brain units, both modular and gradiental, specific information processing patterns emerge that recognize different computational codes (e.g., analog time, digital time, and mixed time).

Although every module and therefore every brain process exhibits self-organized activity and is equipped with decentralized control, I must emphasize how, in human beings, complex processes of coalitional control emerge, capable of emulating a sense of unity and cohesion among the many different centers. Ultimately, in order to understand the human brain as it is in the present, one must review phylogenetic evolutionary history, since, in order to understand the organization of every single human mind, it is necessary to examine evolutionary history on the ontogenetic and narrative levels. When observing only the here and now, as is typically done by those applying the standard cognitive orientation, little can be understood about a creature like *Homo sapiens*, originating from history.

2
Clinical Psychophysiology and its Parameters

7
Psychophysiology and Clinical Psychophysiology

Psychophysiology is the discipline that studies the dependency relationships between mental activity and biological parameters. In the short space of little more than a hundred years, it has experienced tremendous development, from the methodological as well as theoretical and epistemological points of view, becoming one of the most promising areas of neuroscience research today.

Once again, I must emphasize how the conceptual origins of the psychophysiological method, as Andreassi noted (1989), can be traced back to ancient Greek philosophy and medicine. Erasistratus of Ceos, who lived in the third century BCE, is identified by Andreassi as the first author to experimentally document mind–body interactions clinically, making a diagnosis and successfully implementing a therapy that could be considered the archetype for the application of the neuroscientific method in the clinical setting.

Erasistratus had been called to consult with King Seleucus to try to resolve the intricate clinical case of his son, Antiochus. Having no strength, the young prince remained in his bed, presenting with a psychosomatic crisis characterized by negative feelings of anxiety and sadness, the main symptoms being palpitations, cold sweats, and a deathly pallor. None of the illustrious physicians called in by his father was able to resolve this clinical case. Erasistratus, however, was the first to implement a methodology that could be defined today as psychophysiological. In fact, he realized that the young man's crises were intermittent and therefore decided to isolate him in a room where he regularly and consistently had those close to him come to

Neuroscience-based Cognitive Therapy: New Methods for Assessment, Treatment, and Self-Regulation, First Edition. Tullio Scrimali.
© 2012 John Wiley & Sons, Ltd. Published 2012 by John Wiley & Sons, Ltd.

visit. Erasistratus monitored his symptoms of sweating (the process at the foundation of electrodermal recording), paleness, and tachycardia during the visits. By measuring the prince's heart rate at the wrist, palpating his sweaty hands, and observing his facial pallor, Erasistratus thus determined that the attacks occurred when his very beautiful stepmother entered the room. After a long private consultation, Antiochus admitted to being in love with his stepmother and in despair about the conflict he was experiencing between his desire for a woman, respect for his father, and social rules.

Two thousand three hundred years ago, Erasistratus thus made the first diagnosis based on historically documented psychophysiological data. He then advised King Seleucus, who consented to a divorce from his wife in order to wed the woman to his son. Once the son was finally able to marry the woman he loved, he soon recovered to live in happiness. As you can see, study of the somatic correlates of emotion in medicine and psychology has quite a long history.

Now that we have paid proper homage to the contribution of ancient Greece to the development of science in the western world, let's return to our own time period. Modern psychophysiology developed in the twentieth century. During its period of rapid growth, attributable to a certain extent to the technological progress that provided tools and then progressively more effective and reliable techniques, differentiation in the epistemological background was witnessed. These developments were so far-reaching that the first authors faced opposition to their reductionism and associationism (Pavlov, 1903), with an opposing viewpoint couched in terms of motor theories of the mind, and new directions in contemporary interactionist epistemology that re-elaborated the mind–brain connection theme, based on new neuroscientific contributions in a dimension that was not strictly biologistic and reductionist (Popper and Eccles, 1977).

This definition of psychophysiology demonstrated an evolutionary process. Mangina redefined this discipline as: "The science that studies the physiology of mental functions through the relationships between brain, body, and behavior in the living human being that interacts with the environment" (Mangina, 1983). Subsequently, Andreassi proposed the following formulation: "Psychophysiology constitutes the study of the connections between manipulation of psychological variables and resulting physiological responses measured in the living human being, with the goal of advancing the clarification of the links between mental processes and somatic functions" (Andreassi, 1989).

It appears evident, then, that psychophysiology is the discipline that most directly involves the problem of the mind–brain connection. The development of psychophysiology articulated over the twentieth century started from a reductionist standpoint, subsequently reaching a more complex dimension. I personally provided, recognized at least in Italy, an original contribution from study and research.

In the strict sense of the word, psychophysiology should be broken down more accurately into experimental and clinical psychophysiology. In the second of these, the study of modifications in biological processes is implemented over the course of specific mental and psychosomatic disorders, working with patients afflicted with mental and psychosomatic distress in a clinical setting rather than with healthy subjects in a laboratory setting. Clinical psychophysiology interacts with and contributes to various contexts such as clinical psychology, psychiatry, psychotherapy, social psychology, health psychology, behavioral medicine, and psychosomatic medicine. The development of a true clinical psychophysiology called for the resolution of complex technical and methodological problems, as well as of those relating to economic issues associated with the possibility of acquiring low-cost systems to record specific biological parameters, for the purpose of making them usable in both the clinical and psycho-educational settings (Furedy, 1983).

The last ten years of the twentieth century were branded the decade of the brain, with an international agreement directed at developing lines of research. Based on the work of numerous researchers and remarkable amounts of investment, very intriguing results were obtained, leading to a better comprehension of the mind's processes and the brain's functions, an explanation of the clinical reality within mental disorders, and, above all, mechanisms for treatment and recovery (Scrimali and Grimaldi, 1991). From the start of the new millennium, for the first time it was feasible to document, via both structural and functional brain imaging techniques, how effective cognitive psychotherapy treatments could contribute to building new cerebral networks and furthering the development of additional synapses (Cozolino, 2002; Scrimali, 2008). As we will see in Chapter 8, some methods today, such as quantitative EEG, digital recording of EDA, and study of frontal cognitive processes implemented with laser light spectrography, have become so simple to apply and at such a low cost as to make them practical not just in large research laboratories but also in the clinical setting.

8

Electroencephalography and Quantitative Electroencephalography

8.1 Electroencephalography

The surface of the brain produces a series of spontaneous electrical potentials that change according to mental state. The first observation of electrical signals originating from the nervous system dates to 1848, when Emil du Bois-Reymond detected the presence of such action potentials as activity markers on the part of a peripheral nerve. Later, in 1875, Richard Caton made a similar discovery of electrical activity in the brain through studies with monkeys and rabbits (Caton, 1875).

The breakthrough discovery that electrical brain activity recorded on the scalp could correspond to cognitive functions, or emotional activation, came thanks to the German psychiatrist Hans Berger, who published an article in 1929 describing an oscillatory-type electrical activity model recorded from a human brain (the subject was his own son, Klaus). Berger was the first to hypothesize that the electroencephalography (EEG) used in this technique might be used as a biological marker for mental disorders and, therefore, could have potential for clinical implementation and use, from both the diagnostic and therapeutic standpoints (Berger, 1929).

The huge initial enthusiasm the new technique inspired in the psychiatric community, who were delighted to have found a new marker for mental disorders from recording EEG, is quite understandable. Nevertheless, this enthusiasm soon waned, as the study of simple, spontaneous EEG activity could not make use of the complex statistical analysis that would allow identification of any significant mental disorder data until the subsequent

Neuroscience-based Cognitive Therapy: New Methods for Assessment, Treatment, and Self-Regulation, First Edition. Tullio Scrimali.
© 2012 John Wiley & Sons, Ltd. Published 2012 by John Wiley & Sons, Ltd.

advent of computers able to analyze data to make the activity understandable. EEG nevertheless provided important data about the basic conditional functionality of the CNS. It then became a very useful tool in neurology, with particular application to the study of epilepsy.

A real revolution has taken place in recent years with the introduction of computerized EEG. The most important variables in an EEG are set out below.

8.1.1 Frequency

The frequency is the number of times that a wave repeats its oscillatory cycle in one second, and it is measured in hertz (Hz). More precisely, it is the number of cycles per second (or Hz) of a much "faster" wave. Today, we use systems based on automatic frequency analysis (Fourier transform) that allow analysis of the EEG spectrum subdivided into its different frequencies. Brain waves are thereby classified into four types based on their frequency:

- delta: 0–4 Hz;
- theta: 4–8 Hz;
- alpha: 8–12 Hz; and
- beta: > 12 Hz.

Delta and theta waves are also described as slow waves while alpha and beta waves are described as fast waves. The delta rhythm is comprised of low-frequency and high-voltage waves: the EEG in this case is rather synchronous, as the various parts of the brain seem to oscillate in unison. On the other hand, the EEG appears to be asynchronous when the beta rhythm is present. The delta rhythm presents mainly during sleep, although it is present to a varying degree in normal EEGs during awake periods.

The theta rhythm, which also consists of slow waves, can be physiologically recorded from the parietal and temporal lobes of young subjects. In the first weeks of life, a baby displays only theta- and delta-type activity; the alpha waves first appear around 18 months. As an infant grows, the alpha increases until it becomes the dominant rhythm observed in most adults with eyes closed. In the sleep state, theta and delta waves are physiological, yet they assume clear pathological significance in other circumstances, as when they are recorded during coma. In addition to during sleep, the theta rhythm is also found in semi-sleep states and has been shown to play a role in strengthening memory processes.

The alpha rhythm is characteristic of an EEG from an adult in a relaxed state, with eyes closed, and is especially evident in recordings from the temporal and occipital lobes. The alpha rhythm appears during progressive relaxation with eyes closed or during meditation, that is, when the mind is not committed to specific tasks, and sight and sound inputs are absent or reduced to a minimum. The alpha rhythm is also associated with multitasking. Anxious subjects can show difficulty in producing an alpha rhythm. In each individual, however, the dominant alpha frequency is rather constant over time, varying to a maximum of 1 Hz.

It is assumed that an attentive brain that is not occupied with any specific task may produce an alpha rhythm, or that it occurs in multitasking when subjects simultaneously execute many tasks without specifically focusing on any one. When a subject producing an alpha rhythm is asked to open their eyes (provided they are closed until that moment) to make a mental calculation, or when they hear a sudden noise, the alpha rhythm is rapidly replaced by the beta rhythm. This EEG modification is called an arrest reaction or alpha block.

Beta is the most rapid rhythm in the EEG. It appears during periods when the individual is awake, in addition to during a specific phase of sleep, defined as paradoxical sleep or the REM (rapid eye movement) phase. Despite being asleep, the individual exhibits an electrical rhythm similar to that of an awake state and also produces eye movement. The beta rhythm indicates the presence of mental activity influenced by sensory stimulation, as it does in pure mental processing. Where excessive, the beta rhythm indicates the presence of anxiety states associated with negative recursive mental processes such as rumination and worry.

All regions of the brain exhibit each of the electrical activity frequencies, although each specific band is found primarily in particular regions of the brain's surface. For example, alpha waves are found predominantly in the occipital region while beta waves are more typical of the frontal region.

8.1.2 Amplitude

The amplitude of an EEG wave is quantified by its voltage in microvolts and measured from the wave's peak to the lowest point in its trough. EEG amplitude generally includes a comprehensive range of between 20 and 50 microvolts, but there does exist a remarkable degree of variation. In fact, we can observe EEGs with amplitudes of less than 10 microvolts and even as low as 5. Amplitude tends to decrease in response to stimulation. For example, it diminishes in recordings of subjects with eyes open in contrast to those of subjects with eyes closed.

8.1.3 Morphology

The combination of frequency and amplitude in the EEG signal gives rise to the shape of the tracing, or what is referred to as the EEG's morphology. An EEG's morphology fluctuates continuously according to the study subject's state (alert, asleep, etc.). If lasting less than 70 milliseconds, a specific morphology that differs from surrounding EEG activity is described as a spike, while one lasting from 70 to 200 milliseconds is called a wave.

A complex describes two or more waves that present together and repeat at more or less regular intervals. In a monomorphic complex the waves are similar, while in a polymorphic complex they have different morphology.

8.1.4 Symmetry

Symmetry is the degree to which electrical activity in a specific hemispheric region is uniform with that of the corresponding region in the contralateral hemisphere. In principle, the electrical activity in one region should be similar to that of its corresponding region in the contralateral hemisphere.

8.1.5 Coherence

The EEG can be analyzed by comparing the patterns it shows at two points on the scalp. Symmetry between frequency patterns shown at the two recording sites is defined as coherence. Coherence therefore reflects, both quantitatively and qualitatively, the existing functional connections between two separate cerebral areas from two separate regions. In other words, the level of coherence represents a measure of how and how much two regions of the brain are able to communicate. The level of coherence identified between various areas of the brain in one sample of healthy subjects will indicate optimal levels of communication in the regions analyzed. As a clinical example, the levels of coherence in rapid rhythms in the anterior regions of the scalp are altered in psychotic patients who exhibit more activation in areas of the right hemisphere.

8.1.6 Artifacts

One problem that needs to be considered is the potential occurrence of artifacts during EEG recording. Artifacts introduce errors and inaccuracies that the clinician must learn to recognize in order to obtain accurate and secure data. Obtaining a high-quality recording is not an easy task, as multiple factors can cause artifacts.

Firstly, it should be remembered that electrodes are affixed to the skin during the process and they therefore record activity coming from it, as in the example of EDA. Second, the electrodes record electrical activity coming from beneath the skin, where we find various layers of muscle endowed with their own electrical activity. Positive electrodes also record electromyographical (EMG) activity coming from these muscles. Additionally, EEG activity is recorded through thick skull bone, so thick as to substantially reduce the electrical signal intensity, especially at higher frequencies. The principal artifacts you might encounter, and must avoid, can be schematically classified as follows.

First, common artifacts arise from the subject's movement and are caused by activity in the muscles of the eye, face, and neck. Every time a muscle contracts, in fact, it generates weak electrical signals that at least partially fall within the EEG's frequency bands. Over the years, there have been extensive efforts by various authors to try to define which frequency bands are most involved in myographical artifacts. Some authors, such as Davidson (1988), maintained that the comprehensive band of 13 to 20 Hz was the one most involved in this type of artifact. O'Donnell, Berkhout, and Adey (1974) indicated a high degree of correlation between EMG recordings on frontal muscles and EEG artifacts in the 8–19 Hz bandwidth, identifying this as an increase of alpha rhythm intensity in the EEG during frontal muscle contraction. Other researchers discovered that facial muscle activity manifests at lower frequencies (Nunez, 1982). More recent studies (Thornton, 1996) have demonstrated that artifacts of muscular origin involve all frequency bands, perhaps with the exception of the delta. For such reasons, if "cleanly recorded" EEG signals are required, the subject being tested must not move (or move as little as possible) the muscles in the head, neck, face, and eyes.

Second, common artifacts from cardiac electrical activity occur if the positive electrodes are recording from a region on the scalp over large pulsatile blood vessels. This type of artifact is more frequent in recordings made on older subjects, as the amplitude of EEG waves decreases with age. This is because bone in the skull, the meninges (intermediary connective tissue between the skull and skin), and connective tissue in the skin itself become thicker and less conductive.

Third, common artifacts can occur due to dried-out electrodes, poor contact from insufficient conductive paste on an electrode, inadequate saline saturation of the same, or where an electrode becomes too dry during a long recording. The result is that signals become too weak or excessive interference is captured at 50 Hz. For the same reason, the skin must be cleaned with a cotton ball containing a cleanser that will remove cutaneous sebum, which can block electrical signal conduction.

Finally, common artifacts occur due to a secondary 50–60 Hz signal where commonly used electrical cables running at 110 or 220V are present, creating an electromagnetic field at about 60 or 50 Hz. This electromagnetic field spreads in every direction and is noticeable even at a distance of just a few meters from electrical cables. The intensity of this field can be greater than the intensity of electrical brain signals and the electrodes record this interfering signal along with real EEG signals, giving rise to artifacts.

The two methodological principles for eliminating artifacts are online and offline elimination. The online method avails itself of representative EEG samples that are free from artifacts, used as a model to eliminate those recordings that deviate significantly from the samples. The offline method consists instead of particularly suitable stratagems for removing any evidence of artifacts after the EEG has been digitized. In this case, much care must be taken to avoid eliminating real EEG events mistaken for artifacts.

8.2 Quantitative Electroencephalography

The study of quantitative EEG (QEEG) constitutes a recent development in psychophysiological research that presents interesting prospects for the complex diagnosis of various mental disorders. QEEG does not differ substantially from traditional EEG. Computerized quantitative analysis, however, permits us to calculate some statistical variables that can then be compared with one of the various databases developed over the years, allowing the comparison of the same variables from clinical subjects and data collected in studies on healthy control subjects. The areas of research that have been opened with the advent of QEEG are represented by the work of Duffy *et al.* (1994) and described here.

- *Objectification of a biological vulnerability*: evaluate the extent to which certain functional bases exist for a specific disorder that you are studying.
- *Therapeutic planning*: identify the weak and strong points in the organization and electrophysiological state of a subject's brain in such a way as to select and plan the optimal type of therapy.
- *Therapeutic evaluation*: objectively document effective treatment, comparing the EEG data before and after treatment.

8.2.1 Technical and Methodological Aspects

The implementation of QEEG techniques requires a hardware unit consisting of a series of channels (from 1 to 20 or more) and amplifiers able to analyze the EEG from each site on the scalp. A reference database is then necessary to allow comparison of control data with patient information for diagnosing and monitoring therapeutic progress. A good EEG database should cover all age groups from birth to average lifespan of the population, in such a way as to be applicable to all subjects, independent of age (Skeidsvoll, 1999).

Research over the years has used a number of recording modalities and diverse methods, including recording with eyes open, with eyes closed, or during the execution of certain mental tasks. Currently, the most widely accepted modalities for a reference database are recordings made with eyes open and eyes closed, due to their simplicity and relative reproducibility of recording conditions. Data coming from different laboratories and different samples can thereby be compared with adequate reliability. Recordings made during the execution of certain mental tasks are instead bound by numerous variables that are not always controllable. The criteria for developing a QEEG reference database that is clinically useful are described by Thatcher (1998):

- accurate evaluation of demographic data, sampling procedures, and technical details;
- presence of a representative sample, with the certainty that only healthy subjects who don't present with physical or mental illnesses are included;
- adequate sample range, including all age groups so as to be able to measure potentially excessive deviations attributable to the development process;

- clean EEG samples, that is, free from artifacts; and
- accurate statistical analysis of samples.

It is now time to reflect on this methodology's level of maturity and the possibility that it may soon become a commonly used method in the clinical psychology setting.

The first aspect to consider is that of equipment, software, and a database. Enormous progress has taken place in recent years in this area. I can assert that QEEG is now a technique that is within the practical reach of the clinical setting. This aspect includes the availability of affordable equipment, relative ease of use, and finally, the usefulness of results obtained in the clinical setting.

The best 20-channel hardware, software, and sophisticated databases that can very effectively implement the morphological and functional assessment of brain function, and intuitively summarize potential functional deficiencies, are today available commercially. For example, a particularly advanced tool, available for research as well as for clinical work, such as the Mindset NP-Q 10/20, now costs only about \$5,600 (€4,000) and is available from www.np-systems.com. Specific software for quantifying the record and complex statistical post-processing must accompany this device. The program can implement cerebral morphological and functional assessment and can even offer a narrative report of possible diagnoses.

Neuroguide, one of the most powerful pieces of software of its type, can be purchased today at a cost of around \$2,995 (€2,100). As you can see, the total investment is relatively small, at around \$8,400 (€6,000) including accessories, and is within the reach of any private specialized center. In terms of training, a two-day course in the United States where you can learn complete mastery of Mindset NP-Q 10/20 and Neuroguide software costs only \$215 (€150).

It's possible, nevertheless, to familiarize yourself with QEEG with less sophisticated equipment that operates with just two channels and less powerful software. For example, such a tool as the Atlantis II hardware from BrainMaster can be coupled with a simpler version of the Neuroguide software. In that case, total cost falls to around \$2,800 (€2,000). I should point out that all quantitative encephalography systems can be equipped with specific software for neurofeedback, and I will address this methodology in Chapter 18.

A device I developed in my laboratory, in collaboration with Villiam Giroldini, is the NeuroLAB (Figure 8.1 and Figure 8.2), a four-channel EEG

Figure 8.1 NeuroLAB.

Figure 8.2 NeuroLAB at work.

analyzer. NeuroLAB is equipped with powerful software for QEEG called NeuroSCAN & Neurofeedback.

To conclude this topic, I would like to point out that a one-channel EEG system could also be used, both for the assessment and for neurofeedback, in the context of a cognitive therapy. In accordance with the goal of neuroscience-based cognitive therapy, it is important to have simple methods that allow any psychotherapist to easily assess the patient's EEG data, and then to apply some neurofeedback techniques, as I will illustrate in Chapter 17. In this regard, a one-channel EEG analysis, carried out at the Cz place, which is located on the vertex of head, according to the international 10–20 system (Demos, 2005), could be a good solution. In such a case it is possible to obtain a simple analysis of the most important three EEG rhythms, such as beta, alpha and theta.

The Cz place is chosen because it allows analysis of the area of the brain known as the "cingulated gyrus," which gives a lot of information about emotional and tacit activities (Damasio, 1994). For example, the presence of many beta rhythms in this area can be related to the presence of OCD (obsessive-compulsive disorder) and ADHD (attention deficit hyperactivity disorder). When the same kind of analysis is carried out twice, at C3 and at C4, in a depressed patient we find an increase of alpha which exceeds beta and which is higher at the level of the right hemisphere. For this analysis a single-channel Capscan-80 as developed by Expanded Technologies, Inc. could be an ideal option (Demos, 2005; Scrimali, 2011b).

In conclusion, in neuroscience-based cognitive therapy, I would say that the assessment of EEG using a two-channel computerized system, able to make some quantitative analysis and then allowing for the application of Neurofeedback, is the best solution. This is the type of system I have largely used in my experimental research, and which I strongly recommend.

QEEG and Neurofeedback are the "second-level methods" I propose in the area of neuroscience-based CT. A "first-level approach" would be to assess EDA (see Chapter 9) and to train patients using Psychofeedback (see Chapter 18), and this is useful for any patients we treat. Once this first level is complete, we can go ahead and apply the second level of QEEG and Neurofeedback, if it seems appropriate.

Electrodermal Activity and Quantitative Electrodermal Activity

9.1 Electrodermal Activity and its Recording

The recording of Electrodermal Activity (EDA) is the technique that boasts the longest history and the most extensive literature in the area of psychophysiology. It deals with a measurement of characteristics of the skin tissue on specific areas of the human body, typically the fingers. Superficially, it may seem strange that information collected from the fingers could refer to what takes place in the brain (Prokasy and Raskin, 1972), but when you begin to think about some of the functional aspects of skin on the hands and fingers in particular, you may start to understand the link that ties brain, emotional, cognitive, behavioral, and relational activity together. In fact, the epidermis of the fingers is our first point of contact with the external world, allowing us to handle it effectively. To *Homo sapiens*, touching and handling means learning and taking action.

For the surface of the skin on the hands and fingers, in particular, to best carry out its function, flexibility and skin resistance must always be regulated effectively. This occurs when the sweat glands continuously and liberally hydrate the horny layer of the skin (Figure 9.1). Specific experiments have demonstrated that when micro-perspiration is inhibited by the injection of anticholinergic substances, the skin on the hands becomes less sensitive, is less resistant to abrasions, and has reduced capacity for handling. Moreover, we commonly observe that when hands are dry and dehydrated (e.g., during the winter and with frequent use of harsh detergent soaps) the skin cracks more easily and small wounds occur more readily. Another

Neuroscience-based Cognitive Therapy: New Methods for Assessment, Treatment, and Self-Regulation, First Edition. Tullio Scrimali.
© 2012 John Wiley & Sons, Ltd. Published 2012 by John Wiley & Sons, Ltd.

Figure 9.1   Sweat gland showing: 1) Glandular Pore; 2) Horny Layer of the Skin;
3) Clear Layer of the Epidermis; 4) Granular Layer of the Epidermis; 5) Prickle-Cell
Layer of the Epidermis; 6) Germinal Layer and Basal Membrane; 7) Convoluted
Capillaries; 8) Sudoriparous (Sweat) Gland Duct; 9) Capillary Plexus of the Duct;
10) Sympathetic Vegetative Fibers; 11) Capillary Plexus of the Secretory Portion
of the Gland; 12) Myoepithelial Fibers.

common observation is that dehydrated skin on the fingertips decreases
sensitivity and handling ability. Try to identify a small object or thread a
needle with dehydrated hands!

Continuous modulation of micro-perspiration in the hands is therefore
a process that is essential to identification, handling, taking action, and
relating. Offering your hand when you meet someone is a relational act that
transmits a lot of information to the brain. I am certain that shaking a hand
when it is warm, dry, soft, and smooth makes quite a different impression
on the receiver than does a cold and sweaty or rough and chapped hand.
As you can see, even social relations are conditioned by skin perspiration in
the hands!

Since the production and utilization of perspiration to hydrate the skin
of the hands is a very expensive process, both from the energy viewpoint
and due to loss of valuable salts, we expect the nervous system to closely and
accurately regulate this process. The cognitive and executive brain (frontal

cortical system) and emotional brain (limbic and hypothalamic systems) in fact work together to achieve this (Boucsein, 1992).

It is apparent, then, that perspiration of the fingertips can represent an optimal "track of the mind," to use the metaphor I coined many years ago to describe specific psychophysiological parameters (Scrimali and Grimaldi, 1991). But how do we transition from perspiration in the hands to recording the electrodermal parameter? We can begin to determine the answer to this question by considering that, as with many other biological systems, the skin of the hands exhibits a behavior similar to that of a resistor, whose conductance modifies continuously with variation in the functional states of the skin tissue and nervous system that controls it. In fact, when we apply a low voltage to the skin of the hands, the electrical current will encounter elevated resistance due to the significant insulating strength of dead cells in the horny layer. However, the epidermis is not a dense structure, as the excretory ducts of many sweat glands intersect with it (Figure 9.1, number 8).

Perspiration is a solute that is rich in the salt sodium chloride. It is therefore an electrolytic solution that can severely lower electrical conductance of the skin, which depends, at any time, on the level of activity in the sweat glands. The more perspiration the glands produce and slowly distribute into the horny layer, the lower skin conductance will be.

A drop in the electrical resistance in some areas of the skin follows about two seconds after a sudden noise, a deep breath, a question posed, or a movement by the subject. This transitory response was called the psychogalvanic reflex in the past but is more accurately described today as the phasic electrodermal response. This response has a characteristic waveform with a rise time of 1–2 seconds and a substantially longer fall time (Edelberg, 1970). The downward slope in the waveform can assume various shapes, such as a curve that slopes slightly or instead descends sharply. An average latency time for a response recorded on the palm of the hand in a room at a comfortable temperature (20° C) is around 1.8 seconds (Edelberg, 1972).

I should specify, however, that since electrodermal resistance varies in inversely proportional terms to the level of emotion, it is preferable to utilize the conductance that changes in direct proportion to the emotional process as a physical measurement of the electrodermal parameter. In essence, the higher the conductance value, expressed in microsiemens (μs), the more elevated the subject's or patient's emotional activation. In 1966, Johnson and Lubin proposed the term "electrodermal activity" to describe the various electrical phenomena tied to cutaneous sudomotor activity, distinguishing two principle types of electrodermal processes in their own field as phasic and tonic (Lacey, 1947). The terms "psychogalvanic activity" and "psychogalvanic reflex" were ultimately dropped from the scientific literature in the 1960s (Venables and Martin, 1967) but, unfortunately, they are still frequently used in lay publications and on the internet today.

Phasic responses are indicative of rapid and transitory moments of activation, resulting from an anxious response, emotional disturbance, conflict situation, or digital and semantic mental activity provoking tension (worry) or readiness to act. These phasic responses seem to be due to rapid contraction of the myoepithelial fibers surrounding the sudoriparous gland duct that cause rapid sweat discharge from this duct. Such phasic responses were described as skin conductance responses (SCRs) by Edelberg (1967; see also Benedek and Kaernback, 2010) and this is the most accurate definition, in accordance with the international scientific literature.

Traceable to the contraction of the duct's myoepithelial fibers (Figure 9.1, number 13), the production of such responses apparently responds to action on the part of the adrenaline mediator (Fowles, 1973). Some studies nevertheless suggest that the duct's myoepithelial fibers are also sensitive to catecholamines (adrenaline and noradrenaline) in the bloodstream (Goodall, 1970).

These phasic responses can be recorded in diverse circumstances, both clinical and experimental. From the clinical point of view, recording anxious responses provoked by exposure to or imagination of a fearful situation holds particular interest. It is thereby possible to objectively evaluate the real emotional resonance of disturbing situations (Davis, 1929). Among those associated with phasic-type electrodermal responses, the parameter that has been the subject of the most in-depth analysis is the so-called orienting reaction, namely a phasic response evoked by the consecutive presentation of equivalent tonal acoustic stimuli patterns (Sokolov, 1963). This procedure of eliciting and recording phasic electrodermal responses evoked by acoustic stimuli takes on particular value in the study of human information processing. In fact, the task of listening to and even counting acoustic stimuli activates signal processing as well as other cognitive functions, such as working memory and executive competencies, when the patient is asked to perform a task (e.g., pressing a key) in response to the sounds. In ADHD, for instance, the patient demonstrates elevated arousal (higher values of skin conductance level, or SCL) but, while listening to the acoustic pattern, provides responses that are reduced to sound only and records a declining recognition performance. This shows a deficiency in the concentration processes and attention focus (O'Connell *et al.*, 2004).

An assessment methodology of this type allows the monitoring of the trend of habituation, that is, the process by which phasic responses tend to switch off with repetition of the stimulus. If the same stimulus typology is always administered to the subject, their interest will progressively diminish until phasic electrodermal response falls off. The speed with which the habituation process occurs varies from individual to individual and, in any one subject, depends on their emotional and cognitive conditions. So the study of phasic electrodermal responses evoked by monotonous sensory inputs (stimuli) or by more complex cognitive inputs (events) is an instrumental methodology for the study of human information processing (Berlyne, 1961; Scrimali and Grimaldi, 1991).

The study of another type of EDA similar to that of the evoked phasic response is also remarkably important, yet manifests in the absence of external stimuli. These spontaneous phasic responses are described in the English-language literature as nonspecific-skin conductance responses (NS-SCRs). These responses are provoked by mental activity characterized as intense and apprehensive, such as that observed in obsessive patients or those afflicted by a generalized anxiety disorder. The mental activity is typically described as worry (Davey and Wells, 2006).

We now move on to the description of tonic EDA, expressed as a baseline level of electrodermal conductance or SCL, an index for the general state of activation and vigilance (Malmo and Shagass, 1949). A reduction in SCL is indicative of progressive psychophysical relaxation and a general relaxation process in the individual (Mathews and Gelder, 1969). Recording the baseline level of electrodermal conductance, then, seems particularly useful where substantiating the degree of psychophysical relaxation achieved through learning and practicing various self-control techniques is desired. Paul demonstrated that the psychophysical relaxation produced via a brief relaxation technique training session completely corresponds to modifications in SCL (Paul, 1969). Daily monitoring of this parameter ultimately proves able to provide the anticipated indicators of stress level that the subject experiences.

To conclude this description of the electrodermal parameter, I should add that everything discussed up to this point refers to exosomatic EDA. This term indicates that the electrodermal parameter under analysis generates from external application of voltage to the body so as to record the conductance passing through the skin and its variations.

Another type of EDA exists in which no voltage is applied. Instead, two electrodes are placed, one on an area where there are few sweat glands, for example the back of the hand, and the other on an area with many such glands, such as the palm of the hand (Wilcot, 1966). In this way, a potential differential of about 50 millivolts can be recorded using an operational amplifier. Modifications in the emotional situation provoke variations in potentials that immediately change polarity. In endosomatic terms, measurements are more accurate and information-enhanced because they can show the difference between an orienting reflex and a defensive reflex. However, rather complex tools and methodologies are required, making these measurements more useful in the scope of research than in a clinical setting.

The regulation of EDA involves structures in both the peripheral and central nervous system and is complex. In the CNS, we can largely distinguish three different systems that are capable of regulating EDA: a cortical system identified in the premotor cortex of the frontal lobe (Area 6 from Brodmann, 1909); a second system localized in the anterior limbic structures (Isamat, 1961); and a third system consisting of the amygdala, hippocampus, and thalamus.

As you can see, EDA reflects multiple processes. Planning and executive processes find a home in the frontal lobe, a structure that is therefore among the most evolved and sophisticated in the entire nervous system; emotional processes are primarily accomplished in the limbic system; the memory processes involve the hippocampus; and the regulation of sensory input plays out within the thalamus. In addition to that, the study of EDA implemented simultaneously on both hands can provide interesting structural and functional information about the hemispheric specialization processes. Some research, in fact, has demonstrated that functional asymmetry between the right and left hands can be accentuated or reduced depending on emotional condition, in addition to being influenced by pathological states such as schizophrenia and depression. One such study, from Bob *et al.* (2007), showed that, in schizophrenia and depression, patterns of hemispheric coherence analyzed via the bilateral recording of EDA are related to symptomatic presentations observed in the clinical situation. In particular, these authors observed that right-handed control subjects recorded some slightly higher SCL values, while in left-handed subjects the condition inverted in those who were depressed and worsened in schizophrenics.

From the biochemical viewpoint, catecholamines influence EDA, as adrenaline can activate the myoepithelial cells in the sudoriparous gland duct, thus generating phasic responses. The last mediator released from the nerve endings that stimulates the sweat gland is acetylcholine. This explains why anticholinergic substances tend to diminish electrodermal conductance.

The relative simplicity of recording the electrodermal parameter and the remarkable amount of valid and accessible information that it can provide about mental, emotional, and cognitive activity explain the notable quantity of studies and research on this subject in the literature. The first observations on EDA, in fact, began in the second half of the nineteenth century with Tarchanoff, who was the first to record and systematically study this psychophysiological parameter in humans (Tarchanoff, 1890). The tool was quite simple, largely consisting of a Wheatstone bridge, which Charles Wheatstone fabricated and fully described for the first time in 1843 for the general purpose of measuring resistance in materials, an application that is still used in industry today. In brief, it is a system comprised of an electric current source, ordinarily in the form of a battery, a series of electrical resistance elements, and a galvanometer. The galvanometer measures the current that flows through the circuit, which is dependent on the value of resistance. The movement of the galvanometer's needle signals each variation in resistance (Wheatstone, 1879).

With this device, Tarchanoff did indeed demonstrate variable resistance from the skin on the hands of patients. The galvanometer signaled every change in electrodermal resistance via oscillations in its needle. Tarchanoff's tool therefore represents one of the origins of neuroscience. Figure 9.2 shows the schematic drawing for an original psychogalvanometer, which I

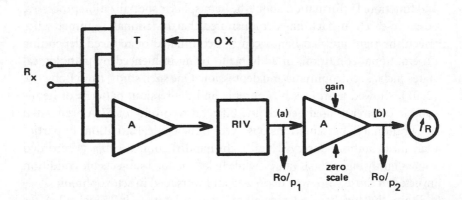

Figure 9.2 Schema of the first apparatus for recording EDA, which I designed at the end of the 1970s.

fabricated at the end of the 1970s in my laboratory in the Department of Psychiatry at the University of Catania.

In psychotherapy, the study of EDA made its entrance with Jung's research, which called on Freud's assumption that therapy should identify the unconscious processes that were causing the patient's suffering. Jung thus applied the recording of EDA to the analytical technique by preparing a list of words that he read to the patient as he recorded. Where a word was tied to topics critical to the patient's psyche, he observed evident phasic electrodermal responses. His experiments with EDA were published in 1906 in the article "Studies in word analysis" (Jung, 1906). This contribution can therefore be considered the first important stage in integrating EDA recording into the psychotherapeutic setting.

In recent years, developments in digital electronics and information technology have provided renewed motivation for recording EDA, making data measurement not only more reliable but also more easily recorded and subjected to post-analysis. Today, the components of an efficient recording system for this parameter are generally three: a measurement tool, software for recording information, and a computer for processing collected data.

The goal of one important part of my research has been that of developing a reliable yet economic methodology that is easy to use while maintaining verifiable data, collected in a methodologically sound way. This method can then be disseminated on a wide scale, providing reliable clinical as well as scientific results, and therefore facilitating replication of experimental studies. My work in developing equipment for EDA recording and biofeedback started more than thirty years ago. In the 1970s, the Dermometer, connected to an analog plotter, permitted me to launch the first systematic recordings of exosomatic EDA. With Psychotrainer, in the 1980s, I initiated a research project directed at producing a compact, economic, and easy-to-use device for clinical recording of EDA and biofeedback. And then with MindLAB Set (see Section 9.2), I advanced to fully digital technology, achieving at the start of the 2000s a comprehensive, stand-alone tool suite for recording EDA and biofeedback.

9.2 Computer-Aided Analysis of Electrodermal Activity and Quantitative Electrodermal Activity

The use of a computer, together with specific software, for monitoring electrodermal data today allows the development of a new approach to the study of this parameter. For this reason, by analogy with what happened in the field of EEG, I would like to propose the new term "quantitative electrodermal activity" (QEDA) for the computer-aided analysis of electrodermal activity. QEDA is a new tool for recording, by computer, electrodermal data and elaborating this data with specific software. For example, BIOPAC Systems Inc. produces an interactive and intuitive program that lets you instantly view, measure, analyze, and memorize electrodermal data. This program is called AcqKnowledge and includes a fully automated scoring system for EDA data (www.biopac.com). The program's features include options for deriving phasic EDA from tonic EDA, locating spontaneous SCR, and carrying out an event-related EDA analysis.

AcqKnowledge and the BIOPAC instrumentation are ideal for research. In light of the goal of neuroscience-based CT, however, I would like to suggest something simpler and less expensive: the Personal Efficiency Trainer (PET) GSR Recorder, which is economical and can be used for EDA recording and biofeedback (www.biof.com). The (PET) GSR Recorder is powered by PC software, called BioExplorer, which is very intuitive and offers high flexibility for reviewing the data saved in the PET. The whole recorded session is always shown in one graph. The data can also be played back, especially if audio is recorded with the data.

In my laboratory, I developed a new tool, the MindLAB Set (Figure 9.3), which includes the software MindSCAN and Psychofeedback (Figures 9.4, 9.5 and 9.6). MindLAB Set is an integrated system for clinical psychophysiology aimed at recording exosomatic EDA, and permits instrumental psychodiagnostics, as well as the implementation of emotional self-regulation techniques such as psychofeedback and Biofeedback-Based Mindfulness (Scrimali, 2010a). MindLAB Set allows the implementation of some of the processes that constitute the basis for clinical psychophysiological activity, such as recording exosomatic, tonic, and phasic EDA. This device is distributed by Psychotech (www.psychotech.it).

Both the Personal Efficiency Trainer (PET) GSR Recorder and MindLAB Set allow any clinician to obtain accurate and objective information on the subject's level of emotional activation (arousal) as well as on information processing (spontaneous evoked and phasic responses). Continuous biological feedback to the patient (biofeedback) about EDA is provided.

Recorded psychophysiological data can be saved and pulled up later for the purpose of constructing a narrative record of therapeutic process development. It is important for the patient to observe the gradual changes that occur over the course of treatment.

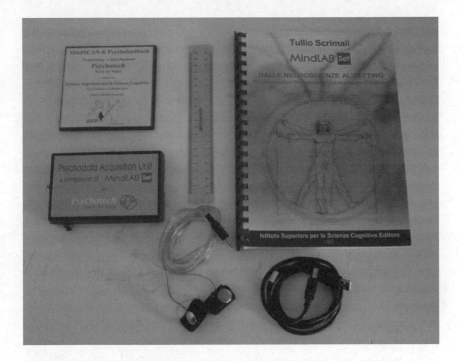

Figure 9.3   The MindLAB Set apparatus.

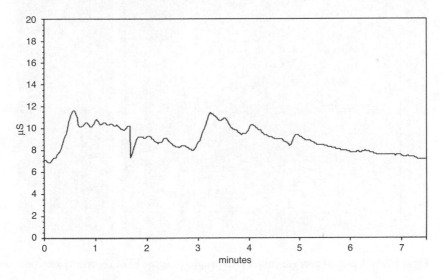

Figure 9.4   A plot of EDA recorded by a MindLAB Set.

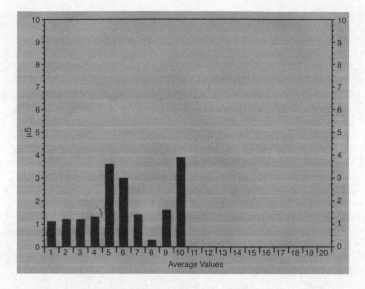

Figure 9.5 A plot of average values of many sessions of EDA recording.

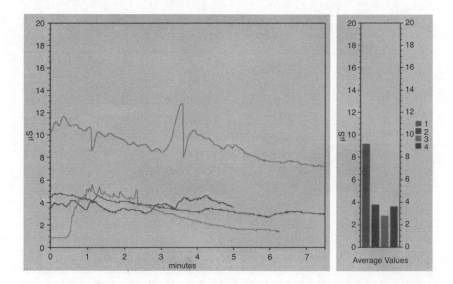

Figure 9.6 A plot of average values plus graphs of some EDA recording sessions.

9.3 Reference Database

Once we had produced and extensively tested the MindLAB Set system, it was necessary to collect a series of standard data that would act as a reference database for comparing records obtained from patients afflicted with various pathological conditions. This procedure is analogous to that followed for the creation of the various existing databases based on the recording of EEG activity analyzed through computer-managed programs. The reference database I created for EDA and which I describe in this book is the Katane, named in honor of the city where I was born. Katane is in fact the Greek name for the city of Catania and means "grater." The first Greek settlers chose the name because they were impressed by how the lava terrain in their new city looked quite similar to a cheese grater. Figure 9.7 is a photograph I took of a section of the Catania coastline in front of my home, in which you can see the shape of a grater quite clearly, much as it must have appeared to the first colonists arriving from the Aegean Sea. Furthermore, the electrodermal records of anxious patients with numerous

Figure 9.7 The rocky shore of Catania.

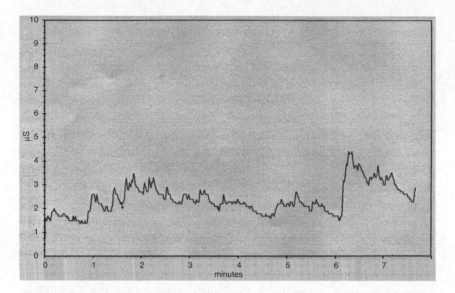

Figure 9.8 A graph of the EDA of an anxious patient which shows a profile similar to that of a cheese grater.

phasic responses look just like teeth, or the profile of a grater. Thus Katane is a fitting name for the database (Figure 9.8).

To develop the Katane standard reference database, we started by asking for participants who were not afflicted with mental disorders. We interfaced a portable laptop computer with MindLAB Set. This allowed us to implement a true mobile lab setting that we could set up each time in different environments:

- the University of Catania (Department of Psychological Sciences, Department of Political Science, Faculty of Legal Sciences, Department of Communication Sciences, Faculty of Medicine and Surgery);
- the private homes of friends and acquaintances; and
- the headquarters of a healthcare company specializing in care for the elderly population (which allowed us to build up a database group of advanced age seniors).

In order to exclude any psychopathological conditions that were not clinically evident, we administered the Middlesex Hospital Questionnaire

(Crown, 1966) to each member of the control group. A total of 536 people were tested. Via MindLAB Set, we implemented the recording method as follows. Subjects were seated comfortably for 10 minutes. After they were acclimatized and calm, we conducted a 4-minute recording. We used control sampling of one piece of data every 0.25 seconds. We provided the following instructions to the subject: "We will now measure a parameter connected to your emotional condition. Do nothing for two minutes but remain calm."

Our first evaluation focused on data deriving from the Middlesex Hospital Questionnaire. We identified subjects who had recorded elevated values on the four scales referring to the emotional activation parameter when filling out Crown's questionnaire. The four scales are: anxiety, phobias, obsessions, and somatizations. We also later studied the depression parameter. Twenty-four subjects in the group recorded dysfunctional scores on these scales and were therefore excluded from the database. We made a preliminary evaluation of the data obtained from the group of subjects that had not shown dysfunctional psychological parameters. We wanted to establish whether the SCL measured with MindLAB Set was in fact influenced by the age variable, as is reported in some of the research literature. For this purpose, control subjects were subdivided into four age groups: 11–15, 16–25, 26–60, and over 60. For each age group, we calculated the average and standard deviations from the three parameters under consideration, as reported in Table 9.1.

Using a Student's t-test statistical analysis method, we compared the average and standard deviations of measurements in different samples. We first analyzed the gender variable. Comparison of data relating to gender obtained from the three age groups did not show significant differences. Subsequently, we calculated the average and standard deviations for each age group without considering the gender variable (overall values in the tables). We made further comparisons with these data. The first and second age groups were not significantly different, so I decided to consolidate the data into a new 11–25-year-old age group. The average and standard deviations for the combined age group of 11–25 years were 5.4 and ±4.4 respectively. We compared these values with ones from the combined sample from subjects in the 26–60 age group. Comparison showed a statistically significant difference between the average and standard deviations ($p < 0.01$). Finally, we compared data pertaining to the second and third age groups. The results showed a highly significant statistical difference ($p < 0.001$).

Table 9.1 Average values of SCL showing
the effect of the ageing process.

Age group 1		SCL
(11–15)	Overall	8.0 ± 5.6
	Males	8.0 ± 5.0
	Females	8.0 ± 6.4
Age group 2		SCL
(16–25)	Overall	6.8 ± 4.9
	Males	7.2 ± 4.8
	Females	6.4 ± 4.9
Age group 3		SCL
(26–60)	Overall	3.8 ± 3.3
	Males	3.9 ± 3.8
	Females	3.6 ± 2.5
Age group 4		SCL
(over 60)	Overall	2.0 ± 1.1
	Males	1.9 ± 1.1
	Females	2.2 ± 1.2

Ultimately, we can assert that the electrodermal conductance measured with MindLAB Set does not differ by gender but decreases with age. This is apparently attributable both to physical characteristics of the skin, which tends to dehydrate with age, and to brain activation modalities, which tend to diminish during the ageing process. The reference data for SCL in the Katane database, obtained from research, which we used to compare the data from patients, are reported in Table 9.2.

Since the lowest data values from the three groups were similar, we simplified the interpretation to state that the comprehensive normal values in the young age group were within 10 microsiemens, within 7 microsiemens in the adult group, and within 3 microsiemens in the senior adult group (over 60 years of age).

Table 9.2 Average values of SCL for three different age groups.

Age group	SCL	Comprehensive values
11–25	Average: 5.4	1 to 10
26–60	Average: 3.8	0.5 to 7.1
Over 60	Average: 2.0	0.9 to 3.1

9.4 Evoked Electrodermal Responses

When considering electrodermal activity, we are usually dealing with the spontaneous, tonic and phasic activities, which are the epiphenomenon of general brain activity, for example, arousal.

If we decide to administer some sensorial stimuli to the patients, while registering EDA, we are monitoring the "Evoked Electrodermal Responses" (EEDRs). This kind of paradigm is called "stimulus-related" and it is strictly linked with information processing (Grings and Dawson, 1978).

If we administer to the patient some acoustic stimuli, using headphones, after any stimulation we can observe a specific phasic response at EDA level. When we repeat the stimulation a total of ten times, for example, according to Humphrey (1933) and Harris (1943) we observe a process called habituation, whereby the amplitude of the responses decreases until finally it disappears.

The characteristics of this process of habituation are closely linked with the activities of human information processing, of the subject, and with the subject's personality (Coles, Gale, and Kline, 1971).

The study of the electrodermal index of habituation is a very interesting and promising area of research and clinical application. For this reason, the programs MindSCAN and Psychofeedback that I developed for MindLAB Set include some specific tools for eliciting the "Evoked Electrodermal Responses" using acoustic, controlled stimuli (Psychotech, 2008). Habituation is retarded in anxious patients and in schizophrenics affected by positive symptoms (Gruzelier, 1976; Gruzelier and Venables, 1972).

9.5 Effects of Psychoactive Drugs on Electrodermal Activity

Since patients with whom we use MindLAB Set for assessment or psychotherapy quite often take medication, we have to know the effect of various drugs on the electrodermal parameter, for the purpose of accurately interpreting data recorded. Like any other physiological system, the electrodermal parameter does in fact show the effects of both the direct and indirect influence of psychoactive drugs introduced into the human body. EEG specialists are well aware of this issue and advise a psychotropic drug washout of several days before subjects present themselves for a recording, as it is known that many drugs can demonstrate a pronounced effect on the recorded morphology. With regard to EDA, drugs administered can also affect this parameter, and there is an acknowledged necessity to consider peripheral activity, therefore, in the skin or control centers, that is, in the CNS.

Every drug capable of producing anticholinergic effects reduces electrodermal conductance, as it is recognized that the final chemical mediator in perspiration is acetylcholine. Anticholinergic drugs can therefore reduce electrodermal conductance with a peripheral mechanism beyond their potential effect on the CNS. Among these drugs are:

- anti-epileptics;
- anti-Parkinsonians;
- neuroleptics, primarily phenothiazine compounds; and
- tricyclic antidepressants.

In addition to these, other psychoactive drugs affect EDA, as they modify some mental processes such as anxiety and arousal, mood level and thymic activation, or information processing. In this case, modification in EDA depends on the drug's symptomatic and therapeutic effect.

Among everyday drugs ingested, we also have to consider coffee, tea, tobacco, and alcohol. The first three activate the nervous system, therefore causing increased electrodermal conductance. Alcohol manifests a biphasic effect that is activating in smaller amounts while it reduces EDA in larger amounts, simultaneously demonstrating a sedative effect.

We'll now summarize the effect of some frequently taken drugs on the electrodermal parameter.

9.5.1 Beta-Blockers

Due to their adrenolytic effect, beta-blockers can reduce the perception of physical symptoms of anxiety and can contribute to restructuring both tonic and phasic EDA. This is therefore a correlate of the therapeutic effect of such drugs and can be utilized for monitoring the anxiety condition (Gruzelier *et al.*, 1981). In hypertensive patients, a certain correlation has been observed between decreased blood pressure obtained with a beta-blocker and reduced electrodermal conductance values.

9.5.2 Benzodiazepines

These psychotropic drugs can counteract anxiety and are the drugs most prescribed and consumed on the planet today.

The effect of benzodiazepines on the therapeutic parameter has been widely documented, with regard both to decreased SCL and a reduced number of nonspecific skin conductance responses (NS-SCRs). A clear connection with the therapeutic effect of benzodiazepines was demonstrated both in the short term (just a few minutes with quick-acting benzodiazepines like lorazepam) and in the medium term (a few days) with systematically implemented therapy (Frith *et al.*, 1984). This serves to document the pharmacodynamic and therapeutic effect. Figures 9.9 and 9.10 show two recordings in which both the short-term (Figure 9.9) and medium-term

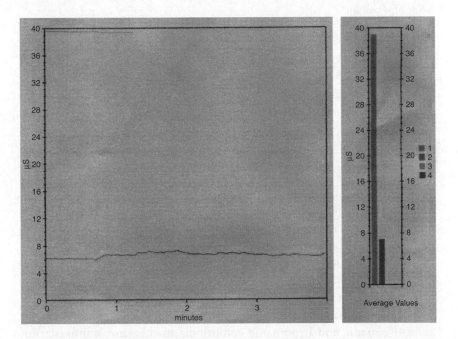

Figure 9.9 Graph showing the dramatic change on EDA when lorazepam is administered after a panic attack.

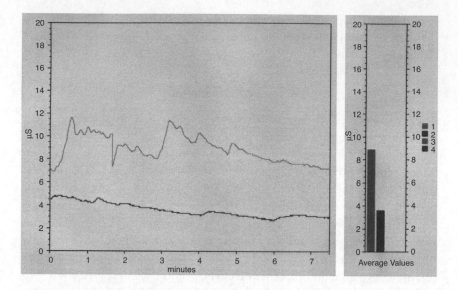

Figure 9.10   The change in values and shape of EDA after some days of treatment using alprazolam.

(Figure 9.10) effects of anxiolytics on anxious patients are documented. The difference in SCL (upper record and left bar in the histogram/bar chart) is very clear. In Figure 9.10, the decreased number of spontaneous phasic responses (nonspecific electrodermal responses, or NS-EDRs) is also evident.

9.5.3 Neuroleptics

Two widely used neuroleptics are chlorpromazine and haloperidol. Chlorpromazine exhibits a certain peripheral anticholinergic-type effect that can reduce electrodermal conductance beyond a potential central-type therapeutic effect. Haloperidol, on the other hand, acts on electrodermal conductance only as a result of its symptomatically therapeutic effect on psychoses (Gruzelier and Hammond, 1978). Therefore, recording tonic and phasic EDA can serve as an index for the symptomatic activity and pharmacodynamic effect of haloperidol, as demonstrated in the schizophrenic as well as in the manic and hypomanic conditions. In this case, administering haloperidol leads to a gradual reduction (over several days) in SCL and the number of nonspecific skin conductance responses (NS-SCRs).

9.5.4 Antidepressants

The tricyclics influence EDA on the skin's surface due to their anticholinergic effect, as shown in a study that I conducted at the beginning of the 1980s (Scrimali, Grimaldi, Rapisarda *et al.*, 1982). This does not occur with selective serotonin re-uptake inhibitors (SSRIs), which influence the electrodermal parameter only via their mood-lifting effect (Thorell, Kjellman, and D'Elia, 1987). The effect of SSRIs on electrodermal conductance can therefore be used as an evaluation parameter for the therapeutic effect of the administration of the drug. In a depressed patient, for example, administering fluoxetine activates a progressive increment in conductance as it improves the mood level.

I would like to specify, however, that when I talk about the therapeutic effect of an SSRI, I do not mean a true antidepressive effect, as it is acknowledged that, for genuine therapeutic progress to occur in depression, the modification of dysfunctional patterns and automatic thought as well as relational patterns (internal operative models) are processes that no so-called antidepressant can alter, and which can only be achieved through psychotherapy. In reality, the so-called antidepressants should more accurately be called mood lifters, as it is recognized that the only effect they are capable of manifesting is that of improving asthenia, abulia, anhedonia, and the somatic symptoms of depression.

Treatment with these drugs was paradoxically linked to a certain number of cases of suicide (Teicher, Glod, and Cole, 1990). I say paradoxical perhaps inaccurately, since such a phenomenon can be explained when we consider that when the patient is feeling very bad, they have suicidal ideation but not the strength and executive capacity to follow through with their plans. With the administration of the drug, which acts as a mood lifter, comes this strength and capacity and in a sense we can say that the patient dies from improvement.

9.5.5 Anti-Epileptic Drugs, or "Mood Stabilizers"

The anti-epileptics Valproic acid, sodium valproate, and carbamazepine reduce tonic and phasic EDA as they affect mood level in the manic and hypomanic condition (Keck and McElroy, 2002).

10

Complex Psychological Diagnosis and Instrumental Psychodiagnostics

10.1 Introduction

The use of methodologies borrowed from neuroscience, such as Atlantis II and MindLAB Set, must first confront the issue of classification and the nosographic framework for the various mental disorders. This is a controversial topic currently taking center stage in the scientific debate. Today, we can identify diverse orientations in the area of mental disorder classification methodology that embody various patient evaluation systems. In fact, we can speak of potential conceptions of the clinical condition according to the following approaches: categorical, dimensional, and structural.

The best-known approaches to the diagnosis of mental disorders are still *categorical*. Such models derive directly from biologistic medicine methodology. Via a diagnosis, a series of subjects suffering with a specific illness are identified. Important corollaries of such an approach are based on the belief that an equally specific etiopathogenetic dynamic and characteristic pathophysiological framework correspond to each specific disease. Consequently, the categorical model indirectly posits that equally ad hoc therapies must exist, corresponding to specific diagnostic frameworks (Scrimali, 2008).

The category system most used today is the *Diagnostic and Statistical Manual of Mental Disorders* (DSM), currently in its fourth edition (American Psychiatric Association, 1997). We observed a classic example of the categorical standpoint when, at the start of the 1980s, within the scope of DSM III, a new nosographic classification of "panic attack disorder" was created (American Psychiatric Association, 1987). Immediately afterward,

---

Neuroscience-based Cognitive Therapy: New Methods for Assessment, Treatment, and Self-Regulation, First Edition. Tullio Scrimali.
© 2012 John Wiley & Sons, Ltd. Published 2012 by John Wiley & Sons, Ltd.

a "specific" pharmacological therapy was proposed for this new disorder, utilizing alprazolam. A recent shining example of such a simplistic yet effective marketing strategy was encountered with the new diagnostic label of "dysthymia," which would admit a specific therapy based on amisulpride. In category-type classification systems, various different symptoms are concentrated into specific disorders that refer to equally pathological conditions.

Another important nosographic classification system is that developed by the World Health Organization as the International Classification of Diseases (ICD), now in its tenth edition (World Health Organization, 1992). It seems important to point out how the DSM progressively supplanted the ICD due to intense pressure from multinational pharmaceutical companies, the overwhelming majority of them American, and based on the currently still strong economic and cultural hegemony of the United States.

According to its official intent, the DSM is a diagnostic system formulated for the purpose of making diagnoses more uniform worldwide, transcending the cultural differences of various nations. As previously stated, the American Psychiatric Association developed this diagnostic system in the United States. It is a multiaxial diagnostic system that codes the patient's clinical condition on the following five axes:

I.   Clinical Syndromes;
II. Personality Disorders and Mental Retardation;
III. Medical Conditions;
IV. Psychosocial and Environmental Factors (stressors); and
V.   Global Assessment of Functioning Scale.

Though useful in giving a global picture of the clinical case, the DSM ended up being used as if it were a patient labeling modality. In fact, I must emphasize that a categorical and nosographic approach is strictly descriptive, that is, it is one that gives an overall description of the patient's situation, without attempting to understand and explain the dysfunctional conditions present within the individual.

Starting from a similar critique, *dimensional* approaches were then developed. Within the dimensional orientation, an assessment system that proposed the study of a series of dimensions took the place of the conception of a pathological condition in terms of diagnostic categories. The model derives from psychology research methods instead of from medicine. The study of various dimensions allows the identification of symptom clusters as opposed to patient clusters. The dimensional approach is discretionary and not categorical, therefore more dimensions can be analyzed simultaneously. Specific implementation of the approach takes place through gathering information via specific assessment tools, based on a certain number of variables.

Whereas categorical and dimensional models form the foundation of the more biologistic approaches, standard and constructivist cognitive psychotherapy authors introduced the *structural* approach. Beck developed the conception in which significant processes are organized on the basis of patterns that constitute the fundamental structures of the knowledge system (Beck, 1979). The task of psychotherapy, then, is that of identifying such dysfunctional patterns and correcting them. According to this orientation, various patients differ substantially not due to specific symptoms or even characteristic dimensions, but rather because of the existence of idiosyncratic dysfunctional patterns.

The constructivist approach to patient assessment is included in part in structural models and in part in categorical models. Regarding the first, descriptions of specific groups of constructs then identify a series of diagnostic categories described as individually significant organizations (Guidano, 1988; 1991). Great emphasis is put on the identification of the individually significant organizational category in which each patient, and indeed each individual, must be included.

This is an aspect of Guidano's thinking that has always left me rather confused, since it gives the impression that he wished to propose another new nosography that was no longer based on symptoms but rather on organizations. The idea that, in every individual, complex nervous system and mental coalitional processes were organized on the basis of one specific constraint traceable to specific organizational classifications (phobic, obsessive, depressive, prone to eating disorders) to me seems not at all reflective of the real clinical situation. In fact, we can quite frequently observe, in one patient, multiple dysfunctions traceable to diverse dysfunctional processes of the self and to different pathological aspects of the nurturing process experienced.

10.2 Functional Diagnosis

The functional orientation encompasses the examination of various mental functions and processes. In accordance with this orientation, I recently developed a conception that proposes studying a series of processes, which are:

- exploration, search for security;
- order–disorder, expectation, control;
- pleasantness, positive outlook toward the future;
- body image and sensitivity to criticism;
- search for some hedonistic reward;
- relational patterns and social cooperation; and
- connection with reality and mental coalitional activity.

These processes can develop positively and adaptively when the individual has a moderately balanced foundation, positively nurtured within a functional parenting process. In this case, the subject will develop flexible patterns that can evolve within the tacit, explicit, procedural, and Machiavellian knowledge processes. When this does not occur, dysfunctional knowledge patterns and coping mechanisms are structured, which I intentionally defined as constraints. In that case, knowledge process functioning is hindered and slowed down as if the knowledge processes were themselves constraints.

This is summarized in Table 10.1:

Table 10.1 A summary of the correspondences between processes, constraints, and disorders.

Process	Constraint	Disorder
Exploration, Search for Security	Phobic	Anxiety, Panic, Phobias
Order-Disorder, Expectation, Control	Obsessive	Obsessions and Compulsions
Pleasantness, Positive Outlook toward the Future	Depressive	Depression
Body Image, Sensitivity to Criticism	Eating Disorder	Anorexia, Bulimia
Search for Hedonistic Reward	Dependency	Addictions
Relational Patterns and Social Cooperation	Difficult Interpersonal, Relationships	Personality Disorders
Connection with Reality, Mental Coalitional Activity	Entropy of the Mind	Schizophrenia

Every single process can exhibit dysfunctional constraints, and therefore we cannot evaluate the clinical framework according to categories identified on the basis of symptoms, but only with an accurate functional analysis founded on the study of multiple mental processes and research into idiosyncratic constraints. We can thereby implement an assessment that is apparently complex and discretionary, as opposed to formulating a reductive and categorical diagnosis.

10.3 Instrumental Psychodiagnostics

With this term, I described the use of equipment stemming from neuroscience methodologies to acquire information on the biological functioning of the human brain (Scrimali, 2008). Within this definition, I implicitly considered that these methodologies must be able to be easily introduced into a clinical setting. As an example, fMRI could not be included today within the scope of instrumental psychodiagnostics, as its high cost means it is applicable only to large laboratories and therefore only suitable for small patient samplings with the sole purpose of research. According to my conception, qualifying methodologies would instead be such typically instrumental psychodiagnostic methods as Atlantis II for QEEG (Brainmaster, 2010) and MindLAB Set for QEDA (Psychotech, 2008), and in the near future fNIR (Biopac, 2009).

10.4 The Contribution of Neuroscience to a Complex Diagnosis

In the clinical setting, the utilization of effective methodologies such as Atlantis II and MindLAB Set can contribute to the acquisition of additional evaluation elements that move in the direction suggested by recent studies. In the near future, the diagnostic process will advance on different levels. With neuroscientific development, it will be both possible and necessary to obtain information on a different level that should be (Evian, 2007):

- genetic (genome research techniques);
- about brain structures (morphological brain viewing techniques);
- about cerebral functions (cerebral functional viewing techniques);
- about psychophysiological parameters (with primary reference to EEG and EDA);

- neuropsychological (memory, attention, executive functions); and
- Machiavellian (recognition of facial expression mimicking).

Although the theory of complex diagnosis now seems mature and methodologies that could make it viable are available, active efforts in the area of information and dissemination of these must occur. This book aims to provide a small contribution to that effort.

3

Neuroscience-based Methods in the Clinical Setting

11

Complex Psychological Diagnosis with Quantitative Electroencephalography

11.1 Introduction

Today, Quantitative Electroencephalography (QEEG) techniques can make a relevant contribution to a complex diagnosis by supplying morphological and functional indications about the conditions of the CNS in the patient being examined. For example, Neuroguide software provides the clinician with an almost incredible amount of information. First and foremost, it will supply morphological information, identifying the area of the brain that seems to be malfunctioning, and it must be said that the visual impact of this EEG brain mapping is truly remarkable. Then, the software provides a detailed report describing the cerebral structure that seems to be responsible for the ongoing psychopathological process, with in-depth information on its dysfunctional state. Finally, Neuroguide describes the actual functional relationships of the modular structures identified as inactive, along with the gradiental cortical areas charged with specific coalitional control.

Imagine showing these data to your patient and then developing an integrated pharmacological, psychotherapeutic, and neuropsychological treatment plan based on neurofeedback. If, after several months of therapy, you repeated the QEEG, you would be able to observe some quite striking modifications in the new functional patterns documented by the recording. As you can well imagine, this is a real Copernican revolution in psychology, as, for the first time, rather than epiphenomena such as symptoms and tests, we can observe the direct impact of our therapeutic methods on the brain.

Neuroscience-based Cognitive Therapy: New Methods for Assessment, Treatment, and Self-Regulation, First Edition. Tullio Scrimali.
© 2012 John Wiley & Sons, Ltd. Published 2012 by John Wiley & Sons, Ltd.

11.2 Dementia

The analysis of the signal spectrum and the evaluation of the amplitude and strength in different wave frequencies are being put forward as particularly useful methods for the evaluation of cognitive patterns (Widagdo, Pierson, and Helme, 1988) and a range of research underlines how diagnostic differentiation between normal seniors and those with dementia may be possible through EEG quantitative analysis and evoked potentials (Mattia *et al.*, 2003). In dementia and senile cognitive deterioration, it is clearly of the utmost clinical importance to consider the ageing population.

The rest of this section is comprised of reports on some dementia research I was involved in, given here in detail as an illustrative example of what current EEG tools can achieve. As you can see, easy-to-use research tools are now available not just in large university laboratories but also through simple and low-cost equipment suites, such as Atlantis II or NeuroLAB Set, that permit you to examine cerebral patterns and integrate them with your neurological investigation, allowing functional diagnosis of dementia-related disorders. With these suites, you can evaluate those senior patients that begin to present with memory disturbances and assess whether their EEG profiles show initial anomalies that could be indicative of a developing dementia process.

In our study, we enlisted a total of 16 subjects aged 65–70 years, 8 of whom were patients with Alzheimer's diagnoses according to National Institute of Neurological and Communicative Disorders and Stroke/Alzheimer's Disease and Related Disorders Association (NINCDS-ADRDA) criteria (McKhann *et al.*, 1984) and 8 of whom were control subjects. The Alzheimer's group was made up of 4 males and 4 females (average age = 74.25, SD = 3.37, average education = 8.25 years, SD = 4.8). The control group comprised 5 males and 3 females (average age = 73.87, SD = 4.64, average education = 10.12 years, SD = 4.15).

11.2.1 Materials

The subjects were evaluated using a battery of neuropsychological tests, including the Mini Mental State Examination (MMSE), the Rey Auditory Verbal Learning Test (RAVL), and the Frontal Assessment Battery (FAB).

- The Mini Mental Status Examination (Folstein, Folstein, and McHugh, 1975) is used for the evaluation of impairment in intellectual efficiency in the presence of cognitive deterioration. Comprehensive scoring ranges from a minimum of 0 and a maximum of 30 points.

- The Rey Auditory Verbal Learning Test of immediate and deferred recall (Rey, 1958) is used to evaluate both short- and long-term memory. The test consists of 5 presentations of a list of 15 semantically uncorrelated, frequently used, and highly understandable words with immediate recall from the subject. The deferred recall test is completed after a 15-minute break, providing evaluation of the capacity to recall the material learned. Scoring for immediate recall ranges from 0–75 and scoring for deferred recall from 0–15.

- The Frontal Assessment Battery (Dubois *et al.*, 2000) is a brief battery of tests that allows assessment of the executive functions. It consists of six subtests, each of which explores the relative function of the frontal lobe: conceptualization, mental flexibility, motor planning, sensitivity to interference, inhibition control, and environmental autonomy. The scoring ranges from 0–18.

Subsequently, the two groups were administered a Quantitative EEG recording using a NeuroLAB Set device by Psychotech. (Psychotech, 2007)

11.2.2 Method

In our work, we focused on the analysis of the amplitude, frequency, coherence, and symmetry of the brain signal at four different points on the scalp (F1, F2, T5, T6), according to the international 10–20 system for electrode placement. All research participants were initially subjected to the battery of neuropsychological tests. Their neuropsychological assessment showed the following differences between the two groups: Alzheimer's patients presented with spatial-temporal disorientation, working memory deficit, and memory and executive functions deficit (MMSE = 19.8, FAB = 9.3, RAVL R.I. = 27, RAVL R.D. = 4.75) while healthy control subjects presented with an optimal cognitive state (MMSE = 29, FAB = 17, RAVL R.I. = 48. 2 RAVL R.D. = 10.3).

A NeuroLAB Set was used, with electrodes placed at areas F1, F2, T5, and T6 on the subjects' scalps. Oil was lightly removed from the skin with a cotton ball and alcohol, and a conductance gel applied to the electrodes. We first soaked the two reference electrodes in a saline solution of 5% sodium chloride, spreading EEG conductance gel on them and applying them to the auricular lobes of both ears. Subjects were asked to close their eyes and relax for approximately 8 minutes. Subjects were seated on comfortable chairs, in a silent room, and were asked not to speak or move during those 8 minutes.

11.2.3 Results

After an 8-minute recording, the average results were obtained. We completed the statistical tests by first analyzing the amplitude variance via a multivariate analysis of variance (MANOVA) and then evaluating the delta-, theta-, alpha-, and beta-rhythm values present. We identified statistically significant differences between the control and Alzheimer's groups.

Specifically, we noted very high delta output in the frontal areas of the Alzheimer's subjects compared to in the posterior areas of the control subjects ($F = 38.08$, $p < 0.001$; $F = 39.62$, $p < 0.001$; $F = 7.967$, $p = 0.014$; $F = 37.615$, $p < 0.001$). Similarly, theta rhythms in subjects within the Alzheimer's group showed a statistically significant difference compared to the control group ($F = 55.747$, $p < 0.001$; $F = 51.772$, $p < 0.001$), as the phenomenon was less evident primarily in the right posterior temporal areas ($F = 19.556$, $p = 0.001$; $F = 1.613$, $p = 0.225$).

Additionally, we found higher amplitude in the alpha rhythm of normal subjects compared with those with dementia, both in the frontal ($F = 35.174$; $p < 0.001$; $F = 21.880$, $p < 0.001$) and posterior temporal areas ($F = 47.987$, $p < 0.001$; $F = 23.435$, $p < 0.001$). There was an inversion in the alpha rhythm between the posterior and anterior areas in the subjects with Alzheimer's, while in the control group the alpha rhythm was higher in the posterior regions ($F1 = 12.7$, $F2 = 12.8$, $T5 = 14.3$, $T6 = 15.1$). In the patients with dementia, the same rhythm was more represented in the anterior regions ($F1 = 5.8$, $F2 = 5.7$, $T5 = 4.8$, $T6 = 5.5$). In the subjects with Alzheimer's, a low inter-hemispheric coherence of the theta rhythm was also shown. On the other hand, there were no statistically significant differences in beta rhythm in the frontal areas between the control and Alzheimer's groups ($F = 0.158$, $p = 0.697$; $F = 0.564$, $p = 0.465$) while there were differences evident in the temporal areas ($F = 22.167$, $p < 0.001$; $F = 6.811$, $p = 0.021$).

Emerging data emphasize lower inter-hemispheric coherence between subjects with Alzheimer's with respect to the healthy control group subjects, showing less inter-hemispheric communication in patients with dementia compared to their same-aged peers who did not show cognitive deterioration. The loss of cerebral coherence could be determined by atrophy in the corpus callosum regions, as the literature acknowledges, and emphasizes that inter-hemispheric coherence may be appreciably decreased in neurodegenerative diseases such as dementia (Jelica *et al.*, 2000).

Our research showed a significant increase in the delta and theta bands in subjects afflicted with dementia, and this increase could be connected to the loss of neurons in the hippocampus and posterior areas that are stimulated by cholinergic inputs; to degeneration of the mesial temporal cortex that can affect the functional connectivity between the hippocampus and temporo-parietal cortex (Killiany *et al.*, 1993), causing delay in synaptic, cortical, and subcortical communication (Thatcher, 1998); or, finally, to decreased mass of the hippocampal and entorhinal cortex gray matter (Fernandez, Arrazola, and Maestu, 2003).

A different alpha-rhythm pattern with anteriorization of the same was shown in the dementia patients compared to the healthy control subjects. However, the literature stresses the normality of a posterior alpha amplitude greater than anterior alpha amplitude (Lubar *et al.*, 1995). On the other hand, no significant change in reference to beta frequencies in the frontal areas was shown, although a decrease in frontal beta activity is sometimes reported in studies of Alzheimer's patients (Mattia *et al.*, 2003). We may perhaps assume that, with increased beta oscillation rhythm and amplitude observed when engaging in cognitive tasks (Cohen, Elgar, and Fell, 2009), we could have observed an Alzheimer's/control group difference where subjects were asked to perform cognitive exercises during recording.

11.3 Schizophrenia

From the end of the 1960s, experimental evidence from neuroscience began to attract the attention of researchers. One of the discoveries of this research was potential malfunctioning of the left hemisphere in schizophrenic patients (Rodin, Grisell, and Gottlieb, 1968). Etevenon and collaborators were the first to conduct an exhaustive review of all the experimental data then available, evaluating the link between symptoms typical of schizophrenia and pathological lesions present in the left hemisphere. These researchers arrived at the conclusion that catatonia and delirium could frequently be connected to lesions on the left temporal lobe (Etevenon *et al.*, 1983).

Flor-Henry then documented that in patients presenting with epilepsy types traceable to lesions present in the left temporal lobe, psychotic syndromes that are quite similar to the clinical presentation of schizophrenia can frequently be observed (Flor-Henry, 1988). Another hypothesis correlating with the previous one is that which takes into consideration potential alteration in inter-hemispheric communication mechanisms due to problems that appear to be localized to the corpus callosum. A number of studies were carried out on schizophrenic patients for the purpose of analyzing hemispheric functional coherence patterns with specific reference to EEG activity coherence. Recall that coherence can be defined as the degree of similarity between two EEG signals recorded at different sites on the scalp (Evans and Abarbanel, 1999).

In schizophrenic patients, significantly higher coherence values were identified than in the control group (Wexler *et al.*, 1998). Such increased coherence could be interpreted as a vulnerability marker for schizophrenia, representing an alteration tied to neuronal development. One study conducted by Tauscher and colleagues at the University of Vienna got its start with detection of dysfunction in the prefrontal cortex of schizophrenic patients (Tauscher *et al.*, 1995). These data seem to agree with those of other studies that have shown an alteration in the neural development processes, primarily in the frontal cortex of schizophrenic patients.

Cortical development during adolescence is normally characterized by a remarkable decrease in synapses. Completing post-mortem studies on tissue obtained from the frontal cortex of normal subjects, Huttenlocher found that synaptic density reaches a peak during infancy, with a subsequent 30–40% drop during adolescence, then stabilizes in adulthood (Huttenlocher, 1979). Such synaptic rarefaction, better described as synaptic pruning or trimming, reflects a reduction in the cortico-cortical connections. The typical age of schizophrenia onset (late adolescence and young adulthood) and the importance of synaptic pruning suggest that this disorder may develop from a pathological extension of the pruning process. A similar hypothesis was supported by post-mortem studies that evaluated the number of dendritic spines in the frontal cortex of schizophrenic and normal control subjects' brains.

At the Cognitive Psychophysiology Laboratory at the University of Catania's Department of Psychiatry, with the collaboration of Katia Polopoli, I completed experimental research for the purpose of evaluating potential anomalies in hemispheric functional patterns of schizophrenic patients. We conducted recordings with NeuroLAB Set in comfortable surroundings with no distractions of a visual (e.g., excessive light) or auditory nature (anechoic headphones for noise elimination were used). All the subjects we studied were recorded at 9 a.m., lying on an examination couch in such a position as to minimize any artifacts due to neck muscle contraction.

Within the scope of the research that I am about to describe (Scrimali, 2008), we studied the index of functional coherence in the frontal lobes. For the analysis of EEG patterns of hemispheric functional coherence, we recruited 10 patients (6 males and 4 females, average age 33) who were afflicted with paranoid schizophrenia (according to DSM-IV), had at least a 5-year history of the disorder, were being treated with traditional neuroleptics (haloperidol, 5 mg/day), and were in the clinical compensation stage. Patients with neurological problems or auditory dysfunction were excluded. Ten healthy control subjects (5 males and 5 females, average age 26), comparable in age and gender to the other patients, were also enlisted.

In our research, the recordings were obtained over three time periods: a first phase with eyes closed for one minute, a second with eyes open for one minute, and a final phase during which subjects performed serial subtractions of 7. For each of the three recording phases, we analyzed the data relating to EEG inter-hemispheric coherence (F1/F2; T5/T6) and anteroposterior intra-hemispheric coherence (F1/T5; F2/T6).

We next examined the values relating to alpha rhythm present. We subjected the data to statistical analysis via the application of the t-test to a two-sample distribution. The results we obtained are summarized below.

When subjects were examined with their eyes closed, we observed a significant increase in frontal inter-hemispheric coherence (F1/F2) and in left intra-hemispheric coherence (F1/T5), in addition to an increase in right intra-hemispheric coherence (F2/T6) in schizophrenic patients compared to control subjects. When the eyes were open, both in patients and in control subjects, coherence values were lower than with eyes closed. However, we saw a significant increase in right intra-hemispheric coherence as well as an increase in left intra-hemispheric coherence in schizophrenic patients when compared to control subjects. During execution of serial subtractions, there was greater difference between control subjects and schizophrenic patients, with a remarkable drop in coherence between the two hemispheres in normal subjects, while in schizophrenic patients, coherence values were higher at all locations, with significant increases in both frontal and temporal inter-hemispheric coherence. We also found a greater reduction in alpha-rhythm values in schizophrenic patients than in control subjects.

This research allowed us to demonstrate a series of different hemispheric functional patterns in schizophrenic patients when compared to healthy subjects. Consistent with the data in the literature reporting slow rhythms present in schizophrenia, decreased alpha rhythm was shown in our sample. Additionally, coherence patterns showed less hemispheric functional differentiation. This data allows us to corroborate the increasingly supported theory that, in schizophrenic patients, a functional gap occurs in the left frontal lobe. The research also demonstrated that our methods and equipment are functional for routine use in the psychiatric clinical setting. This presents an opportunity for new and interesting prospects with important implications for schizophrenia psychopathology and therapy. With regard to the latter, we can assume that modifications in EEG coherence patterns and the presence of alpha rhythm could be utilized as indices in clinical development.

11.4 Depression

Prichep, Lieber, and John (1986) described the QEEG abnormalities associated with depression. A typical feature of QEEG in depression is the presence of slower than normal activity in the frontal area.

One of the problems relating to positive implementation of pharmacological treatment to a depressed patient is the ability to identify the drug to which the patient responds. I must further emphasize, to avoid any misunderstanding, that when I talk about "response," I personally do not mean a true therapeutic response, as I do not consider pharmacological treatment of depression (in truth, of any other mental disorder) truly therapeutic, but only "symptomatic." A positive symptomatic or mood-lifting effect can be expected in seriously depressed patients, even for two months (Leuchter *et al.*, 2009). However, much valuable time is lost while trying to identify the most effective drug. Recent studies apparently demonstrate the potential for utilizing QEEG as a methodology that can manifest a positive psychophysiological response to the drug much sooner than the symptomatic and therapeutic effect appears, or that can much earlier document the inadequate effect of the drug tested.

Leuchter *et al.* identified a real biological marker of response to depression treatment that described antidepressant treatment response (ATR) in recorded frontal patterns via a rather simple QEEG technique based on a four-channel recording. The study involved some 375 patients of between

18–75 years old. Their research demonstrated that the theta and alpha bands they recorded from the frontal regions, and quantified using the simple methodology they adopted, are adaptable and can within a week manifest a positive psychophysiological response to the administration of an SSRI antidepressant such as escitalopram.

11.5 Mania

The clinical condition of mania is associated with the presence of high-frequency activity in the right orbital frontal area or the inferior parietal lobules. Furthermore, an excess in frontal beta is considered a trait marker for mania (Walker, Lawson, and Kozlowski, 2007).

Frontal EEG asymmetries, recorded during an experiment of exposure to an anger-evoking event, have been demonstrated to be a possible EEG marker of mania and ipomania (Harmon-Jones and Allen, 1998). In fact, patients prone to hypomania/mania symptoms show an intense left frontal activation when confronted with an anger-evoking situation, whereas individuals prone to depression symptoms evidenced stronger withdrawal motivation (Harmon-Jones *et al.*, 2002).

11.6 Attention Deficit Hyperactivity Disorder

The clinical implementation of QEEG methods for a complex diagnosis of ADHD appears particularly promising. Snyder and Hall recently conducted a meta-analysis that included new studies and data on a total of 1,498 patients. The pattern they identified involves an increase in theta rhythms and a decrease in the beta band (Snyder and Hall, 2006).

Complex evaluation of ADHD can be implemented with the introduction of QEEG, which allows integrated treatment planning that includes neurofeedback and psychofeedback techniques, as we will see in Chapter 12.

11.7 Obsessive-Compulsive Disorder

A recent study examined the power of delta, theta, alpha, beta1, and beta2 bands with high-resolution EEG data in patients with obsessive-compulsive disorder (OCD) and compared it with that of normal controls (Desarkar *et al.*, 2007). OCD patients showed significantly higher power than controls, which was widespread in the theta frequency, predominantly left-sided fronto-temporo-parietal in delta and alpha bands, and only left frontal in beta2 bands.

According to this data it seems that there is an increased band power in OCD patients in all these bands, which have been shown to be associated with cognitive processing. This may reflect increased processing load in this group of patients, with recruitment of a wide area of the cerebral hemisphere. Neurofeedback seems to be a very promising technique to be applied to treating this disorder (Hammond, 2004), as I will show in Chapter 15.

12

Complex Psychological Diagnosis with Quantitative Electrodermal Activity

12.1 General Aspects

In this chapter I give some information about how to use MindLAB Set for monitoring and registering Quantitative EDA. MindSCAN is the procedure I developed, as part of MindLAB Set, in order to evaluate EDA at the beginning of assessment with a patient. It consists of recording the tonic and phasic EDA implemented with MindLAB Set for a total time of about seven minutes. Within the scope of recording, there are three distinct phases:

- three minutes baseline;
- two minutes cognitive activation (serial subtractions of seven); and
- two minutes recovery.

MindSCAN is very easy to implement and provides valuable indications as to psychodiagnosis and integrated treatment planning. You can conduct a MindSCAN routinely with all patients during their first session. Overall, it requires about ten minutes, including output of results and printing the record. I will now provide a summary of the MindSCAN procedure.

12.1.1 Setting

After completing the initial session with the patient using MindLAB Set in a face-to-face setting, you may proceed with MindSCAN. Launch MindSCAN and the Psychofeedback program without turning the acoustic feedback on.

Neuroscience-based Cognitive Therapy: New Methods for Assessment, Treatment, and Self-Regulation, First Edition. Tullio Scrimali.

The monitor turned toward the patient should be turned off for now (see Chapter 13 on sets and settings).

12.1.2 Advising the Patient

Tell the patient what will happen, as follows:

> I would now like to complete a simple recording of a physiological function that is related to your mental condition. Due to developments in neuroscience, we can now measure and quantify mental conditions with this equipment.
>
> It is somewhat like EEG in neurology or electrocardiography in cardiology. We are trying to obtain objective records about how your physiological processes are functioning.
>
> Specifically, we can obtain documentation of your mental condition. Acquiring this measure is very simple and will not have any harmful effect on you. The equipment is safe, as it is battery-powered and isolated from the computer. And you will not feel a thing. It is quite similar to taking your temperature when you might have a fever.
>
> Instead of the thermometer, I will apply two small pads to two fingers of your dominant hand. The recording will take place in three phases and will last a total of about seven minutes. In the first phase, you should not do anything and should try to remain calm. I will then ask you to do some mental arithmetic for two minutes and then for the remaining two minutes you will try to relax and clear your mind of any thought.

12.1.3 Testing

Gently wipe the index and middle fingers of the patient's dominant hand with a dry tissue and affix the electrodes to the fingertips without gripping too hard, at the same time ensuring that the electrodes do not move. After applying the electrodes, turn on the equipment and start the recording (PLAY button). Wait about one minute to allow the equipment to calibrate the patient's conductance value and set the data acquisition value to 0.5 seconds. This way, the graph will set an x-axis of seven minutes. At this point, stop the recording and then restart it. For the first three minutes, you need not do anything. When the graph reaches the end of the third minute, activate the "mark event" and tell the patient: "The number you should start with is 350! Going backward, subtract out loud by 7 and tell me the result of each calculation until I tell you to stop."

After two minutes of serial subtractions of seven, tell the patient to stop and reactivate the "mark event," asking the patient to mentally relax and to try to stop thinking about the cognitive test just completed or its outcome.

12.1.4 Assessing and Reviewing Results with the Patient

At this point, you can print the recording, show it to the patient, and provide comment or start the second recording session. In the first case, you can use the mouse pointer to indicate the various aspects of the recording. Note the values recorded (minimum, average, and maximum) and comment on them. Where the age-group values are higher than indicated by the Katane database, point out to the patient that this proves their mental condition is altered.

Look at and point out the patient's recorded morphology where there are more than three spontaneous phasic responses in the first two minutes and, where the recording displays a saw-tooth contour, indicate that this demonstrates sustained excessive mental activity. Also comment on what occurred during both the serial subtractions of seven and recovery periods.

You should see just a small increase in conductance during the cognitive task and a rapid recovery in the previous value. A marked increase in values during the serial subtractions of seven and a lack of recovery show an elevated level of anxiety and worry.

12.1.5 Planning Treatment

Now tell the patient that this equipment is not only designed for psychodiagnosis but is also helpful to integrated therapy. Then offer psychofeedback sessions for the purpose of learning new strategies for mental self-regulation. Explain to the patient that a positive outcome of integrated treatment (pharmacological and psychotherapeutic) will lead to a modification in the recording and that new measurements will be made on an ongoing basis for the purpose of documenting progressive clinical improvement.

As you can see, the procedure I've described is highly innovative and can favorably motivate the patient, who will be happy to leave the session with a record and objective evaluation of their condition. I have carried out in-depth testing of this methodology with hundreds of patients, always obtaining clinically positive results and a high degree of patient satisfaction.

Instrumental psychodiagnostics represents a new orientation in clinical psychology that I have developed in recent years. It involves attempting to use psychophysiological techniques within the assessment process, with the added purpose of acquiring biological information that will supplement psychological and relational information. The concept of instrumental psychodiagnostics fits into the complex bio-psychosocial model of mental disorders and promotes the consideration of the human condition in the disorder and in therapy at a biological level. The brain, and the mind, are conceptualized at a psychological level as well as within the scope of inter-human relations, as we all acknowledge that humans, from the ethological viewpoint, are social animals (Scrimali, 2010a).

Instrumental psychodiagnostics therefore provides assessment procedures capable of documenting the active functioning of mental processes available in the clinical setting. Recording EDA with MindLAB Set (or some other device such as a Personal Efficiency Trainer (PET) GSR Recorder, powered by PC software, called BioExplorer) can be integrated into the broader scope of instrumental psychodiagnostics that also includes the study of EEG, EMG, cardiac, and thermal activity, as well as, in the future, biochemical activity.

Over the lengthy course of my active research at the ALETEIA Clinical Center's Institute for Cognitive Sciences, I compiled the Katane database to provide standard values extracted from an adequate sample of control subjects, as described above. I subsequently tested ample groups of patients afflicted with the following clinical problems:

- generalized anxiety disorder;
- panic attack disorder;
- post-traumatic stress disorder;
- phobias;
- OCD;
- depression;
- eating disorders;
- addictions;
- schizophrenia;
- mania;
- ADHD;
- stuttering;
- hypertension;
- irritable bowel syndrome;

- premenstrual syndrome; and
- psychogenic impotence.

12.1.6 Use of Recorded Data for Constructing a Narrative on the Self-Regulation Process

The ability to recall saved recordings from storage is an important element of the therapeutic process. In therapy, it is very helpful for the patient to develop a positive narrative, describing the continuous progress in their clinical condition. Often, patients tend to deny the progress they've made due to an excessively pessimistic view tied to their dysfunctional patterns. Using software functions that allow them to view all the recordings obtained over the course of the various phases of treatment, we can facilitate the development of a new, more positive and adaptive narrative that is forced to acknowledge the ongoing process of change, as unequivocally documented in the recordings.

We can uncover an important aspect of this topic within the procedure that I describe in Chapter 14, called the "strange family situation" procedure. Reviewing with the patient and family the recordings made in the presence of the operator and family allows you to objectively point out that the family's highly expressed emotion creates stress in the patient, which MindLAB Set fully records. This information can form the starting point for building a narrative based on establishing that family interaction is objectively negative.

Another potential use of this procedure is to document the effect of a fast-acting benzodiazepine like lorazepam during the session. Before and after administration, the patient can objectively observe in an EDA recording the efficient and rapid effect of the drug. Because the drug has been documented as unequivocally effective, this observation will form the basis for developing a new narrative based on coping processes, which the patient then has at their disposal.

12.2 Data Regarding Specific Clinical Disorders

12.2.1 Generalized Anxiety Disorder

In generalized anxiety disorder, elevated SCLs have been observed with oscillations that appear to be in line with the development of anxious symptomatology over time (Birket-Smith, Hasle, and Jensen, 1993).

12.2.2 Panic Attack Disorder

In panic attack disorder, recent targeted experimental research documented elevated values in SCL that increase remarkably when a panic attack trigger is presented. Some research linked this data with high levels of plasma noradrenaline recorded in these patients (Braune *et al.*, 1994).

12.2.3 Post-Traumatic Stress Disorder

In post-traumatic stress disorder, a specific activation response characterized by an increment in EDA has been demonstrated when patients are shown vignettes illustrating the traumatic event, while a similar reaction does not manifest when the patients observe drawings illustrating stressful situations that are unrelated to the specific trauma they have experienced. Another piece of interesting information regarding the behavior of EDA in this disorder is that the recorded electrodermal arousal response changes in response to subsequent integrated pharmacological treatment and CT (Tarrier *et al.*, 2002).

12.2.4 Phobias

Research has shown that in phobic patients existing elevated values of SCL further increase when the patient thinks about the fearful situation or watches a video relating to it (Lader and Wing, 1964).

12.2.5 Obsessive-Compulsive Disorder

In OCD, the characteristic presence of numerous and extensive spontaneous phasic responses is connected to the worry phenomenon (Zahn, Insel, and Murphy, 1984; Hofmann *et al.*, 2005).

12.2.6 Depression

In depression, low conductance values and the presence of spontaneous phasic responses are recorded where anxious phenomenology and prominent rumination are also present in the clinical context (Lader and Wing, 1969).

12.2.7 Eating Disorders

With anorexia, an increase in SCL is recorded when food is presented to the patient, serving to demonstrate the fact that the sight of food activates a conditioned stress response, with resulting interference in digestion (Scrimali, 2003). Some recent studies have tended to demonstrate that QEEG can be altered in eating disorders, as is the EDA (Smith, Sams, and Sherlin, 2006).

With anorexic and bulimic patients, using a video image of the patient results in an increase in SCL. Applying cognitive restructuring, it is possible to get the patient to understand how viewing their own body generates an elevated arousal with consequent avoidance (self-observation phase). Patients can understand that avoidance feeds the vicious circle that forms the basis for maintaining the body image disorder (Scrimali, 2003).

12.2.8 Addictions

In addictions, elevated levels of arousal during craving are shown by records that have high values in SCL (Taylor, 2004; Taylor *et al.*, 1999).

12.2.9 Schizophrenia

In schizophrenia, with positive symptoms present, we can observe numerous spontaneous phasic responses as well as remarkable levels of arousal (conductance values often reach levels higher than 30 microsiemens). When negative symptoms prevail, very little spontaneous phasic activity is recorded. An increase in SCL can also be monitored as a warning sign of possible relapse, or rather a new crisis, as I have described (Zahn, Frith, and Steinhauer, 1991; Scrimali, 2008).

12.2.10 Mania

In the hypomanic or the manic phase of bipolar disorder, electrodermal conductance increases remarkably. The systematic recording of such a parameter can then be used as a warning sign of a change in the thymic condition (Iacono *et al.*, 1983).

12.2.11 Attention Deficit Hyperactivity Disorder

ADHD is a complex syndrome involving both cognitive and mental functions as well as behavioral and relational patterns. It is characterized by impairment in the neuropsychological attention process and a marked tendency to maintain elevated levels of arousal and motor hyperactivity that make learning in class very difficult, and in some cases impossible. These dysfunctions also compromise Machiavellian intelligence, producing relational problems. Numerous studies have demonstrated the usefulness of the electrodermal parameter in evaluating ADHD.

During a cognitive task requiring attention, one research study showed that children afflicted with ADHD exhibited a pronounced reduction in electrodermal orienting response when presented with stimuli, but more marked differences were observed than in a peer control group in terms of errors made. This data is consistent with a suspected difficulty in allocating adequate cognitive resources in the presence of cognitive stimuli (O'Connell *et al.*, 2004).

Overall, the EDA pattern in the patient afflicted with ADHD is characterized by elevated arousal levels in addition to decreased specific phasic responses relating to stimuli to be intercepted and analyzed (Constantine *et al.*, 2000).

12.2.12 Stuttering

Stuttering is a clinical condition that afflicts millions of people. It has been calculated that there are between 40 million and 50 million children with stuttering issues in the western world (Coleman, 1976). Various studies demonstrate the critical role of anxiety and a socially phobic mind-set that establishes and maintains the disorder (Weber and Smith, 1990; Craig, 1990). Arousal is elevated and even more accentuated at the time when the patient begins to stutter.

Recently some research into stuttering has been carried out using QEEG. The results of QEEG analysis demonstrated an increased slow-wave, especially delta, activity of the recordings both from resting state and in hyperventilation in the children with a stutter compared to the controls (Ozege, Toros, and Comelekoglu, 2004).

12.2.13 Hypertension

Numerous research studies, focused on the analysis of biological response patterns to stressors of various types (e.g., unpleasant and intense sounds), have demonstrated some specific patterns in hypertensive patients. In fact, the hypertensive patients demonstrate significantly greater changes in response than do normotensive peer group subjects. In particular, higher blood pressure, increased heart rate, greater electrodermal activity, and higher levels of plasma noradrenaline, cortisolemia, and free fatty acids are observed (Baumann *et al.*, 1973).

In such research situations, recorded EDA is consistent with higher values in SCL and a response characterized by its elevated level compared to control subjects. The recovery from levels following introduction of the stressor also appears delayed (Fredrikson *et al.*, 1980).

This data is interesting, suggesting that MindSCAN can be useful in studying the mental components connected to the recent onset of potential minor hypertension. In Chapter 15, in fact, we'll see that psychofeedback can be a useful resource in the integrated treatment of hypertension. A series of research projects completed by our work group and using MindLAB Set allowed us to identify higher values of SCL in hypertensive subjects and to observe a drop during pharmacological and integrated treatment, a reduction that was in line with lowering blood pressure.

12.2.14 Irritable Bowel Syndrome

Irritable bowel syndrome is a rather widespread problematic issue that is remarkably incapacitating and difficult to resolve in disorders that include colic, diarrhea, and constipation, as it is acknowledged that it has to do with an issue that is typically functional and closely connected to emotional dynamics. In patients afflicted with irritable bowel syndrome, experimental research has demonstrated high values in the base level of electrodermal conductance, which rise remarkably in stressful situations (Walter, 2006).

12.2.15 Premenstrual Syndrome

Premenstrual syndrome is a dysfunctional condition that can occur in women during the time immediately preceding menstrual flow. It is characterized by both somatic and mental distress. With regard to the latter aspect, emotional tension, irritability, impulsiveness, and aggression appear to occur. In this syndrome, EDA records elevated values in SCL (Van Den Akker and Steptoe, 1980).

12.2.16 Psychogenic Impotence

The process of penile erection is disturbed by any negative emotion. Anxiety, for example, can make some males unable to obtain an erection (Ansari, 1976). When dealing with a patient affected by psychogenic impotence, the monitoring of electrodermal activity can be a good way to complete the assessment procedure.

Very frequently in such a clinical condition, it is possible to find some high levels of SCL and the presence of many spontaneous and evoked phasic responses. In this case, my clinical experience, together with some data from the literature, demonstrated that EDA-biofeedback could be a good therapeutic approach to the treatment of psychogenic impotence when integrated with cognitive therapy (Benson, Greenwood, and Klemchuk, 1975).

13

Sets and Settings when Applying a Neuroscience-based Clinical Methodology

Sets and settings are crucial topics, both in the sphere of medicine and, to a larger extent, in psychotherapy. The set describes the material aspects of the context in which the bond between therapist and patient is developed; in other words, the physical environment, namely the room and more generally the offices where clinical work is performed, the equipment used, micro-climactic conditions, furniture, ambient sound, and proxemics. The setting describes the relational aspects and, therefore, the interaction between therapist and patient. It is obvious that sets and settings mutually influence each other. For example, a white coat is a part of the set but strongly influences the setting. Rubber gloves and a mask influence it even more.

During my long service at the University of Catania's Department of Psychiatry, I always avoided wearing the white coat that immediately connoted the clinical-type setting, and I related to the patient by wearing everyday or sportswear-type clothing. When vagrants and alcoholics visited in a pitiful hygienic condition due to a long life on the street, I always refused to wear a mask and rubber gloves, unlike many of my colleagues.

Do I believe it's possible to initiate a nurturing relationship by introducing oneself in a mask and rubber gloves? Imagine the good mother who, just to change her baby's diaper, first puts on a mask, a sterile green gown, and surgical rubber gloves. The question hardly needs to be answered. Nevertheless, colleagues who dress like this believe they're being good psychiatrists, and perhaps they are, but only in the sense of biological psychiatry, the orientation that gave us lunatic asylums, shock treatments, lobotomies,

Neuroscience-based Cognitive Therapy: New Methods for Assessment, Treatment, and Self-Regulation, First Edition. Tullio Scrimali.
© 2012 John Wiley & Sons, Ltd. Published 2012 by John Wiley & Sons, Ltd.

indiscriminate neuroleptic therapies, and the concept of so-called chronic illness. No, thank you!

Within the scope of psychotherapy, Freud dealt with sets and settings in a very specific way. Moreover, to Freud, who was somewhat obsessively acting from the viewpoint of an exasperatingly deterministic conception, everything was important and held meaning. I am always moved when visiting his offices in Vienna (I return whenever possible to spend an hour in this fantastic and quite magical place, where modern psychotherapy was born), especially by his attention to detail, as seen in the positioning of the patient couch and the armchair in which Freud sat, famously behind the patient.

Now, after almost two centuries of modern psychiatric history and more than a century of psychotherapy, we are living in an era of revolution. For example, the lunatic asylum set and the institutionalization setting were eliminated (in Italy, at least) due to the work of courageous and ingenious psychiatrists like Basaglia (1964). But have we evolved sufficiently to systematically bring equipment into the psychotherapy and clinical psychology set? Is it feasible to fuse neuroscience and psychotherapy in daily clinical work today? A great contribution toward this has been made by the speed and size of developments in microelectronics and computer science – Figure 13.1 and Figure 13.2 should give you a clear picture of the development of the process of adopting neuroscience methods in clinical practice.

In Figure 13.1 you can see my Laboratory of Clinical Psychophysiology at the Department of Psychiatry, University of Catania. This represents what was state of the art technology from 1980 and 1990. Clearly, the setting on view here cannot be applied in the clinical field!

During the "decade of the brain" which developed from 1990 to 2000, the situation changed and the new lab that you can see in Figure 13.2 has more potential to also be appropriate for clinical work.

But a real revolution took place between 2000 and 2005, when I was able to produce some small and portable devices that could be connected to the computer by powerful software. The new devices, which I called NeuroLAB Set and MindLAB Set (see Chapter 9), enabled me to travel east and west from Italy, reaching countries such as Japan, Canada, the United States, Brazil, and Argentina, taking with me the Mobile Neuroscience Lab that you can see in Figure 13.3.

The miniaturization of devices enabled us to use them in everyday clinical practice, but it was still necessary to develop a new setting for CT when using the neuroscience-based methods described in this book.

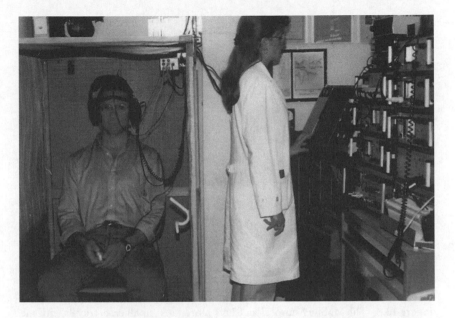

Figure 13.1 The Laboratory of Clinical Psychophysiology at the Department of Psychiatry, Medical School, University of Catania, from 1980 to 1990.

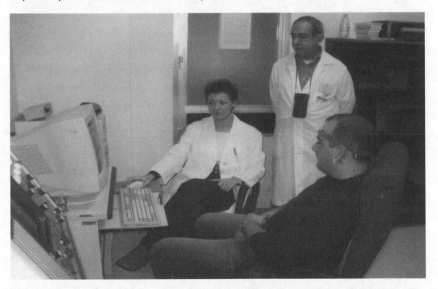

Figure 13.2 The Laboratory of Clinical Psychophysiology at the Department of Psychiatry, Medical School, University of Catania, from 1990 to 2000.

Figure 13.3 The Mobile Neuroscience Lab, stored in a small case, travels with me from Tokyo to Kobe for an invited workshop on neuroscience-based CT during the World Congress of Behavioral and Cognitive Therapies in 2004.

I have examined this issue in depth for some years. For example, if the psychophysiology set consists of a laboratory and if, right in the middle of a session, we are compelled to ask the patient to follow us into the laboratory to make a recording, that would trigger specific emotional dynamics in the patient (and potentially in any family members present, who, in Sicily at least, are usually both apprehensive and plentiful) and remarkable resistance in the therapist who is forced to move, during their work, from one environment to another and deal with complex and challenging equipment. Thus with time, I understood that the ideal solution was to subtly and ergonomically incorporate MindLAB Set into the typical clinical session and psychotherapy setting. In this way, after completing part of the session, we can offer to measure the patient's electrodermal parameter without either patient or therapist having to move from their armchairs, and while maintaining the same positions as during the rest of the session. Equipment and computers thereby enter subtly into play, while the application of electrodes without the need for any specific preparation or conductive paste makes everything more relaxed and less dramatic. Even describing electrodes as sensors when you address the patient helps, as we all know that the term

Figure 13.4 Some Japanese colleagues at work using neuroscience-based CT.

"electrode" can evoke the disturbing idea of shock treatments and, more commonly, the risk of receiving an electric shock.

In light of these considerations, I would like to propose two different setting types that, for the sake of clarity, I will refer to as methodologies: computerized QEEG and computerized recording of EDA. In the first methodology, there is no question that we must work in a dedicated setting: a small laboratory where electromagnetic interference is at a minimum, and EEG equipment and ancillary accessories are available for use. We must also ask the patient to thoroughly wash their hair on the morning of the examination and inform them that, after the recording, their hair will have conductance gel in it, so requiring yet another wash.

Here, we are dealing with a specific setting that we would define as dedicated, like that of psychodiagnostics for instance. The real work environment is yet another setting, and both the laboratory itself and staff are almost always different. At the ALETEIA Clinical Center I founded in Enna and of which I am director (www.centroclinicoaleteia.it), for example, we have one manager for psychodiagnostics, one for neuropsychology, and yet another for clinical psychophysiology, specifically targeted at QEEG. These specialists carry out examinations scheduled on different days and which are specific to their own specialized settings, and they set aside time for the full evaluation of collected data and the return of the summary narrative, from which planning and subsequent monitoring of the clinical condition can develop.

When I developed MindLAB Set, I achieved a small but substantial revolution, bringing the new methodology into the clinical setting, thereby removing it from the large laboratory (Figure 13.1) and bringing it into a more simple clinical situation (Figure 13.5). Using the MindLAB Set system is so intuitive and the MindSCAN software's graphic interface is so easy to understand that the therapist will not be distracted, but instead will be able to continue focusing attention on the patient and maintaining eye contact while launching the assessment procedure within the usual settings of

Figure 13.5 A side-by-side setting.

Figure 13.6 A face-to-face setting.

clinical sessions and consultations in medicine, psychology, psychiatry, and psychotherapy. The operator is seated at their desk while the patient and their companions are positioned in front of the operator.

To create this type of setting (Figure 13.6), you must make use of a second monitor with the screen turned toward the patient. During the standard clinical session, the patient monitor is turned off, just as it would be when performing a baseline EDA evaluation according to the MindSCAN assessment methodology. You should turn on the second monitor only when reviewing the recording and providing comment to the patient.

The new setting that I am proposing, then, permits the transition from the usual psychological consultation to implementation of computerized psychobiological procedures that will allow you to employ instrumental psychodiagnostics and/or psychotherapy integrated with psychofeedback techniques without ever having to change your position. My associates and I have systematically tested this new and original setting at the ALETEIA Clinical Center, while students and specialists at the ALETEIA School have used it in their professional education for some years now. And the results are very positive.

14

Multimodal Assessment of Family Process and the "Family Strange Situation"

Attachment theory examines the patterns related to the parenting and attachment process, both in animals and in humans (Harlow, 1958; Bowlby, 1988; Ainsworth, 1989). The attachment dynamic is a component that is critical to the development of the human relational mind (Guidano, 1987; Siegel and Hartzel, 2003). In recent years, a new science called the neuroscience of human relations has gained substantial strength by bridging social psychology and neuroscience (Cozolino, 2006). Within the scope of this neuroscience of human relations, the specialized branch of psychophysiology, or social psychophysiology, occupies an important position (Andreassi, 1989). In this field, recording of EDA has been utilized to monitor attachment processes where elevated SCL has been shown in both the caregiver and the child who exhibited resistant anxious attachment patterns (Lemche *et al.*, 2005).

At the University of Catania's Medical School, Department of Psychiatry, I developed a line of research in social psychophysiology studying the psychophysiological correlates to level of EDA in the family emotional climate (Scrimali and Grimaldi, 1991). I implemented this line of research with reference to a series of studies that provided encouraging results (Gruzelier and Venables, 1975).

In 1981, after having made a complete review of the literature, Ohman reached the conclusion that the electrodermal parameter was closely correlated to the status of schizophrenic patients' clinical condition, with particular regard to relapses and episodes of clinical decompensation (Ohman, 1981). Vaughn and Leff also demonstrated that environmental stress, in

Neuroscience-based Cognitive Therapy: New Methods for Assessment, Treatment, and Self-Regulation,
First Edition. Tullio Scrimali.
© 2012 John Wiley & Sons, Ltd. Published 2012 by John Wiley & Sons, Ltd.

Figure 14.1 The psychophysiology of expressed emotions. Two hostile and over-involved relatives provoke high electrodermal responses in the patient.

the form of both life events and family relationships characterized by high expressed emotion, could increase arousal in schizophrenic patients. These authors confirmed this data over the course of experimental research now considered classic (Vaughn and Leff, 1976). The link between arousal shown in EDA recordings and the exposure of schizophrenic patients to the emotionally expressive family was then reconfirmed in subsequent research (Tarrier *et al.*, 1988). This is therefore, a potentially very interesting aspect of the use of psychophysiological techniques in the multimodal study of the family emotional climate, in terms of reaching an objective evaluation of the emotion expressed by the family about schizophrenic patients (see Figure 14.1 and Figure 14.2).

Figure 14.2 The psychophysiology of expressed emotions. Two under-involved and not hostile relatives do not activate intense EDA responses.

Experiments completed at the University of Catania's Department of Psychiatry Psychophysiology Laboratory yielded encouraging results in this area (Scrimali and Grimaldi, 1991). From such preliminary data, I developed a new multimodal assessment procedure for family relational patterns defined as the "Family Strange Situation."

On the whole, the procedure consists of evaluating not just the patient's EDA, both in the absence and in the presence of the family, but also their ability to potentially control the electrodermal parameter in a biofeedback scenario. The Family Strange Situation will now be explained in more detail.

14.1 The Family Strange Situation Procedure

To begin, the patient provides a Five Minute Speech Sample (Magana *et al.*, 1986) for the purposes of evaluating expressed emotion with all the cohabiting family present. Then the patient is subjected to a procedure summarized as follows.

- *Trial One*: The patient receives a succinct description of the biofeedback dynamic. The patient tries to decrease acoustic feedback from the equipment by relaxing as deeply as possible, with the family out of the room (7 minutes). The EDA is recorded via computer.
- *Trial Two*: The procedure is repeated as in the first trial, this time with the family in attendance. In this phase, the following guidance is provided to the patient: "Repeat what you did the first time, trying to achieve the best possible result." Briefly explain to the family what the patient should be trying to do ("Your family member will try to reduce the sound level and modify the analog visual display. This will occur when they are able to relax"). Specific guidance to the family is: "Watch what they do and try to work together to get the best possible result."

Video recording monitors the family dynamic (spatial proximity, behavior, verbal and nonverbal communication).

With regard to the more technical aspects of this methodology, we utilize MindLAB Set and Psychofeedback software with the Family Strange Situation. This software allows you not only to save the two trial recordings but above all to analytically and summarily compare them. Once the evaluation procedure is complete, you can show the patient and family the results you've obtained.

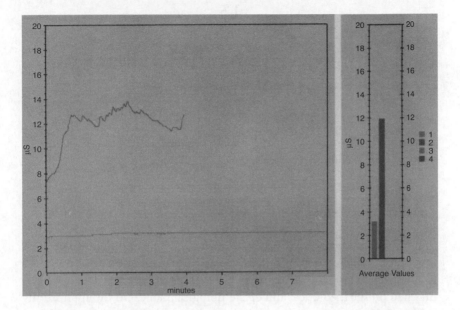

Figure 14.3 A graph registered during a Family Strange Situation procedure.

In Figure 14.3 you see a graphed recording of a patient during a Family Strange Situation procedure. The figure shows the effect that the relatives' presence has on the patient's SCL during the trial (upper graph in the record and right bar in the histogram). It appears evident that when a dysfunctional and stressful interaction activates in the presence of family, the patient's arousal experiences a sharp rise.

Data deriving from the research can be summarized as follows. First, the Family Strange Situation methodology proved easy to manage, reliable, and viable. MindLAB Set functioned well and can be adopted for systematic implementation of the Family Strange Situation. With testing, we extracted baseline values to which we will be able to refer in subsequent phases of research when using the Family Strange Situation procedure to systematically test patients afflicted with mental disorders.

15

Biofeedback, Neurofeedback, and Psychofeedback

15.1 Theoretical Foundation and Historical Development

Biofeedback is one of the most interesting and motivating new developments in the field of therapy in recent years. The inspiration this innovative technique has brought to neuroscience and psychotherapy has not been matched on the theoretical and epistemological plane. On the applications side, its ease of use means it can be a tactical, effective, and practical tool for change. In the cognitivist sphere, biofeedback stimulated a remarkable amount of reflection, research, and application (Pancheri, 1979; Scrimali and Grimaldi, 1982; 1991; Baumeister and Vohs, 2006).

The conceptual elaborations and research I developed over more than thirty years have spanned the evolution of behavioral and cognitive psychotherapy, with a personal history in which I can clearly identify four stages: behavioralist (second half of the 1970s), standard cognitivist (the 1980s), constructivist (the 1990s), and oriented to the logic of complex systems (the 2000s). In the context of this short book, it is not possible to thoroughly examine the biofeedback topic (for such purpose, consult specialized texts such as Scrimali and Grimaldi, 1982; 1991; Scrimali, 2003; Baumeister and Vohs, 2006). I will instead briefly analyze biofeedback and self-control from a psychophysiological, cognitivist, constructivist, and complex systems-oriented viewpoint.

Biofeedback, whose name derives from the combination of the terms "biology" and "feedback," is both an experimental and a clinical procedure consisting largely of presenting, with the assistance of suitable equipment,

Neuroscience-based Cognitive Therapy: New Methods for Assessment, Treatment, and Self-Regulation,
First Edition. Tullio Scrimali.
© 2012 John Wiley & Sons, Ltd. Published 2012 by John Wiley & Sons, Ltd.

information relating to the dynamic development in biological functions measured from the subject's body (Fuller, 1977). The objective we strive for is that of instructing the individual about the potential for regulating and controlling biological functions that are normally all or partially involuntary, or that are no longer voluntary due to a pathological condition. The first step is to "install" a new mode of biological regulation; the second step is to improve it; and the third, to restore it. Examples of the three different dynamics are presented below.

In general, one is not aware of development in biological variables such as heart rate, systolic and/or diastolic blood pressure, or micro-perspiration of the fingertips. Information regarding the dynamic status of these parameters is, however, obtainable via electronic equipment. When patients are provided with this information (Figure 15.1) via visual displays or acoustic feedback, they can identify, through a process of trial and error, which cognitive and emotional tactics may be effective in gaining control over biological variables and which may not. They can then electively employ the mechanisms that lead to regulation of the parameter in question.

In this case, this goal is to instill, or "install" if you will, voluntary control over the parameters that are normally regulated automatically at the subcortical level.

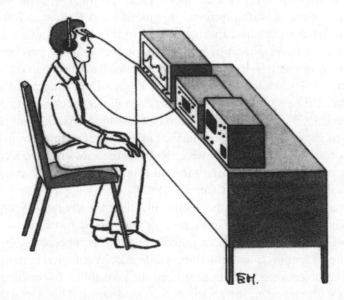

Figure 15.1 A biofeedback setting.

In the case of EMG (electromyography) biofeedback, where the goal is to induce a state of deep relaxation, we must acknowledge that a certain awareness of the degree of muscular tension or dysfunctional tension is present in physiological conditions with effective mechanisms of proprioceptive feedback (neuromuscular spindles). Here, effective feedback does not introduce information from scratch, but rather makes it more detailed and therefore more useful in developing control.

Finally, in the case of a loss of physiologically informative feedback due to a pathological process, the biofeedback technique replaces the lost function of the damaged physiological channels. This occurs in rehabilitative medicine when utilizing biofeedback mechanisms on parameters such as the disposition of a limb that is no longer properly communicating with central control mechanisms.

Biofeedback first developed in the United States at the end of the 1960s, when Miller demonstrated the potential for teaching an animal to control biological functions regulated by the neurovegetative nervous system, such as heart rate and peripheral cutaneous vasomotor activity (Miller, 1969). Also in the United Stated during the same period, another group of researchers demonstrated that it was possible for humans to achieve self-control of parameters such as heart rate, cutaneous vasoconstriction, and EEG rhythms (Snyder and Noble, 1968). In the 1970s, biofeedback techniques were in widespread use in America and Europe. Advances in microelectronics undoubtedly contributed to this rapid progress, as they enhanced the development of increasingly more compact, practical, and low-cost equipment. In Italy, the history of biofeedback began in the second half of the 1970s, mainly at University of Rome's Department of Psychiatry, where Pancheri and his group formed the Biofeedback Society of Italy (Pancheri, 1979). Then, over the course of just ten years, the biofeedback paradigm experienced a remarkable shift in perspective, transitioning from reductionist conceptions to more articulated theories characterized by a human information processing viewpoint and influenced by cognitivist epistemology (Scrimali and Grimaldi, 1991).

Both experimentally and therapeutically, the first stage of development in biofeedback was strongly influenced by behaviorist principles of learning through operant conditioning. According to this conception, feedback performed a reinforcement function, stabilizing physiological responses via a training objective, and reduced instead the probability of conflicting responses with respect to the anticipated control target. This is exactly why the biofeedback setting was initially set up according to these principles and tended to result in structuring feedback based on devices that could deliver, primarily to animals, rewards (food or more direct stimulation of the brain pleasure centers) or punishment (electric shock).

In these circumstances, however, biofeedback that was framed purely in a traditional paradigm (the conditioning theme) led to new information that threatened an old axiom of reflexological and behavioral psychology, namely the belief that the physiological parameters controlled by the autonomic nervous system could not be the object of operant or effective conditioning but only of Pavlovian conditioning. This solid conviction of Miller and Konorski in 1928 was, after much confusion, later accepted by Skinner, who then became a strong supporter. It was a kind of scientific dogma until the second half of the 1960s (Miller and Konorski, 1928; Skinner, 1976). Then, in 1967, Neal Miller and his work group initiated a series of experiments unequivocally demonstrating that, in animals, a parameter under neurovegetative control, such as heart rate, could be operantly conditioned (Miller, 1969). The dogma of operative nonconditionability of physiological responses through autonomic mediation having thus been contradicted, researchers in the second half of the 1960s also began to demonstrate the potential for gaining control of a whole series of such parameters via the use of biological feedback techniques in humans.

Currently, the biofeedback conceptualization as an application of teaching principles through operative conditioning is still accepted by diverse authors. During the 1980s, a different interpretive model was nevertheless developed, one that was characterized by systems theory and influenced by the cybernetic and computer information processing model of human information processing. Systems theory has experienced rapid and intense interdisciplinary development in recent decades. Within the scope of this theory, the study of the possibilities and modalities of integration and control among systems has played an important role, be they of a physical, chemical, or biological nature (Wiener, 1966; Maturana and Varela, 1980).

The regulation of dynamic processes in the human body, as in the animal, occurs primarily through feedback mechanisms. The regulation of dynamic activities via feedback can be described as a situation in which the final conditions of a process can act to regulate the development of the process itself. In this context, the informational element takes on great importance.

It is essential for some existing mechanism to function as an analyzer of the dynamic development of the process, which communicates information to the effector mechanisms, because they act on the process in the desired way. Thus, the cortical control system could not operate on muscular

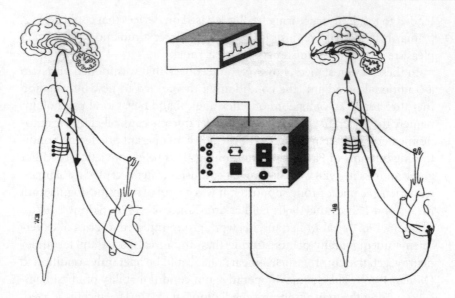

Figure 15.2   The cerebral cortex does not receive any information about heart rate activity unless specific devices are used.

activity if it were not continuously informed of the position of the skeletal areas concerned, the pressure applied to the skin, and the degree of tension and extension of the various muscle groups involved in the movement in question. The gradiental cortical nervous system is not capable of adequately controlling activity such as heart rate, blood pressure, or cutaneous vasoconstriction, not so much due to lacking the mechanisms and effector circuits but because it has insufficient information channels. In fact, data relating to the development of the biological functions cited are channeled at the diencephalic level and do not reach, even to a very minimal extent, the level of the cerebral cortex (Figure 15.2).

The technical components common to all types of biofeedback technique are summarized in the illustration of the set in Figure 15.3.

Biofeedback techniques involve the utilization of a set made up of electrodes or a transducer, a device that can analyze and convert signals of the parameter monitored. Both the acoustic and visual displays are important, as they perform the essential function of providing the sensory channels (typically acoustic and visual) with information on the development of the biological functions monitored. As illustrated in Figure 15.3, it is understood that the acoustic feedback is only analog and synchronic, while we

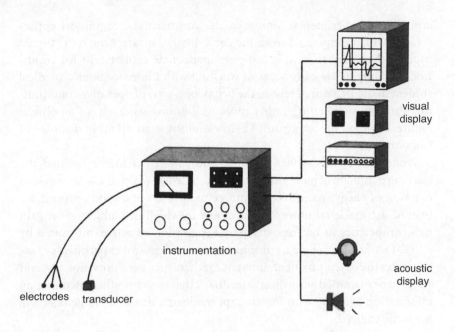

Figure 15.3   **The different components of any biofeedback device.**

describe three different types of visual feedback: diachronic analog (record), synchronic analog (LED bar), and synchronic digital (numeric display).

At this point, we must ask ourselves what really happens once the self-regulation dynamic is initiated via the equipment in the biofeedback setting. In accordance with cognitive biocybernetic logic, the control imposed on normally involuntary functions is expressed within a conscious and voluntary process. The feedback is, then, not a reinforcement but rather a message. One such interpretation of the biofeedback dynamic is at the basis of Brener's theory, which offered an information model of self-control via biological feedback (Brener, 1974). According to Brener's model, the potential for control over a specific biological function correlates with the level of information available and with conscious awareness of that function. Biofeedback is, then, a technical modality to activate or increase control of biological processes by installing or increasing informational feedback that makes the dynamic development of parameters to be managed available to the conscious.

With regard to the interpretation of the biofeedback dynamic, I have personally adhered to the biocybernetic model since the start of my research and clinical experiments. Moreover, the constructivist cognitivist episte-mology which I espoused from the early 1980s considers the reductionist model of learning to be a completely inadequate explanation for condi-tioning. Only in my early years of working with biofeedback as a medical student in the 1970s did I rely on the behavioral view of operative condition-ing. Paraphrasing Lenin's rather more well-known assertion of a political nature, I coined the aphorism: "Behavioralism is an infantile disorder of Cognitivism!"

From the cognitivist viewpoint, it immediately seemed clear that the learning paradigm of biological functions control in which the body was seen as a kind of passive receptor of reinforcements was not a good proposition. Instead, I considered more valid a model in which the subject must gain new competency in self-regulation and is considered active, motivated by a feed-forward to execute a continuous series of control experiments. This promotes the development of different mechanisms, used provisionally, and adopted or discarded according to feedback that conveys either encouraging information agreeing with the attempt made or a denial message rejecting the tactic utilized.

Up to this point, I have described biofeedback as a simple dynamic of self-control over biological parameters. From the time when biofeedback began to be considered a potential therapeutic tool, an additional series of problems occurred that, to date, have resulted in the therapeutic dynamic of biofeedback being in accord with more than one model. On this subject, it is interesting to observe that a similar process to that previously described was reapplied in the same context. In fact, the dynamic of this new, rev-olutionary therapeutic tool was soon framed in a reductionist viewpoint, making reference to the epistemological background of a medical discipline like pharmacology.

For biofeedback, then, the dual issue of specific and nonspecific, or placebo, effects arose in the same way as happened with understanding pharmacological therapeutic tools. Accordingly, a series of research studies attempted to isolate the variables in order to show an unequivocally specific effect (control of the biological function) that acted determinately on the therapeutic process, while for nonspecific effects, such as expectations and modified philosophies, an auxiliary and nondeterminant influence would have had to be demonstrated. In short, biofeedback would have had to act as a technical pill and then demonstrate an unequivocally specific control effect over the biological variables, as a drug must produce a clear and documentable pharmacodynamic effect on a specific physical substrate. The reductionist background of contemporary medicine markedly influenced such a conception.

I must say that, at the beginning of my research work on biofeedback and its applications, I was also vulnerable to similar theories, to the point of planning experiments in which biofeedback training/placebo procedures were expected to show only a specific therapeutic (psychophysiological) effect from an electrodermal biofeedback technique. I later became dissatisfied with this sort of interpretation and developed a more satisfactory one along with Chiari (Chiari and Scrimali, 1984). According to this conception, a dichotomy between specific effect (control of the biological parameter in question) and nonspecific effect is implausible, because cognitive factors are already involved in the control dynamic, as I emphasized when illustrating the biocybernetic model of biofeedback. Therefore, where control cannot exist without the involvement of cognitive factors, a therapeutic effect will not occur without modifications to the patient's knowledge system, on the tacit as well as the explicit level. I believe, then, that the control of monitored parameters progresses toward determining some therapeutic result in step with building new modalities of interpreting external reality and the self, intended in both a biological and a mental sense as well as in the sense of developing new abilities. Different ways of interpreting external reality and building new competencies lead to a more adaptive evolution in personal identity, which would be the most important result in therapeutic change provided by biofeedback training.

15.2 Physiological and Psychophysiological Biofeedback

So far, I have talked about biofeedback techniques, describing how it may be possible to therapeutically install and make use of biological feedback from various parameters. At this point, I must stress that the subject of biofeedback differs according to whether we're dealing with recording physiological or psychophysiological parameters. This distinction requires a certain clarification. Going back to my earlier definition of biofeedback as "both an experimental and a clinical procedure consisting largely of presenting, with the assistance of suitable equipment, information relating to the dynamic development in biological functions measured from the subject's body," I should point out that this can refer to different types of biological functions. In particular, we can distinguish between biological parameters that primarily express somatic activity and psychophysiological parameters that also include mental functions. One biofeedback technique that starts from a biological parameter, such as muscle tone, targets somatic function control, while types of feedback such as EEG rhythms and EDA are aimed at achieving mental and cognitive self-control. On this subject, Pancheri and Chiari worked on distinguishing between direct and indirect feedback techniques (Pancheri and Chiari, 1979).

In 1981, at the Biofeedback Society of Italy's Second Congress, I proposed defining physiofeedback or physiological feedback as direct feedback, and psychofeedback or psychophysiological feedback as indirect feedback. The inherent issues in the two different categorizations are diverse (Scrimali and Grimaldi, 1982). Any issue in physiofeedback is more immediate, involving acquisition of control over a specific function, and therefore only concerned with physiological problems that have already been studied in depth and resolved (e.g., the muscular activity dynamic in EMG feedback). However, any inherent issue in psychofeedback is more complex and intricate, involving psychophysiology. Psychofeedback from EDA is considered a typical example.

It is not unreasonable to think that some biofeedback techniques can take on the connotation of physiofeedback or psychofeedback, depending on their use. A typical example is EMG feedback, which when used for bruxism therapy (data acquisition from the masticatory muscles and control of tone in the same) is physiofeedback, but in other cases (data acquisition from the frontalis muscle and mental control) becomes psychofeedback. The concept of psychofeedback implies that we can use a biological parameter as an indicator of psychic phenomena at the cognitive and mental level. In the current state of study and research, the two biofeedback techniques that satisfy the definition of psychophysiological feedback are biofeedback from EEG activity and biofeedback from EDA.

Purely from its having been extensively utilized to monitor modification in the patient's mental situation, EMG biofeedback performed through recording tone in the frontalis muscle does not seem to me, in light of extensive experimental and clinical data, ideal for use from a psychophysiological viewpoint in the context of cognitivist psychotherapy, and for the following reasons. Thus far, it has not been unequivocally demonstrated that generalized muscular extension corresponds to relaxation of the frontalis muscle in every patient. In any case, the EMG training completed to obtain muscular extension enters into the context of relaxation techniques that do not allow the use of the biofeedback setting, as a situation in which emotional reactions are clearly demonstrated, to consider and analyze dysfunctional cognitive patterns for contradicting inadequate belief systems.

Interpretation of the biofeedback therapeutic dynamic in cognitive psychotherapy draws instead on those factors that are particularly present in biofeedback from EDA and EEG rhythms. These parameters correlate well with mental variations and cognitive activity, therefore, allowing the initiation of a psychotherapeutic treatment plan where the most important objective achieved is not so much self-control, in the reductionist sense, as it is lowering the level of functioning in recorded parameters, or rather, the analysis and modification of maladaptive knowledge structures on the tacit and explicit levels.

15.3 Biofeedback and Cognitive Therapy

The very first stage in biofeedback development, in the psychotherapeutic sense, took place within the scope of so-called relaxation techniques. For many years, different methods were suggested, aimed at achieving psychophysical relaxation for those who practiced them. The best known were Schultz's autogenic training and Jacobson's muscular relaxation training (Schultz, 1960; Jacobson, 1929). Such techniques were used autonomously for the purpose of allowing neurotic patients to reacquire a certain mental control, or in the context of more developed treatments such as Jacobson's progressive relaxation in systematic desensitization. Fully described by Wolpe, and interpreted according to a behavioral, reductionist epistemology that identified its therapeutic rationale in the principle of reciprocal inhibition, the latter technique was already quite well known and widespread in the 1960s (Wolpe, 1958). Thus, when relaxation techniques via biofeedback began to be asserted (EMG feedback, electrodermal feedback), some authors thought about using the new therapeutic tool in their methodologies, but predominantly in their epistemological approaches to systematic desensitization. Preliminary data concerning the use of biofeedback in the scope of systematic desensitization began to be published in the early 1970s (Rappaport, 1972).

In Italy, the first experiments integrating biofeedback into systematic desensitization treatment were completed and published by my work group in the and later by Chiari and Mosticoni (Scrimali, Grimaldi and Aguglia, 1978; Chiari and Mosticoni, 1979). I must emphasize how, in this first stage of biofeedback use in the psychotherapeutic context, we did not formulate a new paradigm, but did observe that the use of biological feedback techniques in the context of systematic desensitization allowed us to make treatment more effective. We saw this increased effectiveness in patients achieving a more profound state of relaxation and a faster learning curve in self-control. In the second stage, the introduction of biofeedback into the paradigm of systematic desensitization unfortunately excluded some cognitive factors.

The two authors who first fully analyzed the biofeedback problem from the cognitivist viewpoint were Lazarus and Meichenbaum (Lazarus, 1975; Meichenbaum, 1976). Lazarus described the biofeedback technique in the psychotherapeutic setting as capable of increasing the patient's coping abilities in the face of fearful stimuli. According to this author, the amount of anxiety an individual experiences when facing any problematic situation is inversely proportional to their consciously being able to make use of adequate behavioral and cognitive tools to effectively manage and resolve it. Awareness of the ability to control emotional reactions, as developed during biofeedback training, would thus increase coping ability in fearful situations.

Lazarus' formulation seemed interesting to me, so much so that I planned an experiment in 1981 with the aim of studying coping styles when normal subjects and anxious patients were faced with unpleasant acoustic stimuli, primarily to show whether electrodermal feedback-based training would modify the coping ability of anxious patients over time, while also modifying their representational style (Scrimali, Grimaldi and Rapisarda, 1983). The research-level results were positive, allowing me to definitively abandon the paradigm of reciprocal inhibition in favor of an epistemological conception of biofeedback in psychotherapy, characterized by a cognitivist approach. Along these lines, I also turned to Meichenbaum's theories about cognitive factors in biofeedback therapies. According to this author, biofeedback training can be completed in three phases: initial conception, ability acquisition and experimentation, and finally transfer of what is learned in treatment to real-life situations. The three phases described in the cognitive theory of self-control, as proposed by Meichenbaum (1976), coincide with these first three phases. In the first, the patient begins to monitor their behavior and physiological responses. In the second, cognitive processes and new behavioral abilities start to develop. In the third and final stage, the patient's belief system is restructured.

Meichenbaum's conception clearly shows that learning the ability of self-control becomes therapeutic to the extent that it allows the patient's knowledge system to be modified. This is the point of reference for my own conception of the biofeedback dynamic in psychotherapy. According to my conception, the patient could achieve the self-observation, instructional modification, and belief systems restructuring phases during biofeedback training. The self-observation phase consists of the attempt to clarify to the patient the precise dynamic of the anxious pathology related to fearful situations, focusing their attention on specific behavior, internal dialogue, and emotional reactions that they demonstrate during the problematic situation. We complete the work through a series of psychophysiological and cognitive-behavioral tests aimed at demonstrating the patient's arousal reactions in relation to simple sensory stimuli, their capacity to manage stressful situations, and their mind-set in trying to resolve these issues constructively, without adopting avoidance tactics.

The results of this assessment phase are communicated to the patient. In most cases, the clinical picture that emerges from these data is characterized by the patient's difficulty in dealing with arousal, and by their profound belief in the present and future impossibility of mental control. A general result is a perceived incapacity to positively confront and manage situations with negative emotional connotations (namely, a decrease in coping skills), and an almost constant condition of poor confidence in their own effectiveness in managing problematic situations.

The objectives in the instructional modification phase include training the patient and then instructing them on mental control, consequently improving their coping skills and self-efficacy. These objectives are achieved, in practice, through biofeedback training. Using the equipment to train the patient gradually counteracts their convictions about the impossibility of controlling arousal, increases their capacity for resilience through practice in coping with experimental stressors, and as a result, improves their self-confidence (self-efficacy).

The new scenario proves incompatible with the patient's prior dysfunctional beliefs, and such incompatibility – a true cognitive dissonance – can lead the patient to a general improvement in self-image. This occurs through the modification of internal dialogue and representational style that derive from a progressive decrease in escape behaviors and a gradual installation of active confrontational behaviors toward fearful situations. We can thus implement a true cognitive restructuring. According to the conceptualization just outlined, the therapeutic dynamic of biofeedback would ultimately be traceable to the following factors:

- controlling the psychophysiological correlates to anxiety;
- restructuring beliefs regarding the emotional issue;
- increasing capacity for coping and resilience; and
- augmenting self-efficacy.

15.4 MindLAB Set-based Coping Skills Training

Coping skills strategies are compromised in many neurotic patients. Phobic patients systematically try to avoid any negative stimuli, in spite of coping with them. For this reason, I developed a specific type of training, made possible by some particular features of MindLAB Set. I also created a new name for this technique: *MindLAB Set-based Coping Skills Training*.

This kind of training consists in administering to the patient, through headphones, some disturbing sounds. This procedure is automatically managed by the programs MindSCAN and Psychofeedback. The patient attends a session of self-regulation by Psychofeedback and receives these negative sounds in a randomized way.

Whenever the patient receives the negative sounds, they should learn to reduce the arousal response as a new way of coping positively with any stressor, rather than adopting any avoidance behavior.

15.5 Relaxation, Self-Control, Self-Regulation

From my own constructivist and complex point of view, I can attest that the newly acquired competencies in emotional self-regulation modify the patient's construction of reality. What occurs (a panic attack, for instance) now loses its threatening and alienating connotations, being transformed into a confrontable and explorable process. Ultimately, a progressive shift in personal identity begins to find motivation. The patient puts the burden of memories, tied to experiencing loss of emotional control, escape and avoidance, then failure, into perspective as they move toward reinforcing representations of a self that is able to regulate the mental process, confront problems, and explore its own world.

My last and most recent conceptual development in biofeedback is that involving the logic of complex systems (Skarda and Freeman, 1990; Scrimali, 2008). In accordance with this conception, biofeedback is not primarily a self-control process but rather one of self-regulation. In the context of the so-called relaxation techniques that include Schultz's autogenic training (1960) and Jacobson's progressive muscular relaxation (1929), the primary preconceived objective is that of reducing the overall activation level of the body. This is pursued via methods aimed at putting into perspective the body's ergotropic posture, namely that which is present when challenging activity must be confronted, in order to promote the so-called trophotropics, which diminish energy output and favor the recovery of optimal levels in body functioning. In order to practice such techniques, a setting is required that supports reduced sensory inputs: soft lighting with eyes possibly closed, soundproofing, and even relaxing music.

In the process systems-oriented viewpoints that I have described, we attribute less relevance to the concept of relaxation, placing more emphasis on self-regulation. In substance, you advise the patient to acquire the ability to self-monitor and manage their emotions vigilantly in a setting similar to that of daily reality. Most patients to whom I offer psychofeedback with MindLAB Set and software methodology tend to want to close their eyes, often complaining that the acoustic feedback from the equipment is stressful, as they describe it. In this case, I have to explain that it has nothing to do with a relaxation technique but is instead a self-regulation process that must be implemented via modalities emulating those in real life. If the patient has a panic attack while driving, they will certainly not be able to relax – that is, close their eyes and recline on the seat – but will instead try to regulate mental processes by modifying the internal dialogue and decreasing emotional activation, exactly as they will have learned to do in the session, using MindLAB Set.

It is understood, then, that self-control is a new competency that allows the emergence of a never-before-encountered balance between the frontal cortical systems and the limbic and hypothalamic structures. Such new equilibria are nevertheless not characterized, according to recent conceptions informed by the logic of dynamic and nonlinear complex systems, by a simple top-down control connection, with the frontal system (top) assuming control over the limbic system (down), but represent a new dynamic in which the cortical regulation process produces an innovative condition of balance distributed among the various systems through recurring feedback mechanisms. Ultimately, the regulation of complex processes within a dynamic and nonlinear system which is far from being in equilibrium does primarily occur in line with a top-down logic, that is, from the more evolved to the more obsolete, but this is according to a recursive dynamic that encounters the emergence of new patterns of balance. In short, it seems too simplistic to think that, during feedback, the frontal cortical structures take control of the more obsolete limbic structures. In reality, a new dynamic equilibrium is created, one that is more adaptive to the dialectic between the frontal cortical centers of the neopallium and the emotional limbic structures of the archipallium. The whole CNS resets in a complex way, with new dynamics, moving toward the more evolved equilibria of a different and new chaotic attractor.

16

Meditation, Mindfulness, and Biofeedback-based Mindfulness (BBM)

16.1 Meditation

According to Walsh, the term "meditation" refers to a variety of practices that train the individual to improve awareness and activate cerebral processes for greater voluntary control. The ultimate objectives of these practices are the development of a more profound awareness of the nature of mental processes, consciousness, identity, connection to reality, and the promotion of optimal states of psychological wellbeing and awareness (Walsh, 1988).

16.1.1 Types of Meditation

Goleman (1982) proposed evaluating various meditation techniques on the basis of the principle processes activated, explained as follows:

- *concentration*: the mind focuses on a specific mental process;
- *awareness*: the mind observes itself; and
- *integration* of both the above processes.

In concentration, the strategy for strengthening attention consists of focusing on one object and constantly bringing the mind back to it, as the mind would otherwise tend to wander. In transcendental meditation, for example, one is advised to begin the mantra softly each time the mind starts to lose focus.

Neuroscience-based Cognitive Therapy: New Methods for Assessment, Treatment, and Self-Regulation,
First Edition. Tullio Scrimali.
© 2012 John Wiley & Sons, Ltd. Published 2012 by John Wiley & Sons, Ltd.

The meditation techniques largely centered on the awareness process are Theravada Buddhism vipassana, zazen shikantaza, Krishnamurti self-awareness and Gurdjieff self-remembering (Lang, 2004). There are a few schools of meditation that focus on just one process, among them transcendental meditation (Nidich and Seeman, 1973) but most schools claim to be eclectic, as they utilize a variety of techniques drawn from two groups (i.e., the group of concentration and the group of awareness), in practice adapting to the individual inclinations of their devotees. In any case, all the schools agree on the necessity to narrow one's field of focus in order to reach a state of altered consciousness by following the path of concentration or that of awareness (or mental presence).

Neuroscience provided a noteworthy contribution to the better understanding of meditation techniques through imaging studies of the modifications of function in processes and, in the long term, brain structures. EEG and, in particular, QEEG made another notable contribution to the study of brain state during meditation. Studies conducted on Buddhist monks during meditation showed the creation of functional hemispheric asymmetry, with transition from left-side dominance to right-side dominance, as well as the simultaneous optimization of cognitive and somatovisceral functions presiding over the right hemisphere.

During meditation, an increased alpha rhythm and a general transition to slower rhythms in the EEG during the initial phases of relaxation are shown, with decreased heart and respiratory rates, transitioning to a different EEG response in progressive profound relaxation. This is characterized by a theta rhythm that seems to correlate with the phase defined as concentration, when meditating subjects focus their attention on a symbol or a mantra (as is typical of Asian meditative practice). In later stages of experiencing satori and samādhi we find intense beta activity in the EEG. Satori is the spiritual goal of Zen Buddhism during which the feeling of infinite space is experienced. Samādhi conists in the contemplation of one of forty different objects such as mindfulness of breathing and loving kindness. This state of consciousness is generally associated with the meditating subject experiencing joy and a profound sense of peace. Another important effect of meditation, in terms of electroencephalography, is the realization of inter-hemispheric synchronization. During the active awake state, the two brain hemispheres instead appear particularly desynchronized, both inter-hemispherically and intra-hemispherically.

Greater synchronization between the two hemispheres is also associated with states of wellbeing and positive emotion, while desynchronization correlates with stressful situations and negative emotion. Shapiro and Walsh (1984) completed a controlled study on synchronization and state of mind, using transcendental meditation. An expert in this technique was asked to press a button when perceiving, during meditation, a state of awareness and profound sense of wellbeing, an experience described as pure awareness. The study showed that the subject pushed the button when the EEG was recording peaks in inter-hemispheric coherence of 100%, that is, when brain activity was completely synchronic. Another aspect of EEG meditation patterns relates to theta rhythms. A variety of research has demonstrated that, during transcendental meditation, the EEG shows an unusually high presence of theta waves (Wallace, 1970).

Use of the electrodermal parameter is largely described in the literature as a marker that can document the specific state of mind connected to the meditative state. Electrodermal response is inked with arousal and, as the subject's mental activity diminishes, electrodermal conductance decreases and spontaneous phasic responses attenuate until they disappear, becoming more analog and iconic as opposed to digital and semantic. I personally employed a method of systematically experimenting with MindLAB Set to evaluate the meditative state in the course of a controlled study conducted with the valuable collaboration of Dr Angela Miccichè (Scrimali and Miccichè, 2010).

The purpose of our research was in part to confirm data in the literature that documents the meditative state as reducing arousal, and in part to use the MindLAB Set methodology for the first time to evaluate the meditative state. Nine volunteer subjects who had been practicing diverse meditation disciplines for some time, and who claimed they were capable of achieving the trophotropic state of consciousness that the state of mind entails, were involved in the study. The resulting group was composed of six males and three females with an average age of 45. We performed the research at ALETEIA Clinical Center's Psychophysiology Laboratory.

We called the subjects in one at a time and, after having acclimatized them to the laboratory and applied the electrodes to the index and middle fingers of the right hand, we asked them to initiate the meditative state. We recorded and obtained the electrodermal parameter via the MindLAB Set system. The electrodermal conductance acquisition channel was a Psychodata Acquisition Unit connected to a computer equipped with the MindSCAN and Psychofeedback software (Psychotech, 2008). We utilized the MindSCAN program. We kept the laboratory quiet and controlled the environmental parameters (22°C, 60% humidity).

Table 16.1 Comparison between EDA during baseline and meditation in a sample of nine subjects.

Subject	Baseline EDA values (in microsiemens)	Meditation EDA values (in microsiemens)
No. 1	6.54	5.17
No. 2	6.50	4.90
No. 3	4.15	3.42
No. 4	8.96	3.56
No. 5	5.08	4.94
No. 6	12.08	11.93
No. 7	2.97	2.22
No. 8	3.07	1.10
No. 9	4.05	2.00
	Total average and s.d.: 6.01 ± 3.19	Total average and s.d.: 4.36 ± 3.18

Student's t-test: $p = 0.01$ (very significant difference)

We made two recordings, one lasting 4 minutes and another 15 minutes, with a 30-minute break in between. During the first recording, the patient was comfortably seated on an ergonomic armchair, doing nothing. We instructed the patient to remain calm but vigilant and not to implement any specific form of physical or mental self-regulation.

During the second recording, we asked subjects to meditate according to their specific abilities. Table 16.1 shows the average EDA values we obtained via the MindSCAN software with a 4-minute recording as a baseline time period and a 15-minute recording of active self-regulation via meditation.

I am also including the graph of an exemplary recording (Figure 16.1) that we carried out on one of the nine subjects in the study, a Thai woman and meditator with about 20 years' experience in the Theravada Buddhist tradition. The baseline recording is the shorter one, ascending (left bar graph) while the meditation recording is the longer one, descending (the right bar graph).

In each of the nine patients, we recorded decreased electrodermal conductance during the meditative state. Analyzed in nonquantitative terms (nonparametric), this result is highly significant (sign test: $p < 0.001$). After the nonparametric analysis, we carried out a quantitative evaluation (parametric) using a Student's t-test. We did this with a computerized

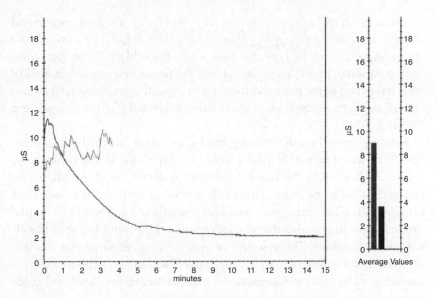

Figure 16.1 EDA values of an experienced meditator during baseline recording compared with those registered during meditation (training).

program called Primer. We made use of the t-test variance for paired data, that is, for recordings repeated on the same subject. As you can see in Table 16.1, the difference proves statistically significant and more accurate. The p-value in fact, ended up at 0.01. The recording technique for the electrodermal parameter implemented via the MindLAB Set system proved easy to implement and did not disturb the meditators.

Our results showed that a meditative state actually reduces arousal and therefore induces a trophotropic state that has therapeutic value for various psychosomatic and mental disorders, as reported in previous chapters. Furthermore, we demonstrated that the MindLAB Set system seems especially suitable for recording and quantifying the real stimulation of a beneficial trophotropic state induced by meditation techniques. In other words, we obtained the anticipated results from our research.

16.2 Mindfulness

Closely connected to the topic of meditation, mindfulness implies the potential for every subject to methodically produce, via study and learning, specific states of mind that have a therapeutic benefit for a wide range of illnesses. The term "mindfulness" literally describes a positive state of mind that can be achieved through progressive learning. It is a state in which the attention focuses on the here and now, where the subject disconnects from the resolution of problems projected into the future or a re-examination of what happened in the past, and includes in a positive and beneficial awareness all the parts of the body that are often neglected (Germer, Siegel, and Fulton, 2005).

Mindfulness techniques are inspired by ancient Asian meditation practices such as vipassana, but have been developed for simpler and more logical application in the western cultural context. One of the important concepts in the scope of mindfulness is that every human often leads a life on automatic pilot, namely one based on stereotypical and repetitive mental processes that impoverish the creative richness of the mind and the individual's own autonomy. The objective of practicing mindfulness is really that of breaking away from automatic mechanical action and negative external conditioning in order to increase awareness of mental processes and guide them in a more harmonious and positive direction.

The author who described a standard mindfulness method was John Kabat-Zinn at the University of Massachusetts, Worcester (Kabat-Zinn, 1994). The enormous development of mindfulness technique applications in many areas, from improvement in quality of life (public health psychology) to medicine and clinical psychology, motivated researchers to document the effect of mindfulness on the CNS via both functional and cerebral morphological imaging methodologies. These studies tend to demonstrate that the right hemisphere is apparently more involved in mindfulness, primarily at the level of the right prefrontal cortex.

In his wonderful book *The Mindful Brain* Daniel Siegel carried out a series of in-depth research studies that tie the theme of mindfulness to the functional and morphological study of the CNS with a scientific approach based on neuroscience (Siegel, 2007). Siegel gives proper attention to the neuronal integration and emotional self-regulation processes that mindfulness seems to activate. The cerebral areas that he identified as involved in the development processes of new neural networks appear to be localized in the medial prefrontal cortical region. Siegel stresses how such areas and connected neural networks may control critical mental processes such as the regulation of physical activity (trophotropic versus ergotropic), functional interhuman communication, emotional regulation, the potential for planning and supplying responses to environmental requirements that are flexible and well thought out, empathy, and the capacity for metacognitive-type self-observation in modulating fear, intuition, and moral ethics. The importance of the many processes in play accounts for the great therapeutic potential of mindfulness and regulation of such neural circuits.

Segal, Williams, and Teasdale integrated mindfulness into the cognitive-oriented treatment of depression for the specific purpose of reducing the rate and seriousness of relapses. The treatment provided the potential for learning, in eight sessions, how to inhibit the distressing symptomatology of ruminating over the past that may initiate and contribute to relapse (Segal, Williams and Teasdale, 2002).

16.3 Biofeedback-Based Mindfulness

My recent research has addressed the theme of mindfulness by combining it with the potential for recording and receiving feedback from EDA in the form of psychofeedback. Along these lines, I developed an original approach to mindfulness, based on neuroscience and fueled by advanced experimental findings that took shape at the University of Catania's Clinical and Experimental Psychophysiology Laboratory at the Department of Psychiatry, as well as at the Institute for Cognitive Sciences. In the context of this area of study and research, I devised an original form of training that I described as Biofeedback-Based Mindfulness. This can also be considered a synchronic mind training, as described below (see also Scrimali, 2010a).

The digital and cognitive mind characteristic of *Homo sapiens* is typically diachronic, able to remember the past, and project, in proactive terms, into the future. In a state of mental health, these two mind systems should function dialectically but harmoniously. In pathological situations, digital activity in the diachronic mind instead produces constant rumination on the past and an incessant pessimistic proaction toward the future. Such a mind-set is quite evident in depression and is also observed in OCD. In the first case, the rumination phenomenon primarily manifests, while worry is exhibited in the second (Davey and Wells, 2006). In such circumstances, synchronic mind training can play a positive therapeutic role when it is permanently integrated into a modification plan that is strategically oriented toward progressive restructuring of the dysfunctional mental processes.

Synchronic mind training can be described as the attempt to actively achieve a state of mind similar to that described as mindfulness and based on positive functional balance in the frontal, limbic, and hippocampal circuits, with the assistance of psychophysiological tools that can supply feedback. Since the EDA parameter has the ability to supply information appropriate to these areas of the brain, recording biological feedback from EDA therefore has the potential to be a method that closely complements the classic techniques of mindfulness.

The mental state produced during synchronic mind training is characterized by the following aspects and related processes:

- *nonconceptual*: arrests the flow of thought (cognitive activity in the left hemisphere) and activates the analog mind (right hemisphere) to search for imagery;
- *centered on the present*: must turn off the diachronic mind, which is usually connected to the past or is proactive toward the future;
- *nonjudgmental*: provisionally accepts and does not debate whatever mental content or state might surface;
- *intentionally focused*: attention must be intensely focused on the acoustic and visual feedback coming from the equipment;
- *comprehensive*: body and mind must be simultaneously (synchronically) taken into account;
- *nonverbal*: activating the tacit mind, the state to be achieved must be primarily nonverbal;
- *tending toward exploration*: new states of mind must be revealed through investigation and positive feedback from the equipment; and
- *liberating*: the training experience must create a sense of liberation from ties to the diachronic mind (past, future) and distressing mental activity.

Biofeedback-Based Mindfulness must teach the patient to achieve a state of mind that can arrest the process of rumination and worry and this goal is achieved using a EDA biofeedback device. The six-session educational training is implemented via MindLAB Set. Once the patient has learned the synchronic state of mind, they must practice attaining it for at least 15 minutes daily and during their everyday routines, so it becomes a fundamental mind-set.

In OCD, this method allows the patient to observe the automatic mental processes related to their obsessions in a nonjudgmental way and with increasing detachment, thereby avoiding any mentally neutralizing activity and ritual on the behavioral level. A series of controlled research studies concerning the application of synchronic mind training is currently taking place at our laboratories in therapy of pain management, OCD, and asthma as well as in gastroenterology, cardiology, and prenatal health.

To allow you to implement Biofeedback-Based Mindfulness yourself, I set out the practical directions below:

> Your first step is to supply the patient with instructions relating to the psychofeedback you are implementing with MindLAB Set (or any other EDA-biofeedback device). Once MindLAB and the Psychofeedback software are launched, read the following preliminary instructions to them.

"This equipment records mental activation. The acoustic and visual displays provide information. The information will be used to regulate your mental condition. During the training, you should focus your attention and state of mind, at all times, on the here and now, avoiding any projection into the future or dwelling on the past."

Once you are confident that the patient has understood the dynamic of mental self-control through psychofeedback, tell them: "The training teaches you how to produce and then maintain a state of mind that is characterized by the following aspects and relative processes." Then provide the list of processes given on page 178.

When the patient successfully produces a synchronic state of mind and reduces emotional activation, they will observe in the record a progressive reduction in the spontaneous phasic responses connected to cognitive mental activity and, at the same time, a progressive decrease in SCL. Once this result is obtained, you must encourage the patient to "photograph" the new state of mind that they have produced, and then reproduce it at home without equipment, devoting at least 15 minutes daily to practicing this style of mindfulness. The newly acquired competency will then be employed as an adequate and positive management process when the patient is faced with the dysfunctional processes of rumination and worry.

17

Neurofeedback and Cognitive Therapy

Neurofeedback is a methodology recently introduced into the practice of integrated therapy of mental disorders, and therefore results are not yet extensively documented, although the literature is growing quite rapidly (Budzynski *et al.*, 2009).

Neurofeedback basically consists in teaching the patient to increase the amount of alpha and theta activity (alpha training and theta training) or the level of beta activity (beta training). The first process makes the anxious patients calmer and more mentally relaxed; the second process can activate people affected by depression (Othmer, Othmer, and Kaiser, 1999; Demos, 2005).

The alpha/theta neurofeedback applications that have been described mostly concern insomnia, OCD, ADHD, depression, mania and drug dependency. With beta training, as mentioned, applications are primarily for depressed patients, who show a reduced beta level together with an increased alpha level.

17.1 Insomnia

As early as the start of the 1980s, Hauri's experimental work showed that using appropriate biofeedback techniques can prove effective in therapy for psychophysiological insomnia (Hauri, 1981). Among the various types of usable biofeedback that are particularly helpful theta feedback training appears, at least on the theoretical level, to be the most promising.

Neuroscience-based Cognitive Therapy: New Methods for Assessment, Treatment, and Self-Regulation, First Edition. Tullio Scrimali.
© 2012 John Wiley & Sons, Ltd. Published 2012 by John Wiley & Sons, Ltd.

In the transition from the awake state to sleep, an EEG phase is described (stage 1) which is characterized by the appearance of the theta rhythm (3–7 cycles per second). In the awake state, theta activity production is associated with a state of deadening the conscious mind and sleeping with the eyes open, a strategy that can prove useful to patients who are unable to fall asleep due to intrusive cognitive activity linked with rapid EEG rhythms (Green, Green, and Walters, 1970).

The ability to increase theta density can be learned quite easily in a suitable recording situation with biological feedback from EEG activity (Brown, 1971). In the light of the seriousness and widespread nature of the insomnia problem and the promising prospects, at least on paper, of theta feedback training, I launched a research program at the end of the 1980s whose purpose was to evaluate the feasibility of theta feedback training in clinical routine and its real efficacy in treating insomnia (Scrimali and Grimaldi, 1991).

The first phase of our experimental work consisted in evaluating whether normal subjects were able to achieve a significant increase in the theta rhythm in a recording and biological feedback situation. Additionally, I decided to experimentally verify the hypothesis that the increased theta performance would correlate with greater ease in falling asleep. In order to evaluate the latter, I resorted to analyzing late-middle latency evoked acoustic potentials and, in particular, recording the N200 wave which is connected with the arousal of the subject.

Evoked acoustic potentials are a parameter which can be recorded when some acoustic stimuli are administered during an EEG registration. In such a case we are studying not the spontaneous EEG but rather the specific pattern evoked by some sensorial stimuli (in this case some acoustic patterns). There are some early, middle latency and late evoked brain potentials, and the N200 is the negative wave that can be recorded 200 milliseconds after the onset of the stimuli.

Some experimental data had already demonstrated that the N200 increased in proportion to the subject's degree of drowsiness (Picton and Hillyard, 1974). I then formulated an experimental ABA design where the two baselines consisted of an attempt at drowsiness by the five subjects who participated in the research, with the N200 recorded in both cases. The experimental variable consisted of theta feedback training in 6–7 sessions lasting about 20 minutes, performed twice a week. If theta training were to be truly effective, first psychophysiologically then therapeutically, we would have had to see a significant increase in the theta band produced in the last as opposed to the first session (learning to increase theta); a significant difference in the amplitude of the theta band produced in the second compared with the first baseline (overall performance learned outside the recording of biological feedback from the parameter in question); and, finally, both an actual increase in the parameter correlating to drowsiness (N200 from the evoked acoustic potentials) and a subjective patient evaluation on falling asleep.

In the second phase, we wanted to study instead the real therapeutic potential of the technique. In this case four insomniac patients participated in theta feedback training, one of whom was hospitalized with depression. The remaining three patients were outpatients and free from any psychiatric pathology. These four subjects had been suffering from severe insomnia for years, and in some cases had been resistant to therapy with benzodiazepine sleeping pills. We evaluated the efficacy of theta training in relation to the following three sleep-related parameters: time taken to fall asleep, duration of sleep, and number of wakings during the night. We also collected data to allow an evaluation of a placebo effect. The sleep-related activity of these subjects was analyzed via an appropriate questionnaire on three occasions: before initiating treatment (baseline), before initiating treatment but after taking a placebo, and at the end of training.

During the first experiment, four out of the five subjects significantly increased theta activity, while we verified during the sessions that one subject was not able to significantly increase the presence of the theta band. The N200 did not increase in this patient, while in the four others it did. All five subjects recorded a significant change from their baselines, although the subject who did not increase theta activity showed the lowest increase on the N200 wave. The patients' subjective evaluation of training was consistently positive. Within the scope of the second experiment, none of the subjects increased the theta to a significant extent, while three out of the four improved their baseline performance.

Evaluations of the training were positive in three subjects. The subject who evaluated it negatively described the experiment as not being very helpful. Improvements in sleep patterns were comprehensively verified in three patients, although in different forms. Only one patient did not experience any effect.

Where there were effects, they were almost always greater than the effects experienced from the placebo, which did not prove helpful. Our research therefore showed a clear relationship between increased capacity to produce theta rhythms and performance in falling asleep, while it did not demonstrate therapeutic efficacy of theta training in the insomnia subjects treated. However, we did obtain a series of useful data in the light of increasing and demonstrating the efficacy of theta feedback training, as follows:

- An adequate number of sessions must occur and end only when significant increase in theta is demonstrated.
- In order to achieve this result, there must be a data acquisition system that operates "online," allowing analysis of historic data series in real time.
- The auditory feedback provided must not be binary or coupled with an arbitrarily fixed threshold, but rather continuously and proportionally correlated with progress in the recording.
- Evaluation of training results must be completed in terms of the recording's depth of content and not based on binary feedback time at the given threshold.

17.2 Obsessive-Compulsive Disorder

The rationale behind using neurofeedback in treating OCD is that of electively teaching the patient to prevent the worry that seems to be connected to increased rapid rhythms in the frontal region. With an acoustic feedback system, the patient is constantly informed about alpha rhythm amplitude in this area.

To perform neurofeedback with OCD sufferers we start with a threshold value and the patient receives feedback every time the amplitude of the EEG signal exceeds the predetermined value in the alpha band. With this training, the patient learns to slow down the frontal electroencephalographic rhythm and consequently to produce non-ruminative mental activity.

Obviously, this new competency is not therapeutic per se, but it becomes so within a cognitive psychotherapy protocol aimed at changing the knowledge structure, as in the Sisifo protocol described below (see also Scrimali, 2003). Without the goal of changing the knowledge structures, the self-control obtained from recording the psychophysiological parameter would remain a goal in and of itself, useless in the sense that it would not be integrated into the necessary evolution of knowledge processes, as occurred in the first experiments on treatment via biofeedback techniques (Scrimali and Grimaldi, 1991). On the tactical level, however, the potential for the patient to acquire control over mental activity, through neurofeedback with biofeedback from EEG frequencies, is a powerful coping tool that increases self-efficacy. That is, knowing that they can inhibit rumination, the patient feels more competent and, therefore, progressively avoids calling on the rituals normally used to reduce anxiety.

This innovative methodology appears extremely promising. For this reason, I decided to embark upon systematic experimentation with neurofeedback in treating patients afflicted with obsessive rumination. I would now like to illustrate a clinical case I treated along with Sonya Maugeri (Scrimali, 2010a).

In this case, a 36-year-old patient afflicted by OCD (diagnosed in agreement with DSM-IV-TR), received neurofeedback treatment within the scope of a cognitivist therapeutic protocol that I developed, called Sisifo. The subject had been tormented by doubts and negative mental imagery that haunted her for many hours each day. Her doubts concerned her past conduct and mistakes she might have made.

We explained to the patient, through neurofeedback training, that she could gradually learn to inhibit such rumination and clear her mind without having to perform the usual rituals which consisted of asking for reassurance from her family concerning her doubts. The patient attended 13 neurofeedback sessions in the Cognitive Psychophysiology Laboratory at the University of Catania's Department of Psychiatry. Each session lasted about 45 minutes, including skin preparation and electrode attachment. We made sure the subject was comfortable in an armchair with a headrest and asked her to clear her mind, guided by the auditory feedback. Every time the alpha rhythm amplitude increased, exceeding the set threshold value, the patient received auditory feedback. In such a way, she learned to establish mind-sets that were useful in implementing the alpha.

The experiment design was as follows: we made a baseline measurement at the beginning of treatment, considering both psychophysiological and psychometric parameters. We first evaluated the average amplitude in the alpha rhythm recorded during the baseline session. We then administered the Yale Brown Obsessive-Compulsive Scale from Goodman, Price, and Rasmussen (1989). We made a new clinical assessment after twelve neurofeedback sessions completed over three months. During the same time period, the patient attended ten cognitive psychotherapy sessions informed by the Sisifo protocol methodology.

The alpha rhythm amplitude values before and after training are documented in Table 17.1 and Figure 17.1. The psychometric data before and after training are documented in Table 17.2 and Figure 17.2. We verified a statistically significant increase in the alpha rhythm.

Table 17.1 Figures showing the change in average alpha rhythm amplitude of EEG following neurofeedback training.

	Baseline	*Training*
Average values and standard deviation	6.15 ± 1.06	9.80 ± 0.28
	p = 0.042 *significant	

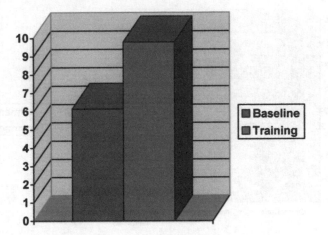

Figure 17.1 Bar chart showing the change in average alpha rhythm amplitude of EEG following neurofeedback training. (Left bar = before treatment; right bar = after treatment.)

We also observed a significant improvement in the psychometric data (Table 17.2, Figure 17.2).

Obsessions, compulsions, and compromised insight all decreased. The differences were evaluated using Student's t-test for repeated measurements, which were shown to be quite significant. The patient's clinical condition also improved, as substantiated by evidence provided by her father. The patient began to carry out activities that she had stopped some time before, such as driving, going out dancing, and looking for a job. The rumination decreased while her sense of self-efficacy improved simultaneously with an improved mood and significantly decreased anxiety. Nevertheless, the patient did not adequately conceptualize precisely how to successfully increase the alpha rhythm. In developing a new overall mind-set, however, she was in fact able to defer and, at times, eliminate the rituals.

Table 17.2 Values of three psychopathological parameters before and after neurofeedback in a 36-year-old sufferer of OCD.

	Pre-treatment	Post-treatment	p
Obsessions	3.80 ± 0.45	1.40 ± 0.55	0.007
Compulsions	3.60 ± 0.55	1.80 ± 0.84	0.004
Compromised insight	3.50 ± 0.58	1.25 ± 0.50	0.001

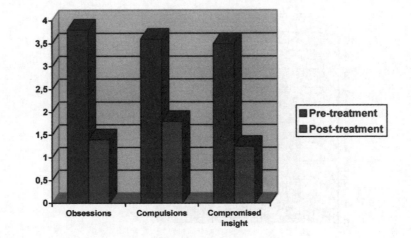
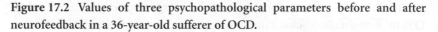

Figure 17.2 Values of three psychopathological parameters before and after neurofeedback in a 36-year-old sufferer of OCD.

The research we completed demonstrated the usefulness of neurofeedback as a tactical tool to manage obsessive rumination in the patient afflicted with OCD. Using NeuroLAB Set, the method proved easy to implement, both efficient and effective. Based on such positive results, we planned a subsequent extensive application of the new methodology for the treatment of obsessive rumination in disorders whose prognosis to date remains poor.

17.3 Attention Deficit Hyperactivity Disorder

Neurofeedback has been reported as a useful method for treating children with ADHD. Recently Gevensleben and colleagues carried out a multisite, randomized, controlled study using computerized attention skills training as a control condition (Gevensleben *et al.*, 2009).

The results obtained show the superiority of the neurofeedback training, indicating the clinical efficacy of this neuroscience-based therapeutic method in children with ADHD. Future studies should focus on the specificity of effects and how to better take advantage of the benefits of neurofeedback when using it as a module of a more complex and integrated CT for ADHD.

17.4 Depression

In accordance with the classic finding that hypoactivation of the left frontal cortex is a marker for depression (Davidson and Irwin, 1999), research has demonstrated that decreasing theta activity (4–7 Hz) and simultaneously increasing beta2 activity (15–18) Hz) at C3 was found to reduce depression in most patients (Hammond, 2005). The possibility of using neurofeedback for treating depressed patients in combination with CT seems to be one of the most promising perspectives in the field of neuroscience-based CT.

17.5 Mania

The first neurofeedback approach to the treatment of mania was proposed by Othmers (1994). This new therapeutical neuroscience-based method was based on the observation that in overaroused patients, such as those affected by mania, it can be very useful to slow the EEG activity of the brain. In this case the goal of neurotherapy will be to lower the beta activity in the frontal lobe (Walker, Lawson, and Kozlowski, 2007).

17.6 Drug Dependency

The first area of drug dependency in which neurofeedback was systematically applied was that of alcohol addiction. Peniston and Kulkovsky, using an alpha-theta training in combination with some imagery, obtained a positive outcome. In fact, they were able to eliminate the addictive behavior in a group of twenty patients who had been heavily dependent on alcohol for more than twenty years (Peniston and Kulkovsky, 1989).

More recently Trudeau, Sokhadze, and Cannon reported some interesting applications with patients affected by dependencies such as heroin addiction, cocaine addiction, and methamphetamine addiction (Trudeau, Sokhadze, and Cannon, 2009). The protocol used in these applications was very similar to the so-called Peniston protocols (Peniston and Kulkovsky, 1990). Patients received acoustic feedback when they were able to slow the EEG rhythms from beta (typical of craving) to alpha and theta, by using some imagery which focused on recovering from addiction and staying healthy.

18

Psychofeedback and Cognitive Therapy

The idea that a critical component of every mental disorder is traceable to the patient's inability to regulate their emotions has been central to the thinking of psychiatrists, clinical psychologists, and psychotherapists from the eighteenth century, beginning with Philippe Pinel's theory on the incapacity of the insane to control their own emotions and therefore on the necessity to create treatments (then largely custodial) that were designed to better manage such problems (Pinel, 1987). It is not possible at this juncture to review the development of the concept of emotional self-regulation, a multifaceted and detailed evolution that crossed the psychoanalytical, behavioral, and cognitive movements. I would just like to emphasize that, within the scope of the complex and systemic cognitivist orientation, emotional self-regulation techniques are merely tactics that make up one part of complex and comprehensive strategies for change.

In addition, I should stress that within the complex, cognitivist orientation we are not just dealing with controlling the emotions, but rather with learning to recognize them and refer them back to the self, as opposed to considering them pathological external symptoms to then be modified. Therefore, the criticism offered by many psychotherapists of a Gestalt or psychodynamic orientation, namely that psychofeedback techniques would only serve to hide the problems, seems ungenerous and inaccurate to me. In the therapeutic work I am proposing within the range of protocols that I developed (see Section 18.1), the potential for self-observation constitutes a crucial component of psychofeedback techniques. It is for this reason that I define it not so much as self-control, but rather as emotional self-regulation.

Neuroscience-based Cognitive Therapy: New Methods for Assessment, Treatment, and Self-Regulation,
First Edition. Tullio Scrimali.
© 2012 John Wiley & Sons, Ltd. Published 2012 by John Wiley & Sons, Ltd.

I have investigated psychofeedback and synchronic mind training in various areas of intervention, as reported below.

18.1 Mental Disorders

Most of my research and clinical experiments have been in the area of mental disorders, introducing the use of MindLAB Set into the diverse protocols of complex and cognitive orientation I developed for the treatment of the disorders below. The protocols are guidelines in which the various techniques are described step by step (Scrimali, 2010a):

- panic attack disorder with or without agoraphobia (Dedalo protocol);
- OCD (Sisifo protocol);
- mood disorders (Galatea and Eolo protocols);
- disorders relating to substance addiction (Baccheia protocols: a set of specific therapeutic programs for the different substances and levels of abuse);
- eating disorders (Fineo and Tantalo protocols);
- personality disorders (Polifemo protocol: in this case, also a family of protocols for specific personality disorders);
- schizophrenia (Negative Entropy protocol);
- attention deficit hyperactivity disorder;
- stuttering.

18.1.1 Panic Attack Disorder with or without Agoraphobia: Dedalo Protocol

New emotional self-regulation competencies acquired via psychofeedback make the patient more capable of competently managing critical situations, increasing their coping ability. Self-efficacy and mastery also increase.

18.1.2 Obsessive-Compulsive Disorder: Sisifo Protocol

Acquiring the capacity to reduce anxiety can render superfluous the behavioral or cognitive ritual the patient habitually uses as a dysfunctional coping mechanism. The synchronic mind training process promotes development in the right hemisphere that is lacking in obsessive patients and improves integration of emotion and cognition.

18.1.3 Mood Disorders: Galatea and Eolo Protocols

In depression, acquiring synchronic mind training competencies makes it possible for the patient to effectively counteract the rumination phenomenon that represents one of the dysfunctional processes present in the pathology. For the bipolar patient, decreased arousal permits a reduction in the excessive level of their activation to better regulate dysphoria and impulsiveness.

18.1.4 Substance Addiction-Related Disorders: Baccheia Protocols

Emotional regulation in the treatment of substance addiction finds its place in the attempt not to consume the substance that is frequently used to self-medicate or to inappropriately manage negative emotions like anxiety, frustration, and sadness. The capacity for self-control acquired through psychofeedback can also be used to effectively manage cravings.

18.1.5 Eating Disorders: Fineo and Tantalo Protocols

In bulimia (Fineo protocol) and anorexia (Tantalo protocol), emotional self-regulation competencies that can be promoted via the psychofeedback and synchronic mind training processes prove helpful in managing the compulsion to overeat and the impulse to vomit, as well as controlling the rumination and worry that follow eating more than was desired.

18.1.6 Personality Disorders: Polifemo Protocol

Personality disorders are primarily characterized by a pronounced difficulty in managing relational dynamics. This dysfunction is attributed to a gap in the emotional regulation processes that activate in the relational dynamic, and also in the difficulty of the frontal lobe to accurately plan operative sequences, which are instead initiated incoherently and chaotically. The psychofeedback and synchronic mind training processes can improve strategic planning and cognitive integration of the frontal structures with the limbic system.

18.1.7 Schizophrenia: Negative Entropy Protocol

In schizophrenia, the patient's potential for learning to regulate arousal through the psychofeedback process represents a valuable coping tool when handling hallucinations and, in general, psychotic decompensation.

18.1.8 Attention Deficit Hyperactivity Disorder

ADHD is still treated primarily with pharmacological interventions, for the most part using methylphenidate. But the increasingly extensive use of this drug is, in my opinion, a worrying development, as it is acknowledged that potential symptomatic improvement causes the family and doctor to disregard the psychological aspects of the clinical problem. Additionally, it has been asserted that methylphenidate and other similar drugs used in the treatment of ADHD have caused a number of cases of death by heart attack or suicide.

Biofeedback from EDA has been extensively researched for this clinical diagnosis in the context of integrated treatment of the cognitive and behavioral orientation. In particular, Alster developed training based on biofeedback from EDA where the patient learns to develop and then maintain one state of mind, described as relaxed attentive focus. This means that the subject learns to decrease arousal while focusing and maintaining active attention on visual and auditory stimuli, in order to experience a positive state of mind rather than distress (Alster, 2009).

18.1.9 Stuttering

Biofeedback techniques are indicated in the literature as a methodology that is helpful in the treatment of stuttering, for the purpose of reducing arousal and providing the patient with proficiency in emotional self-control (Craig and Cleary, 1982).

Clinical and research experiments in this area that we conducted in our laboratories at the Institute for Cognitive Sciences, University of Catania, using MindLAB Set delivered encouraging results. In fact, MindSCAN documented elevated levels of arousal, while psychofeedback permitted the patient to acquire new mental self-regulation competencies that are useful in combating the anxiety that triggers and maintains the speech impediment.

18.2 Psychosomatic Disorders

I have also extensively studied the use of biofeedback for psychosomatic conditions and the positive results confirm data in the literature with regard to the treatment of three important diagnoses: hypertension, irritable bowel syndrome, and premenstrual syndrome (Baumann *et al.*, 1973; Walter, 2006; Peper and Gibney, 2003).

18.3 Meditation, Mindfulness, Music Therapy

In this context, I have carried out a range of research with MindLAB Set, already described in Chapter 16 of this book, confirming the effectiveness of the methodology in documenting modifications in the state of mind that are achievable through meditation, mindfulness, and music therapy techniques (passive listening).

19

Monitoring the Warning Signs of Relapse in Schizophrenia and Bipolar Disorder, and Coping with Them

19.1 Introduction

The consequences of psychotic relapse have been found to be damaging not only to psychiatric patients but also to their families. It is clear from this that an effective program of relapse prevention should be considered a very important component of any program of psychiatric care for schizophrenia and bipolar disorder (Hewit and Birchwood, 2002).

The prodromal phase of a psychosis constitutes an opportunity for a therapeutic intervention based on CT. If we could train our psychotic patients to use self-monitoring techniques, we could influence the outcome of some psychoses. Effective relapse prevention could diminish hospitalization, and consequently, could also save mental health services a great deal of money.

In this chapter I will give some details of a neuroscience-based CT approach to this topic that I have developed and experimented with during recent years.

19.2 Schizophrenia

Since schizophrenia is a mental disorder, characterized by a high risk of relapse, the identification of parameters that furnish premonitory indications of possible relapse is particularly important. In this regard, even if some psychophysiological parameters seem good candidates for this role, undisputable experimental evidence still does not exist to support this. I recently began to develop a new area of research focused on on-field

Neuroscience-based Cognitive Therapy: New Methods for Assessment, Treatment, and Self-Regulation,
First Edition. Tullio Scrimali.
© 2012 John Wiley & Sons, Ltd. Published 2012 by John Wiley & Sons, Ltd.

psychophysiology. This is a new methodology, concerned with the monitoring of psychophysiological parameters in everyday life. In this way, it is possible to gather information, in real time, on the clinical condition of the patient during their daily routines.

The ability to carry out this research is partly due to recent developments in electronic micro-components that permit the use of small, manageable devices. The first methodological problem I had to resolve was the design and production of a compact, robust, trustworthy, and, above all, user-friendly device that could be used at home by the patients themselves, to measure skin conductance.

The original device I set up and called MindLAB Set Home (www.psychotech.it) was intended to be compact, economical, and easy-to-use, by both patients and staff. The device, after a series of trials, proved to be valid and efficient for the scope of the research, in terms of all the above requirements. Once the device was ready to be used, a form to be filled in by the patients was also created to register the different daily readings of electrodermic conductance.

With the instrumentation developed, I used the self-monitoring form to record positive symptoms, particularly correlated to conditions of stress. The patients who participated in the study of the use of MindLAB Set Home in clinic had to self-monitor for arousal using the PsychoFeedback program, and self-evaluate for warning signs using the forms created for this end. Once back at home, the patients in the study were expected to continue the recording themselves.

The work carried out has furnished encouraging preliminary data. The most interesting conclusions can be summarized as follows:

- MindLAB Set Home works perfectly and can be used without difficulty by schizophrenic patients during the period of clinical remission.
- The monitoring of electrodermic activity seems to furnish reliable data regarding the condition of emotional activation and, therefore, the risk of relapse, and may in fact be a candidate to become an important "warning sign."
- In the context of a psychotherapeutic and rehabilitative approach within the cognitive and complex orientation, psychotic patients, in a phase of relative clinical compensation, are able to effect the self-monitoring of warning signs. This procedure can limit the risk of relapse and help the patient achieve an elevated sense of self-efficacy that contributes to the process of self-evolution, which is part of the therapeutic and rehabilitative project.

19.3 Bipolar Disorder

One of the greatest challenges when curing a patient affected by bipolar disorder is monitoring the possible onset of a manic phase during a period of compensation, when the patient's clinical condition is good. Like the schizophrenic patient, the bipolar one must be trained to register EDA every day, in order to monitor this psychophysiological parameter as an early warning sign of a manic phase. Many data have demonstrated that this method, based on the small portable MindLAB Set Home device, is very efficient. Kappeler-Setz and colleagues recently developed a methodology very similar to my MindLAB Set Home and proposed its use for bipolar patients (Kappeler-Setz *et al.*, 2010).

19.4 Coping with Prodromal Symptoms of Relapse in Psychosis

The use of a small personal device such as MindLAB Set Home allows the patient not only to monitor their arousal every day, but also to apply self-regulation techniques based on biofeedback at home. The small device is able to show digital data about electrodermal conductance, which the patients must write on a special card. It also provides some reliable visual (colored LED) and acoustic (via headphones) feedback.

The possibility for the patient to check arousal daily and also to practice some biofeedback-based technique of mindfulness not only reduces activation, with positive consequences for the brain, but also helps develop a higher level of self-efficacy and self-esteem. I remember that when I started to give my psychotic patients these devices to be used at home, some colleagues were convinced that the patients would destroy them. On the contrary, my patients have been so proud of having responsibility for the device and for being actively involved in their own treatment that not one set has been lost or damaged.

20

Get Started with Neuroscience-based Cognitive Therapy

If you want to start to apply the new methods described in this book, plenty of help is at hand. Seminars, workshops, and continuing education training, even residential programs, are scheduled for every calendar year. And you can keep up to date with the scientific developments of neuroscience-based CT by visiting the following websites:

- International Association for Neuroscience-based Cognitive Therapy (www.neurosciencebasedcognitivetherapy.org)
- ALETEIA International (www.aleteiainternational.it)

At ALETEIA International European School of Cognitive Therapy you can take part in courses lasting a week or more. During these courses you can learn and practice the most important methods of neuroscience-based CT such as QEEG, QEDA, neurofeedback, and psychofeedback. Furthermore, a social program, including visits to Catania, Taormina, Syracuse, and Agrigento, can be included as part of the course.

Workshops on neuroscience-based CT will be held during every meeting of the European Congress for Cognitive and Behavioral Therapies (EABCT), during the World Congress of Behavioral and Cognitive Therapies (WCBCT), and during any congress of the International Association for Cognitive Psychotherapy (ICCP).

To start to apply the new methods proposed by neuroscience-based CT in the field of assessment and self-regulation, it would be worth investing in some inexpensive but efficient and scientifically tested apparatus.

Neuroscience-based Cognitive Therapy: New Methods for Assessment, Treatment, and Self-Regulation, First Edition. Tullio Scrimali.
© 2012 John Wiley & Sons, Ltd. Published 2012 by John Wiley & Sons, Ltd.

For QEEG and neurofeedback equipment visit www.brainmaster.com

For MindLAB Set go to www.psychotech.it

For an answer to any questions or for additional information, feel free to contact me at: tscrima@tin.it

References

Ackrill, J. L. (1972–1973). Aristotle's definition of "psyche". *Proceedings of the Aristotelian Society*, new series, volume 73, 119–33. Published by Blackwell Publishing on behalf of The Aristotelian Society.

Adler, A. (1979) *Superiority and Social Interest*, New York–London: W. W. Norton.

Ainsworth, M. (1989) Attachment beyond infancy. *American Psychologist* 44, 709–16.

Alster, J. M. (2009) *A Guide for GSR Biofeedback Techniques for the Natural ADHD Practitioner*, DVD-ROM, CD-ROM, Rainbow Cloud Learning Resources.

American Psychiatric Association (1952) *Diagnostic and Statistical Manual of Mental Disorders First Edition* (DSM-I), Washington: APA Press.

American Psychiatric Association (1968) *Diagnostic and Statistical Manual of Mental Disorders Second Edition* (DSM-II), Washington: APA Press.

American Psychiatric Association (2000) *Diagnostic and Statistical Manual of Mental Disorders Fourth Edition Text Revision* (DSM-IV-TR), Washington, APA Press.

Ammaniti, M. (2009) Quello che resta di Freud (What remains of Freud). *La Repubblica*, August 1, 27–9.

Andreassi, J. L. (1989) *Psychophysiology: Human Behavior and Physiological Responses*, Hillsdale: Lawrence Erlbaum Associates.

Ansari, J. M. (1976) Impotence: prognosis: (a controlled study). *British Journal of Psychiatry* 128, 194–8.

Averill, J. (1980) A constructivist view of emotion, in Plutchik, R. and Kellerman, H. (eds) *Theories of Emotion*, New York: Academic Press.

Bandura, A. (1971) *Social Learning Theory*, Morristown: General Learning Press.

Basaglia, G., (1964) The destruction of the mental hospital as a place of institutionalisation. Thoughts caused by personal experience with the open-door system and part-time service. London: First International Congress of Social Psychiatry.

Neuroscience-based Cognitive Therapy: New Methods for Assessment, Treatment, and Self-Regulation, First Edition. Tullio Scrimali.

© 2012 John Wiley & Sons, Ltd. Published 2012 by John Wiley & Sons, Ltd.

Bateson, G. (1979) *Mind and Nature: A Necessary Unity*, New York: Bantam.

Baumann, R., Ziprian, H., Godicke, H. *et al.* (1973) The influence of acute psychic stress situations on biochemical and vegetative parameters of essential hypertension at the early stages of the disease. *Psychotherapy and Psychosomatics* 22, 131–40.

Baumeister, R. F. and Vohs, K. D. (2006) *Handbook of Self-Regulation*, New York: Guilford Press.

Beck, A. T. (1979) *Cognitive Therapy of Depression*, New York: Guilford Press.

Benedek, M. and Kaernbach, C. (2010) Decomposition of skin conductance data by means of non-negative deconvolution. *Psychophysiology* 47, 647–58.

Bennet, D. and Bennet, A. (2008) Engaging tacit knowledge in support of organizational learning. *VINE* 38 (1).

Benson, H., Greenwood, M. M., and Klemchuk, H. (1975) The relaxation response: psychophysiologic aspects and clinical applications. *International Journal of Psychiatry in Medicine* 6, 87–98.

Berger, H. (1929) Ubes das elektrenkephalogramm des menschen. *Archiv Fur Psychiatric und Nervenkrankneiten* 27, 527–70.

Berlim, M. T., McGirr, A., Beaulieu, M. M., and Turecki, G. (2010) High frequency repetitive transcranial magnetic stimulation as an augmenting strategy in severe treatment-resistant major depression: A prospective 4-week naturalistic trial, *Journal of Affective Disorders* 130 (1–2), 312–17.

Berlyne, D. E. (1961) Conflict and orientation reaction. *Journal of Experimental Psychology* 62, 476–83.

Bettelheim, B. (1976) *The Uses of Enchantment: The Meaning and Importance of Fairy Tales*, London: Penguin.

BIOPAC Systems, Inc. (2009) www.biopac.com [last accessed April 2010].

Birket-Smith, M., Hasle, N., and Jensen, H. H. (1993) Electrodermal activity in anxiety disorders. *Acta Psychiatrica Scandinavica* 88, 350–5.

Bisconti, M. (2008) *Le Culture degli Altri Animali. É Homo l'Unico Sapiens?* (The Cultures of Other Animals. Are Humans the Only Sapiens?), Bologna: Zanichelli.

Black, A. H., Brener, J. A., and Di Cara, L.V. (eds) *Cardiovascular Psychophysiology: Current Issues in Response Mechanisms, Biofeedback and Methodology*, Chicago: Aldine.

Bob, P., Susta, M., Glaslova, K. *et al.* (2007) Lateralized electrodermal dysfunction and complexity in patients with schizophrenia and depression. *Neuroendocrinology Letters* 28 (1), 11–5.

Boucsein, W. (1992) *Electrodermal Activity*, New York: Plenum Press.

Bowlby, J. (1988) *A Secure Base*, London: Routledge.

Brainmaster, (2010). www.brainmaster.com [last accessed April 2011].

Braune, S., Albus, M., Frohler, M. *et al.* (1994) Psychophysiological and biochemical changes in patients with panic attacks in a defined situation of arousal. *European Archives of Psychiatry and Clinical Neuroscience* 244 (2), 86–92.

Breedlove, M., Rosenzweig, M., and Watson, N. W. (2007) *Biological Psychology: An Introduction to Behavioral and Cognitive Neuroscience*, Stanford: Sinauer Associates.

Brodmann, K. (1909) *Vergleichende Lokalisationslehre der Grosshirnrinde*, Leipzig: Johann Ambrosius Bart.

Brown, B. B. (1971) Awareness of EEG-subject activity relationships detected within a closed feedback system, *Psychophysiology* 7, 451–64.

Bruner, J. (1986) *Actual Minds, Possible Worlds*, Cambridge, MA: Harvard University Press.

Bruner, J. (1991) *Acts of Meaning*, Cambridge, MA: Harvard University Press.

Budzynski, T. H., Budzynski, H. K., Evans, J. R., and Abarbanel, A. (2009) *Quantitative EEG and Neurofeedback*, London: Academic Press.

Caton, R. (1875) The electric current of the brain. *British Medical Journal* 2, 278–80.

Chalmers, D. J. (1995) The puzzle of conscious experience. *Scientific American* 273, 80–6.

Chamberlain, L. L. and Butz, M. R. (1998) *Clinical Chaos: A Therapist's Guide to Non Linear Dynamics and Therapeutic Change*, London: Taylor & Francis.

Chiari, G. and Mosticoni, R. (1979) Biofeedback and systematic desensitization in the treatment of agoraphobia. *Journal of Behavior Therapy and Experimental Psychiatry* 10, 109–13.

Chiari, G. and Scrimali, T. (1984) I fattori psicoterapeutici del biofeedback (The psychotherapeutic factors of biofeedback). *Psicologia Contemporanea* 11 (62), 44–9.

Clark, D. M. (1995) Perceived limitations of standard cognitive therapy: a consideration of efforts to revise Beck's theory and therapy. *Journal of Cognitive Psychotherapy: An International Quarterly* 9, 153–72.

Cloninger, C. R. (1994) Temperament and personality. *Current Opinion in Neurobiology* 4, 266–73.

Cohen, M. X., Elger, C. E., and Fell, J. (2009) Oscillatory activity and phase-amplitude coupling in the human medial frontal cortex during decision making. *Journal of Cognitive Neuroscience* 21 (2), 390–402.

Cole, M. G. H., Gale, A., and Kline, P. (1971) Personality and habituation of the orienting reaction: tonic and response measures of electrodermal activity. *Psychophysiology* 8 (1), 54–63.

Coleman, J. C. (1976) *Abnormal Psychology and Modern Life*, Dallas: Scott, Foresman.

Constantine, A., Mangina, C. A., Beuzeron-Mangina, J. H., and Grizenko, N. (2000) Event-related brain potentials, bilateral electrodermal activity and Mangina-Test performance in Learning Disabled/ADHD pre-adolescents with severe behavioral disorders as compared to age-matched normal controls. *International Journal of Psychophysiology* 37 (1), 71–85.

Cooper, M. J. (2009) Imagery and negative self in eating disorders, in Stopa, L. (ed.) *Imagery and the Threatened Self*, London-New York: Routledge.

Costa, E., Corda, M. G., Epstein, B. *et al.* (1983) GABA-Benzodiazepine interaction, in Costa, E. (ed.) *Benzodiazepines: from Molecular Biology to Clinical Practice*, New York: Raven Press.

Cozolino, L. (2002) *The Neuroscience of Psychotherapy*, New York: W. W. Norton.

Cozolino, L. (2004) *The Making of a Therapist*, New York: W. W. Norton.

Cozolino, L. (2006) *The Neuroscience of Human Relationships*, New York: W. W. Norton.

Craig, A. (1990) An investigation into the relationship between anxiety and stuttering. *Journal of Speech and Hearing Disorders* 55 (2), 290–4.

Craig, A. R., and Cleary, P. J. (1982) Reduction of stuttering by young male stutterers using EMG feedback. *Biofeedback and Self-Regulation* 7, 241–55.

Crick, F. (1994) *The Astonishing Hypothesis: The Scientific Search for the Soul*, New York: Scribner Book Company.

Crown, S. (1966) The Middlesex Hospital Questionnaire. *British Journal of Psychiatry* 112, 917–29.

Damasio, A. (1994) Descartes' Error: Emotion, Reason and the Human Brain. New York: Quill.

Damasio, A. (1999) *The Feeling of What Happens*, San Diego: Harcourt.

Darwin, C. (1859) *The Origin of Species by Means of Natural Selection*, London: Murray.

Davey, G. C. L., and Wells, A. (2006) *Worry and its Psychological Disorders*, Chichester: John Wiley & Sons, Ltd.

Davidson, R. J. (1988) EEG measures of cerebral asymmetry: conceptual and methodological issues. *International Journal of Neuroscience* 39 (1–2), 71–89.

Davidson, R. J. and Irwin, W. (1999) The functional neuroanatomy of emotion and affective style. *Trends in Cognitive Sciences* 3 (1), 11–21.

Davis, R. C. (1929) Factors affecting the galvanic reflex. *Archives of Psychology* 18 (115).

Demos, J. N. (2005) *Getting Started with Neurofeedback*, New York: W.W. Norton.

Dennett, D. (1991) *Consciousness Explained*, Boston: Back Bay Books.

Dennett, D. (1996) *Kinds of Minds*, New York: Basic Books.

Desarkar, P., Kumar, V., Jagadheesan, S. K., and Nizamie, S.H. (2007) A high resolution quantitative EEG power analysis of obsessive-compulsive disorder. *German Journal of Psychiatry* 10, 29–35.

Descartes, R. (1984–1991) *The Philosophical Writings of Descartes*, 3 volumes, trans. J. Cottingham, R. Stoothoff, D. Murdoch, and A. Kenny, Cambridge: Cambridge University Press.

De Waal, F. (2006) *Primates and Philosophers: How Morality Evolved*, Princeton: Princeton University Press.

De Waal F. (2008) The thief in the mirror. *PLoS Biology* 6 (8), 201.

Diels, H., and Kranz, W. (1976) *I Presocratici. Testimonianze e Frammenti* (Presocratic Fragments and Testimonials), A. Pasquinelli (ed.), Turin: Einaudi.

Dubois, B., Slachevsky, A., Litvan, I., and Pillon, B. (2000) The FAB: A Frontal Assessment Battery at bedside. *Neurology* 55, 1621–6.

Duffy, F., Hughes, J. R., Miranda, F. *et al.* (1994) Status of quantitative EEG (QEEG) in clinical practice. *Clinical Electroencephalography* 25 (4), VI–XXII.

Eccles, J. C. (1989) *Evolution of the Brain: Creation of the Self*, New York: Routledge.

Eccles, J. C. (1994) *How the Self Controls Its Brain.* New York: Springer-Verlag.

Edelberg, R. (1967) *Methods in Psychophysiology*, Baltimore: Williams and Wilkins.

Edelberg, R. (1970) The information content of the recovery limb of the electrodermal response. *Psychophysiology* 6, 527–39.

Edelberg, R. (1972) Electrical activity of the skin: its measurements and uses in psychophysiology, in Greenfield, N. S. and Sternback R. A. (eds) *Handbook of Psychophysiology*, New York: Holt, Rinehart and Winston.

Edelman, G. M. (1987) *Neuronal Darwinism: The Theory of Neural Group Selection*, New York: Basic Books.

Emery, G., Hollon, S. T., and Bedrosian, R. (1981) *New Directions for Cognitive Therapy*, New York: Guilford Press.

Etevenon, P., Peron-Magnon, P., Campistron, D. *et al.* (1983) Differences in EEG symmetry between patients with schizophrenia, in Flor-Henry, P. and Gruzelier, J. (eds) *Laterality and Psychopathology*, volume 6, Developments in Psychiatry, Amsterdam: Elsevier.

Evans, J. R. and Abarbanel, A. (1999) *Introduction to Quantitative EEG and Neurofeedback*, San Diego: Academic Press.

Evian, G. (2007) Genomics and Neuromarkers are Both Required for the Era of Brain-related Personalized Medicine? www.brainresource.com [last accessed April 2008].

Fernandez, A., Arrazola, J., and Maestu, F. (2003) Correlations of hippocampal atrophy and focal low-frequency magnetic activity in Alzheimer's Disease: volumetric MR imaging magnetoencephalographic study. *American Journal of Neuroradiology* 24, 481–7.

Flor-Henry, P. (1988) LEG spectral analysis in psychopathology, in Giannitrapani, D. and Murri, L. (eds) *The EEG of Mental Activities*, Karger: Basel, 182–200.

Fodor, J. (1983) *The Modularity of Mind*, Cambridge, Massachusetts: MIT Press.

Folstein, M., Folstein, S., and McHugh, P. R. (1975) Mini-mental state: a practical method for grading the cognitive state of patients for the clinician. *Journal of Psychiatric Research* 12, 189–98.

Fowles, D. C. (1973) Mechanisms of electrodermal activity, in Thompson, R. F. and Patterson, M. M. (eds) *Methods in Physiological Psychology*, New York: Academic Press.

Fredrikson, M., Dimberg, U., and Frisk-Holmberg, M. (1980) Arterial blood pressure and electrodermal activity in hypertensive and normotensive subjects during inner- and outer-directed attention. *Acta Medica Scandinavica* 646, 73–6.

Freeman, W. J. (1992) Chaos in psychiatry. *Biological Psychiatry* 31, 1079–81.

Freud, S. (1989) The Basic Writings of Sigmund Freud, New York: Random House.

Friedman, M. (1996) *Type A Behavior: Its Diagnosis and Treatment*, New York: Plenum Press.

Frith, C. D., Stevens, M., Johnstone, E. C., and Owens, D. G. C. (1984) The effect of chronic treatment with amitriptyline and diazepam on electrodermal activity in neurotic outpatients. *Physiological Psychology* 12, 247–52.

Fuller, G. D. (1977) *Biofeedback: Methods and Procedure in Clinical Practice.* San Francisco: Biofeedback Press.

Furedy, J. J. (1983) Operational, analogical and genuine definitions of psychophysiology. *International Journal of Psychophysiology* 1, 13–9.

Gabbard, G. O. (2005) Mind, brain, and personality disorders. *American Journal of Psychiatry* 162 (4), 648–55.

Gazzaniga, M. S., Ivry, R. B., and Mangun, G. R. (1998) *Neuroscience: The Biology of Mind*, New York: W. W. Norton.

Germer, C. K., Siegel, R. D., and Fulton, P. R. (2005) *Mindfulness and Psychotherapy*, New York: Guilford Press.

Gevensleben, H., Holl, B., Albrecht, B. *et al.* (2009) Is neurofeedback an efficacious treatment for ADHD? A randomized controlled clinical trial. *Journal of Child Psychology and Psychiatry* 50 (7), 780–9.

Gintis, H. (2007) A framework for the unification of the behavioral sciences. *Behavioral and Brain Sciences* 30, 1–61.

Goldberg, T. E. (2001) *The Executive Brain: Frontal Lobes and the Civilized Mind*, Oxford: Oxford University Press.

Goleman, D. (1982) Meditation and consciousness: an Asian approach to mental health. *American Journal of Psychotherapy* 30, 41–54.

Goncalves, O. F. (1989) *Advances in Cognitive Psychotherapies: The Constructivist-Developmental Approach*, Lisbon: APPORT.

Goodall, McC. (1970) Innervation and inhibition of eccrine and apocrine sweating in man. *Journal of Clinical Pharmacology* 10, 235–46.

Goodman, W. K., Price, L. H., and Rasmussen, S.A. (1989) The Yale-Brown Obsessive Compulsive Scale. *Archives of General Psychiatry* 46, 1006–11.

Green, E. E., Green, A. M., and Walters, E. D. (1970) Voluntary control of internal states: psychological and physiological. *Journal of Transpersonal Psychology* 2, 1–26.

Grey, N. (2009) Imagery and psychological threat to the self in PTSD, in Stopa, L. (ed.) *Imagery and the Threatened Self*, London-New York, Routledge.

Grings, W. W. and Dawson, M. E. (1978) *Emotions and Bodily Responses: A Psychophysiological Approach*, New York: Academic Press.

Grobstein, P. (2003) Making the unconscious conscious, and vice versa: a bi-directional bridge between neuroscience/cognitive science and psychotherapy? *Cortex* 13, 32–6.

Gruzelier, J. H. (1976) Clinical attributes of schizophrenic skin conductance responders and non responders. *Psychological Medicine* 6, 245–9.

Gruzelier, J. H., Connolly, J., Eves, F. *et al.* (1981) Effect of propranolol and phenothiazines on electrodermal orienting and habituation in schizophrenia. *Psychological Medicine* 11 (1), 93–108.

Gruzelier, J. H. and Hammond, N. V. (1978) The effect of chlorpromazine upon psychophysiological, endocrine and information processing measures in schizophrenia. *Journal of Psychiatric Research* 14, 167–82.

Gruzelier, J. H. and Venables, P. H. (1972) Skin conductance orienting activity in a heterogenous sample of schizophrenics: possible evidence of limbic dysfunction. *Journal of Nervous and Mental Diseases* 155, 277–87.

Gruzelier, J. H. and Venables, P. H. (1975) Evidence of high and low levels of physiological arousal in schizophrenics. *Psychophysiology* 12, 66–73.

Guidano, V. F. (1987) *Complexity of the Self,* New York: Guilford Press.

Guidano, V. F. (1991) *The Self in Process,* New York: Guilford Press.

Guidano, V. F. and Liotti, G. (1983) *Cognitive Processes and Emotional Disorders,* New York: Guilford Press.

Hammond, D. C. (2004) Treatment of the obsessional subtype of obsessive compulsive disorder with neurofeedback. *Biofeedback* 32, 9–12.

Hammond, D. C. (2005) Neurofeedback treatment of depression and anxiety. *Journal of Adult Development* 12 (2 & 3).

Harlow, H. F. (1958) The nature of love. *American Psychologist* 13, 673–85.

Harmon-Jones, E., Abramson, L.Y., Sigelman, Y. *et al.* (2002) Proneness to hypomania/mania symptoms or depression symptoms and asymmetrical frontal cortical responses to an anger-evoking event. *Journal of Personality and Social Psychology* 82 (4), 610–18.

Harmon-Jones, E. and Allen, J. J. B. (1998) Anger and prefrontal brain activity: EEG asymmetry consistent with approach motivation despite negative affective valence. *Journal of Personality and Social Psychology* 74, 1310–16.

Harmon-Jones, E. and Beer, J. S. (2009) *Methods in Social Neuroscience,* New York: Guilford Press.

Harrys, M. D. (1943) Habituatory response decrement in the intact organism. *Psychological Bulletin* 40, 385–422.

Hauri, P. (1981) Treating psychophysiologic insomnia with biofeedback. *Archives of General Psychiatry* 38, 752–8.

Hazan C. And Shaver, P. R. (1987) Romantic love conceptualized as an attachment process. *Journal and Personality and Social Psychology* 52 (3), 511–24.

Hemmen, J. L. and Sejnowski, T. J. (2006) *Problems in Systems Neuroscience,* Oxford: Oxford University Press.

Heraclitus (1954) *Die Fragmente der Vorsokratiker* (ed. Diels, von H.), Berlin: Walter Krantz.

Hewit, L. and Birchwood, M. (2002) Preventing relapse of psychotic illness: role of self-monitoring of prodromal symptoms. Wolters Kluwer Health. *Adis* 10 (7), 395–407.

Hobbes, T. (1994) *Leviathan*, Curley, E. (ed.), Indianapolis: Hacket (original edition 1651/68).

Hofmann, S. G., Moscovitch, D. A., Litz, B. T. *et al.* (2005) The worried mind: autonomic and prefrontal activation during worrying. *Emotion* 5 (4), 464–75.

Holyoak, K. J. and Morrison, R.G. (eds) (2005) *The Cambridge Handbook of Thinking and Reasoning* (Cambridge Handbooks in Psychology), Cambridge: Cambridge University Press.

Hounsfield, G. (1973) Computerized transverse axial scanning (tomography). Description of system. *British Journal of Radiology* 46, 1016–22.

Humphrey, G. (1933) *The Nature of Learning*, New York: Harcourt Brace.

Huttenlocher, P. R. (1979) Synaptic density in human frontal cortex – developmental changes and effects of aging. *Brain Research* 163 (2), 195–205.

Huxley, T. H. (1874) On the hypothesis that animals are automata, and its history. *Science and Culture, and Other Essays* 1, 199–250.

Iacono, W. J., Lykken, T. D., Peloquin, L. J. *et al.* (1983) Electrodermal activity in euthymic unipolar and bipolar affective disorders. A possible marker for depression. *Archives of General Psychiatry* 40 (5).

Isamat, F. (1961) Galvanic skin responses from stimulation of limbic cortex. *Journal of Neurophysiology* 24, 176–81.

Izhikevich, E. M. (2007) *Dynamical Systems in Neuroscience*, Cambridge, Massachusetts: MIT Press.

Jacobson, E. (1929) *Progressive Relaxation*, Chicago: University of Chicago Press.

James, W. (1997) *The Writings of William James: A Comprehensive Edition*, New York: Phoenix Books.

Jelica, V. S. E., Johansson, O., Almkvista, M. *et al.* (2000) Quantitative electroencephalography in mild cognitive impairment: longitudinal changes and possible prediction of Alzheimer's Disease. *Neurobiology of Aging* 21, 533–40.

Johnson, L. C. and Lubin, A. (1966) Spontaneous electrodermal activity during sleeping and waking. *Psychophysiology* 3, 8–17.

Jung, C. G. (1906) Studies in word analysis. *The Journal of Abnormal Psychology*, volume 1, June.

Jung, C. G. (1991) *The Archetypes and the Collective Unconscious*, London: Routledge.

Kabat-Zinn, J. (1994) *Wherever You Go, There You Are. Mindfulness Meditation in Everyday Life*, New York: Hyperion.

Kandel, E. R. (1998) A new intellectual framework for psychiatry. *American Journal of Psychiatry* 155, 457–69.

Kandel, E. R. (2001) The molecular biology of memory storage: a dialogue between genes and synapses. *Science* 294, 1030–8.

Kappeler-Setz, C., Schumm, J., Kusserow, K. *et al.* (2010) Towards long term monitoring of electrodermal activity in daily life. *UbiCom* September 26–29.

Keck, P. E. and McElroy, S. L. (2002) Carbamazepine and valproate in the maintenance of bipolar disorder. *Clinical Psychiatry* 63, Supplement 10, 13–17.

Killgore, W. B., Britton, J. C., Price, L. M. *et al.* (2011) Neural correlates of anxiety sensitivity during masked presentation of affective faces. *Depression and Anxiety* 28, 243–9.

Killiany, R. J., Moss, M. B., Albert, M. S. *et al.* (1993) Temporal lobe regions on magnetic resonance imaging identify patients with early Alzheimer's Disease. *Archives of Neurology* 50, 949–54.

Kosslyn, S. (1994) *Image and Brain. The Resolution of the Imagery Debate*, Cambridge, Massachusetts: MIT Press.

Lacey, O. (1947) An analysis of the appropriate unit for use in the measurement of level of galvanic skin resistance. *Journal of Experimental Psychology* 37, 449–557.

Lader, M. H. and Wing, L. (1964) Habituation of the psycho-galvanic reflex in patients with anxiety states and in normal subjects. *Journal of Neurology, Neurosurgery and Psychiatry* 27, 210–18.

Lader, M. H. and Wing, L. (1969) Physiological measures in agitated and retarded depressed patients. *Journal of Psychiatric Research* 7, 89–100.

Lang, P. J. (1979). A bioinformational theory of emotional imagery. *Psychophysiology* 16, 495–512.

Lang, D. (2004) *Opening to Meditation*, Novato: New World Library.

Lazarus, R. S. (1975) A cognitively oriented psychologist looks at biofeedback. *American Psychologist* 30, 553–61.

LeDoux, J. (1996) *The Emotional Brain. The Mysterious Underpinnings of Emotional Life*, New York: Touchstone.

Lemche, E., Giampietro, V. P., Surguladze, S. A. *et al.* (2005) Human attachment security is mediated by the amygdala: evidence from combined fMRI and psychophysiological measures. *Human Brain Mapping* 27 (8), 623–35.

Lenin, V. I. (1952) *The State and the Revolution*, Foreign Languages Publishing Houses: Moscow.

Lepage, M., Sergerie, K., Benoit, A. *et al.* (2011) Emotional face processing and flat affect in schizophrenia: functional and structural neural correlates. *Psychological Medicine* 41 (9), 1833–44.

Leuchter, A. F., Cook, I. A., Marangell, L. B. *et al.* (2009). Comparative effectiveness of biomarkers and clinical indicators for predicting outcomes of SSRI treatment in major depressive disorder: results of the BRITE-MD study. *Psychiatry Research* 169 (2), 124–31.

Leventhal, M. (1979) A perceptual-motor processing model of emotions, in Plinier, P., Blankstein, K. R., and Spigel, I. M. (eds) *Perceptions of Emotions in Self and Others*, New York: Plenum Press.

Lindsay, P. H. and Norman, D. A. (1977) *Human Information Processing*, New York: Academic Press.

Liotti, G. (2009) Attachment and dissociation, in Dell, P. F. and O'Neil, J. A. (eds) *Dissociation and Dissociative Disorders*, New York: Routledge, 53–66.

Lubar, J. F., Swartwood, M. O., Swartwood, J. N. and Timmermann, D. L. (1995) Quantitative EEG and auditory event-related potentials in the evaluation of Attention Deficit/Hyperactivity Disorder: effects of methyphenidate and implications for neurofeedback training, *Journal of Psychoeducational Assessment*, ADHD Special Issue, 143–60.

Luria, A. (1973) *The Working Brain: An Introduction to Neuropsychology*, New York: Basic Books.

Lyddon, W. and Schreiner, G. (1998) Post-modernismo e psicoterapia (post-modernism and psychotherapy). *Complessità & Cambiamento* 7 (1), 17–28.

McCarthy, G., Luby, M., Gore, J., and Goldman-Rakic, P. (1997) Infrequent events transiently activate human prefrontal and parietal cortex as measured by functional MRI. *Journal of Neurophysiology* 77, 1630–34.

McGinn, C. (1991) *The Problem of Consciousness*, Oxford: Blackwell.

McKhann, G., Drachman, D., Folstein, M. *et al.* (1984) Clinical diagnosis of Alzheimer's Disease: report of the NINCDS-ADRDA work group under the auspices of Department of Health and Human Services Task Force on Alzheimer's Disease. *Neurology* 34 (7), 939–44.

MacLean, P. D. (1973) *A Triune Concept of the Brain and Behavior*, Toronto: University Press of Toronto.

Magana, A. B., Goldstein, M. J., Karno, M. *et al.* (1986) A brief method for assessing expressed emotions in relatives of psychiatric patients. *Psychiatric Research* 17, 203–12.

Mahoney, M. J. (ed.) (1980) *Psychotherapy Process: Current Issues and Future Directions*, New York: Plenum Press.

Mahoney, M. J. (1991) *Human Change Processes*, New York: Basic Books.

Malmo, R. B. and Shagass, C. (1949) Physiological studies of reaction to stress in anxiety states and early schizophrenia. *Psychosomatic Medicine* 11, 9–24.

Mangina, C. A. (1983) Towards an international consensus defining psychophysiology. *International Journal of Psychophysiology* 1, 93–4.

Mansell, W. and Hodson, S. (2009) Imagery and memories of the social self in people with bipolar disorders, in Stopa, L. (ed.) *Imagery and the Threatened Self*, London, New York: Routledge.

Mathews, A. M. and Gelder, M. G. (1969) Psychophysiological investigations of brief relaxation training. *Journal of Psychosomatic Research* 13, 1–12.

Mattia, D., Babiloni, F., Romigi, A. *et al.* (2003) Quantitative EEG and dynamic susceptibility contrast MRI in Alzheimer's Disease: a correlative study. *Clinical Neurophysiology* 114 (7), 1210–16.

Mattson, J. and Simon, M. (1996) *The Pioneers of NMR and Magnetic Resonance in Medicine: The Story of MRI*, Jericho and New York: Bar-Ilan University Press.

Maturana, H. R. (1988) Reality: the search for objectivity on the quest for a compelling argument. *The Irish Journal of Psychology* 9 (1), 25–82.

Maturana, H. R. and Varela, F. (1980) *Autopoiesis and Cognition. The Realization of Living*, Dortrecht: Reidel.

Meichenbaum, D. (1976) Cognitive factors in biofeedback therapy. *Biofeedback and Self Regulation* 1, 201–16.

Miller, G., Galanter, E., and Pribram, K. (1960) *Plans and the Structure of Behavior*, New York: Holt, Rinehart and Winston.

Miller, N. E. (1969) Learning of visceral and glandular responses. *Science* 163, 434–45.

Miller, S. and Konorski, J. (1928) On a particular type of conditioned reflex. *Biological Society Proceedings* 99, 1155–7.

Monod, J. (1972) *Chance and Necessity: An Essay on the Natural Philosophy of Modern Biology*, London: Collins.

Morin, E. (2008) *On Complexity (Advances in Systems Theory, Complexity, and the Human Sciences)*, Cresskill: Hampton Press.

Nadarajah, B., Alifragis, P., Wong, R., and Parnavelas, J. (2003) Neuronal migration in the developing cerebral cortex: observations based on real-time imaging. *Cerebral Cortex* 13 (6), 607–11.

Neisser, U. (1982) *Memory Observed: Remembering in Natural Contexts*, San Francisco: W. H. Freeman.

Nidich, S. and Seeman, T. D. (1973) Influences of transcendental meditation: a replication. *Journal of Counselling Psychology* 20 (6), 565–6.

Nunez, P. (1982) *Electrical Fields of the Brain*, New York: Oxford University Press.

O'Connell, R. G., Bellgrove, M. A., Dockree, P. M., and Robertson, I. H. (2004) Reduced electrodermal response to errors predicts poor sustained attention performance in Attention Deficit Hyperactivity Disorder. *NeuroReport* 15 (16), 2535–8.

O'Donnell, R. D., Berkhout, J., and Adey, W. R. (1974) Contamination of scalp EEG spectrum during contraction of cranio-facial muscles. *Electroencephalography and Clinical Neurophysiology* 37, 145–51.

Ohman, A. (1981) Electrodermal activity and vulnerability to schizophrenia: a review. *Biological Psychology* 12, 87–145.

Ornstein, R. (1992) *The Evolution of Consciousness*, New York: Simon and Schuster.

Othmer, S., Othmer, S. F., and Kaiser, D. A. (1999) EEG biofeedback: training for AD/HD and related disruptive behavior disorders, in Tessmer, D. (ed.)

Understanding, Diagnosing, and Treating AD/HD in Children and Adolescents, New York: Aronson.

Othmers, S. (1994) Treating mania by neurofeedback, in Evans, J. R., (ed.) *Handbook of Neurofeedback: Dynamics and Clinical Applications*, London: Routledge.

Ozege, A., Toros, F., and Comelekoglu, U. (2004) The role of hemispheral asymmetry and regional activity of quantitative EEG in children with stuttering. *Child Psychiatry and Human Development* 34 (4), 269–80.

Paivio, A. (1985) Cognitive and motivational functions of imagery in human performance, in Horn, T. S. *Advances in Sport Psychology*, Champaign: Human Kinetics.

Pancheri, P. (1979) *Biofeedback*, Rome: Bulzoni.

Pancheri, P. and Chiari, G. (1979) Biofeedback e psicosomatica (Biofeedback and psychosomatic medicine). *Psicologia Contemporanea* 6, 11–17.

Paul, G. L. (1969) Physiological effects of relaxation training and hypnotic suggestion. *Journal of Abnormal Psychology* 74, 425–37.

Paulus, M. P. and Braff, D. L. (2003) Chaos e schizophrenia: does the method fit the madness? *Biological Psychiatry* 53 (1), 3–11.

Pavlov, I. P. (1927) *Conditioned Reflexes: An Investigation of the Physiological Activity of the Cerebral Cortex*, translated and edited by G. V. Anrep, London: Oxford University Press.

Peniston, E. G. and Kulkovsky P. J. (1989) Alpha-theta brainwave training and beta-endorphin levels in alcoholics. *Alcoholism: Clinical Experimental Research* 13, 271–9.

Peniston, E. G and Kulkovsky, P. J. (1990) Alcoholic personality and alpha-theta brainwave training. *Medical Psychotherapy* 2, 37–55.

Penrose, R. (1989) *The Emperor's New Mind*, Oxford: Oxford University Press.

Peper, E. and Gibney, K. H. (2003) Taking control: strategies to reduce hot flashes and pre-menstrual mood swings. *Biofeedback* 31 (3), 20–4.

Perna, A. and Masterpaqua, F. P. (eds) (1998) *The Psychological Meaning of Chaos*, Washington, D.C.: American Psychological Association Press.

Perris, C. (1989) *Cognitive Therapy with Schizophrenic Patients*, New York: Guilford Press.

Piaget, J. (1954) *The Construction of Reality in the Child*, New York: Basic Books.

Picton, T. W. and Hillyard, S. H. (1974) Human auditory evoked potentials, effects of attention. *Electroencephalography and Clinical Neurophysiology* 36, 191–9.

Pinel, P. (1988) *A Treatise on Insanity*, Bethesda: Gryphon Editions.

Plato (1900–1907) *Platonis Opera* (in 5 volumes) – *The Oxford Classical Texts*, Oxford: Oxford University Press.

Poincaré, H. (1904) The Principles of Mathematical Physics, in Poincaré, H. *The Foundations of Science (The Value of Science)*, New York: Science Press, 297–320.

Polany, M. (1966) The logic of tacit inference. *Philosophy* 40, 300–86.

Polany, M. (1968) Logic and psychology. *American Psychologist* 23, 27–43.

Popper, K. R. (1972) *Objective Knowledge: An Evolutionary Approach*, Oxford: Clarendon.

Popper, K. R. and Eccles, J. C. (1977) *The Self and its Brain*, Berlin: Heindelberg.

Pribram, K. M. (1971) *Language of the Brain*, Englewood Cliffs: Prentice-Hall.

Prichep, L. S., Lieber, A. L., and John, E. R. (1986) Quantitative EEG in depressive disorders, in Shagass, C. (ed.) *Electrical Brain Potentials and Psychotherapy*, Amsterdam: Elsevier.

Prigogine, I. (1980) *From Being to Becoming: Time and Complexity in the Physical Sciences*, San Francisco: W. H. Freeman.

Prigogine, I. (1996) *The End of Certainty. Time, Chaos and New Laws of Nature*, New York: The Free Press.

Prokasy, W. F. and Raskin, D. C. (1972) *Electrodermal Activity in Psychological Research*, New York: Academic Press.

Psychological Assessment Resources (2003) Computerised Wisconsin Card Sort Task Version 4 (WCST), Psychological Assessment Resources.

Psychotech (2008) Psychotech: Tools for Mind, www.psychotech.it [last accessed April 2011].

Rapaport, D. (1971) *Emotion and Memory*, New York: Grune, Stratton.

Rappaport, H. (1972) Modification of avoidance behaviour: expectancy, autonomic reactivity and verbal report. *Journal of Consulting and Clinical Psychology* 39, 404–14.

Reale, G. and Antiseri, D. (1997) *Storia della Filosofia*, Firenze: Editrice La Scuola.

Reda, M. A. and Mahoney, M. J. (eds) (1984) *Cognitive Psychotherapies: Recent Developments in Theory, Research, and Practice*, Cambridge, Massachusetts: Ballinger.

Rey, A. (1958) *L'Examen Clinique en Psychologie* (Clinical Study in Psychology), Paris: Presses Universitaires de France.

Rizzolati, G., Fogassi, L., and Gallese, V. (2000) Cortical mechanism subserving object grasping and action recognition: a new view on the cortical motor functions, in Gazzaniga, M. S. (ed.) *Cognitive Neuroscience*, 2nd edn, Cambridge, Massachusetts: MIT Press.

Rodin, E., Grisell, J., and Gottlieb, J. (1968) Some electroencephalic differences between chronic schizophrenic patients and normal subjects, in Wortis, J. (ed.) *Recent Advances in Biological Psychiatry*, volume 10, New York: Plenum Press.

Russel, R. and Wandrei, M. (1996) Narrative and the process of psychotherapy: theoretical foundations and empirical support, in Rosen, H. and Kuehlwein, K. (eds) *Constructing Realities*, San Francisco: Jossey-Bass.

Safran, J. D. and Muran, Z. V. (2000) *Negotiating the Therapeutic Alliance*, New York, Basic Books.

Savage-Rumbaugh, S. (1999) Perception of personality traits and semantic learning in evolving hominids, in Savage-Rumbaugh, S. *The Descent of Mind: Psychological Perspectives on Hominid Evolution*, Oxford: Oxford University Press.

Schachter, S. and Singer, J. (1962) Cognitive, social and physiological determinants of emotional state. *Psychological Review* 69, 378–99.

Schacter, D. L. (1996) *Searching for Memory: The Brain, the Mind and the Past*, New York, Basic Books.

Schultz, H. J. (1960) *Das Autogene Training*, Stuttgart: Verlag.

Schwartz, H. G. (1937) Effects of experimental lesions of the cortex on the psychogalvanic reflex in the cat. *Archives of Neurology and Psychiatry* 38, 308–20.

Scrimali, T. (2008) *Entropy of Mind and Negative Entropy. A Complex Cognitive Approach to Schizophrenia and its Therapy*, Karnac Books: London.

Scrimali, T. (2010a) *Neuroscienze e Psicologia Clinica. Dal Laboratorio di Ricerca al Setting con i Pazienti* (Neuroscience and Clinical Psychology. From Laboratory to the Clinical Setting), Milan: FrancoAngeli.

Scrimali, T. (2010b) Complex Cognitive Therapy. A post-standard approach to cognitive therapy. Presentation held at the WCBCT of Boston, June, Data on file.

Scrimali, T. (2011) *MindLAB Set: Multimodal Assessment and Self-Regulation in Psychotherapy*, Enna: ALETEIA publications.

Scrimali, T. and Grimaldi, L. (1982) *Il Biofeedback della Attività Elettrodermica* (EDA: Biofeedback), Milan: FrancoAngeli.

Scrimali, T. and Grimaldi, L. (1991) *Sulle Tracce della Mente* (On the Trail of the Mind), Milan: FrancoAngeli.

Scrimali, T. and Grimaldi, L. (2003) Fineo & Tantalo: A complex systems-oriented cognitive approach in the treatment of patients with eating disorders. *Archives of Psychiatry and Psychotherapy* 5 (1), 15–30.

Scrimali, T., Grimaldi, L., and Aguglia, E. (1978) Impiego clinico dello skin resistance biofeedback in un caso di nevrosi d'ansia (The use of EDA biofeedback in treating a patient affected by an anxiety disorder). *Bollettino della Società Medico-Chirurgica di Catania* 46 (1–2), 201–4.

Scrimali, T., Grimaldi, L., and Rapisarda, V. (1983) La ristrutturazione cognitiva mediante elettrodermofeedback ed evocazione sperimentale della risposta neurovegetativa di allarme in paziente ansiosi (Cognitive restructuring by Biofeedback-Based Coping Skills Training). *Formazione Psichiatrica* 1, 67–71.

Scrimali, T., Grimaldi, L., Rapisarda, V. *et al.* (1982) Analisi comparativa tra attivitá elettrodermica e livelli plasmatici di amitriptilina. *Formazione Psichiatrica* 4.

Scrimali, T. and Miccichè, A. (2010) Monitoraggio della attività elettrodermica durante esercizi di meditazione, in: Scrimali, T. *Neuroscienze e Psicologia Clinica. Dal Laboratorio di Ricerca al Setting con i Pazienti* (Neuroscience and Clinical Psychology. From Laboratory to the Clinical Setting), Milano: FrancoAngeli, 199–203.

Searle, J. R. (2005) *The Mind:* A Brief Introduction, Oxford: Oxford University Press.

Segal, Z., Williams J. M., and Teasdale J. D (2002) *Mindfulness-Based Cognitive Therapy for Depression*, New York: Guilford Press.

Shapiro, D. H. and Walsh, R. N. (eds) (1984) *Meditation: Classic and Contemporary Perspectives*, New York: Aldine.

Shevrin, H. and Dickman, S. (1980) The psychological unconscious: a necessary assumption for all psychological theory. *American Psychologist* 35 (5), 421–34.

Siegel, D. J. (1999) *The Developing Mind. How Relationships and Brain Interact to Shape Who We Are*, New York: Guilford Press.

Siegel, D. J. (2007) *The Mindful Brain*, New York: W. W. Norton.

Siegel, D. J. and Hartzell, M. (2003) *Parenting from the Inside Out*, New York: Penguin.

Skarda, C. A. and Freeman, W. J. (1990) Chaos and the new science of the brain. *Concepts in Neuroscience* 1 (2), 275–85.

Skeidsvoll, H. (1999) A new way of building a database of EEG findings. *Clinical Neurophysiology* 110 (5), 986–95.

Skinner, B. F. (1976) *About Behaviorism*, New York: Random House.

Smith, P., Sams, M., and Sherlin, L. (2006) The neurological basis of eating disorders. I: EEG findings and the clinical outcome of adding symptom-based, QEEG-based, and analog/QEEG-based remedial neurofeedback training to traditional treatment plans. Paper presented at the 2006 SNR Conference, Atlanta, June 2006.

Snyder, C. and Noble, M. (1968) Operant conditioning of vasoconstriction. *Journal of Experimental Psychology* 77, 263–8.

Snyder, S. M. and Hall, J. R. (2006) A meta-analysis of quantitative EEG power associated with Attention-Deficit Hyperactivity Disorder. *Clinical Neurophysiology* 23 (5), 440–55.

Sokolov, E. N. (1963) Neuronal models and orienting reflex, in Brazier, M. A. B (ed.) *The Central Nervous System and Behavior*, New York: Josiah Macy Jr Foundation.

Sperry, R. W. (1980) Mind–brain interaction: mentalism, yes; dualism, no. *Neuroscience* 5, 195–206.

Spielberger, C. D., Gorsuch, R. L., and Lushene, R. E. (1970) *Manual for the State-Trait Anxiety Inventory*, Palo Alto: Consulting Psychologist Press.

Squire, L. R. and Paller, K. A. (2000) Biology of memory, in *Kaplan and Sadock's Comprehensive Textbook of Psychiatry*, volume 1, 7th edn, New York: Lippincott, Williams and Wilkins.

Stopa, L. (2009) How to use imagery in cognitive-behavioural therapy, in Stopa, L. (ed.) *Imagery and the Threatened Self*, London-New York: Routledge.

Strogatz, S. H. (1994) *Non-linear Dynamics and Chaos*, Colorado: Westview a Member of Perseus Books Publishing.

Tarchanoff, P. E. (1890) Über die Galvanischen Erschemunger an der Haut des Ameuschen bei Reizung der Sinnesorgane und bei Verschiedenen Former der Psychisohen Tatikkeit. *Pflugers Archive für die Gesamte Physiologie* 46, 46–55.

Tarrier, N., Barrowclough, C., Porceddu, K., and Watts, S. (1988) The assessment of psychophysiological reactivity to the expressed emotion of relatives of schizophrenic patients. *British Journal of Psychiatry* 152, 618–24.

Tarrier, N., Sommerfield, C., Connell, J. *et al.* (2002) The psychophysiological responses of PTSD patients: habituation, responses to stressful and neutral vignettes and association with treatment outcome. *Behavioural and Cognitive Psychotherapy* 30, 129–42.

Tauscher, J., Schindler, S., Rappelsberger, P., and Kasper, S. (1995) EEG changes in schizophrenic diseases. A critical review. *Fortschritte der Neurologie-Psychiatrie* 63 (4), 162–9.

Taylor, J. (2004) Electrodermal reactivity and its association to substance use disorders. *Psychophysiology* 41, 982–9.

Taylor, J., Carlson, S. R., Iacono, W. G. *et al.* (1999) Individual differences in electrodermal responsivity to predictable aversive stimuli and substance dependence. *Psychophysiology* 36, 193–8.

Taylor, J. G. (1992) Towards a neural network model of the mind. *Neural Network World* 2, 797–812.

Teasdale, J. and Barnard, P. J. (1993) *Affect, Cognition, and Change*, Hillsdale: Lawrence Erlbaum Associates.

Teicher, M. H., Glod, C., and Cole, J. O. (1990) Emergence of intense suicidal preoccupation during fluoxetine treatment. *American Journal of Psychiatry* 147, 207–10.

Thatcher, R. W. (1998) Normative EEG databases and EEG biofeedback. *Journal of Neurotherapy* (2–4), 3.

Thorell, L. H., Kjellman, B. F., and D'Elia, G. (1987) Electrodermal activity in antidepressant medicated and unmedicated depressive patients and in matched healthy subjects. *Acta Psychiatrica Scandinavica* 76 (6), 648–92.

Thornton, K. E. (1996) On the nature of artifacting the QEEG. *Journal of Neurotherapy* (1–3), 5.

Trudeau, D. L., Sokhadze, T.M., and Cannon, M.A. (2009) Neurofeedback in alcohol and drug dependency, in Budzynski, T. H., Budzynski, H. K., Evans, J. R., and Abarbanel, A. (eds) *Quantitative EEG and Neurofeedback*, London: Academic Press.

Tschacher, W. and Scheier, C. (1995) Analyse komplexer psychologischer Systeme II: Verlaufsmodelleund Komplexitaet einer Paartherapie. *System Familie* 8, 160–71.

Tulving, E. (1972) Episodic and semantic memory, in Tulving, E. and Donaldson, D. (eds) *The Organization of Memory*, New York: Academic Press.

Van Den Akker, S. and Steptoe, A. (1980) Psychophysiological responses in women reporting severe pre-menstrual symptoms. *Psychosomatic Medicine* 51, 319–28.

Vaughn, C. and Leff, J. (1976) The measurement of expressed emotion in the families of psychiatric patients. *British Journal of Social and Clinical Psychology* 15, 157–65.

Venables, P. H. and Martin, I. (1967) *A Manual of Psychophysiological Methods*, New York: John Wiley & Sons, Inc.

Walker, J. E., Lawson, R., and Kozlowski, G. (2007) Current status of QEEG and neurofeedback in the treatment of clinical depression, in Evans, J. (ed.) *Handbook of Neurofeedback*, Binghampton, NY: Haworth Medical Press.

Wallace, R. K. (1970) Physiological effects of transcendental meditation. *Science* 167 (4), 35–9.

Walsh, R. (1988) Two Asian psychologies and their implications for western psychotherapists. *American Journal of Psychotherapy*, 42 (4), 67–73.

Walter, S. (2006) Irritable bowel syndrome: diagnostic symptom criteria and impact of rectal distensions on cortisol and electrodermal activity. PhD dissertation. Linkšping University Medical Dissertations, no. 974, ISSN 0345–0082.

Waxman, S. (2004) *From Neuroscience to Neurology: Neuroscience, Molecular Medicine, and the Therapeutic Transformation of Neurology*, Salt Lake City: Academic Press.

Weber, C. M. and Smith, A. (1990) Autonomic correlates of stuttering and speech assessed in a range of experimental tasks. *Journal of Speech and Hearing Research* 33, 690–706.

Wells, F. L. and Forbes, A. (1998) On certain electrical processes in the human body and their relation to emotional reactions. *Archives of Psychology* 2 (10), 1–39.

Wexler, B. E., Stevens, A. A., Bowers, A. A. *et al.* (1998) Word and tone working memory deficits in schizophrenia. *Archives of General Psychiatry* 55, 1093–6.

Wheatstone, C. (1879) *Scientific Papers of Sir Charles Wheatstone*, London: Physical Society of London.

Widagdo, M. M., Pierson, J. M., and Helme, R. D. (1988) Age-related changes in QEEG during cognitive tasks. *International Journal of Neuroscience* 95 (1–2), 63–75.

Wiener, N. (1966) *Cybernetics: or Control and Communication in the Animal and the Machine*, Cambridge, Massachusetts: MIT Press.

Wilcot, R. C. (1966) Adaptive value of arousal sweating and the epidermal mechanism related to skin potential and skin resistance. *Psychophysiology* 2, 249–62.

Wolpe, J. (1958) *Psychotherapy by Reciprocal Inhibition*, Stanford: Stanford University Press.

Wolpe, J. (1968) *Behavior Therapy Techniques*, New York: Pergamon Press.

World Health Organization (1992) *The ICD-10 Classification of Mental and Behavioural Disorders: Clinical Descriptions and Diagnostic Guidelines*, Geneva:

WHO Press. Italian editors: Kemali, D., Maj, M., Catapano, F. *et al.*, Milan: Masson.

Young, J. (1999) *Cognitive Therapy for Personality Disorders. A Schema-Focused Approach*, Sarasota: Professional Resource Press.

Zahn, T. P., Frith, C. D., and Steinhauer, S. R. (1991) Autonomic functioning in schizophrenia: electrodermal activity, heart rate, pupillography, in Steinhauer, S. R., Gruzelier, J. H., and Zubin, J. (eds) *Handbook of Schizophrenia*, volume 5, Amsterdam: Elsevier.

Zahn, T. P., Insel, T. R., and Murphy, D. L. (1984) Psychophysiological changes during pharmacological treatment of patients with obsessive compulsive disorder. *British Journal of Psychiatry* 145, 39–44.

Index

Neuroscience-based Cognitive Therapy: New Methods for Assessment, Treatment, and Self-Regulation, First Edition. Tullio Scrimali.
© 2012 John Wiley & Sons, Ltd. Published 2012 by John Wiley & Sons, Ltd.